Resistance Reimagined

UNIVERSITY PRESS OF FLORIDA

Florida A&M University, Tallahassee
Florida Atlantic University, Boca Raton
Florida Gulf Coast University, Ft. Myers
Florida International University, Miami
Florida State University, Tallahassee
New College of Florida, Sarasota
University of Central Florida, Orlando
University of Florida, Gainesville
University of North Florida, Jacksonville
University of South Florida, Tampa
University of West Florida, Pensacola

RESISTANCE REIMAGINED

Black Women's Critical Thought as Survival

REGIS M. FOX

University Press of Florida

Gainesville · Tallahassee · Tampa · Boca Raton

Pensacola · Orlando · Miami · Jacksonville · Ft. Myers · Sarasota

This book may be available in an electronic edition.

First cloth printing, 2017
First paperback printing, 2018

23 22 21 20 19 18   6 5 4 3 2 1

Portions of this text were previously published as "Behind the Scenes of American Liberalism." *The Elizabeth Keckley Reader, Volume 1, Writing Self, Writing Nation*. Ed. Sheila Smith McKoy. Hillsborough, NC: Eno Publishers, 2016. 125–141. Print. Courtesy of Elizabeth Woodman.

Library of Congress Cataloging-in-Publication Data
Names: Fox, Regis M., author.
Title: Resistance reimagined : black women's critical thought as survival / Regis M. Fox.
Description: Gainesville : University Press of Florida, 2017. | Includes bibliographical references and index.
Identifiers: LCCN 2017030400 | ISBN 9780813056586 (cloth : alk. paper) ISBN 9780813064895 (pbk.)
Subjects: LCSH: African American women—History. | African American women—Political activity—History. | African American women civil rights workers—History. | African Americans—Civil rights—History. | African American women political activists—History. | African Americans—Social life and customs.
Classification: LCC E185.86 .F676 2018 | DDC 305.48/896073—dc23
LC record available at https://lccn.loc.gov/2017030400

The University Press of Florida is the scholarly publishing agency for the State University System of Florida, comprising Florida A&M University, Florida Atlantic University, Florida Gulf Coast University, Florida International University, Florida State University, New College of Florida, University of Central Florida, University of Florida, University of North Florida, University of South Florida, and University of West Florida.

University Press of Florida
15 Northwest 15th Street
Gainesville, FL 32611-2079
http://upress.ufl.edu

FOR US

Contents

Figures

Acknowledgments

First, I thank God for so much, particularly for gifting me with the opportunity to do work that I love every single day.

Moreover, I am immensely grateful to all who have touched this project in some way: every contribution, large or small, has been meaningful to me.

I never would have made it to graduate school without the encouragement of faculty and friends in the English department of Clark Atlanta University. It was at CAU that I developed vital intellectual self-esteem. I thrived there, largely because of the taken-for-granted-ness of black excellence. It was in Atlanta that I first learned that my love of African-American literature was important and that I, in fact, had something to say.

This sustained me (though not without challenges) during my study at the University of California, Riverside. I owe my survival, as well as the initial cultivation of this project, to many scholars there, including Emory Elliott, Lindon Barrett, Michelle Raheja, Jennifer Doyle, Keith Harris, and Jayna Brown. Vorris Nunley and Traise Yamamoto influenced my thinking and my spirit, inside and outside of the classroom, more than they will ever know. For letting me be vulnerable, thank you. With her honesty, generosity, consistency, and sheer brilliance, Erica Edwards exemplifies mentorship. I strive every day to live up to her example. Many, many thanks also go to my UCR colleagues, many of whom have become lifelong friends.

Without the support of the Dorothy F. Schmidt College of Arts and Letters and the Department of English at Florida Atlantic University, I don't know what I would have done. A College Advisory Board Faculty Research Award, in addition to a McKnight Junior Faculty Fellowship via the Florida Education Fund, provided crucial funding during the publication process. A heartfelt thanks to Derrick White, Andy Furman, Elena Machado, Rafe Dalleo, Adam Bradford, and Sika Dagbovie-Mullins for shepherding me through those first years in the profession, and to all those colleagues, sorority sisters, and comrades who helped South Florida feel like home. Many thanks as well to my new colleagues at Grand Valley State University for their enthusiastic support of my work, especially Sherry Johnson, and the Center for Scholarly and Creative Excellence for their Book Publication Subvention Grant, as well as my allies and advisors at the University Press of Florida, including Sian Hunter, Ali Sundook, Eleanor Deumens, and Kel Pero. Thanks also to all the artists, librarians, and archivists who have made this book better than I could have ever imagined.

For friends and family who attended conferences, read drafts, brainstormed ideas, but also made cocktails, cooked meals, fielded tears, and loved on me more than I ever felt I deserved, we did it! I hope this book makes you proud, especially: Keenan Norris, Alicia Cox, Sonia Rodriguez, Tracy Zuniga, Talitha LeFlouria, Courtney Harris, Coyea Gurley, Tela'nea Forbes, Lyeah Granderson, Ariel and Brandi Brockman, Ashley Johnson, and Gerina Davis. To my sisters—Kellen, Shamees, and Toni Jr.—I hope you see yourselves in the women in these pages. To my Jima, this book is a testament to your boldness. And Grandad, though you aren't here to read it, your patience and vision have made it all possible. Thank you to Melvin, Cherie, Toni, and Tyronne for welcoming me with open arms into the family, for understanding when the book kept me out of your presence, but knowing you were never out of my heart. And I thank all of my aunts, uncles, cousins, grandparents, godparents, and godchildren for all of the ongoing prayer and advice.

To my mother: there are no words to say how much I value all that you sacrificed for me to be in this position. I am the author, scholar, teacher, and woman I am today because of your deep wisdom and even deeper compassion. I am blessed to be your first-born, but also to be your forever friend.

And Garrett: when we met, I was hastily drafting the last chapters of the dissertation. You gladly lent me your desk. Now, it's our desk! I love you. My hope is that this book is just the first of many things we create to try to change the world for the better.

Prologue

Naming Black Women's Ideology Critique

As a professor of African-American literature and culture, I experience occasional bouts of pedagogical surprise. In a Winter 2013 class, for instance, students analyzed Maria W. Stewart's lecture in Boston's Franklin Hall (1832) in order to evaluate the conventions of argumentative writing. When subsequently tasked with an essay assignment to argue a position on a controversial issue facing his or her community, one student drafted a paper on the effects of employment discrimination in her Los Angeles neighborhood, marshaling Stewart's claims from over a century ago to interrogate decreased employment opportunities in relation to diminished supports for public education and increasing police brutality. Again, in a separate course, class members identified the ways in which the framework of *David Walker's Appeal in Four Articles* (1829) expressly privileges black manhood, not to isolate Walker as singularly patriarchal, but to consider the ways in which masculinity undergirds many of the popular cultural renderings of black empowerment with which they were most readily familiar. With little to no prompting, participants in a more recent, pre-twentieth-century African-American studies course used Frances E. W. Harper's short story "The Two Offers" (1859) and her speech "Woman's Political Future" (1893) to forecast prominent issues in the 2016 U.S. presidential campaigns and debates. Student creativity and inventiveness of this ilk remind me of precisely the sort of intellectual curiosity that propelled me into my profession.

Other instructional encounters are more commonplace, such as when I conclude a unit on early African-American rhetoric and public performance with Sojourner Truth's famed "Ar'n't I a Woman?" speech to the 1851 Women's Rights Convention in Akron, Ohio. As I lecture about the sensational quality long associated with this particular oration, or about Truth's specific deployment of intersectional analyses, I am more often than not met with a sea of contented faces. "We get it," they signal to me, knowingly, unanimously. "Of course," they nod and smile. As I attempt to complicate our discussion by introducing Truth's intricate manipulation of embodied rhetoric and sarcasm, the students' sense of ease and reassurance does not dissipate. On the contrary, it persists. In fact, I seldom come across class members wrestling with the import of the itinerant preacher's words at all. For many of them, Truth's potency, her relevance in the context of black resistance, is self-evident. It's obvious, glaringly so. Bolstered by underdeveloped perceptions of her exotic difference, laboring body, and witty banter, students situate Truth, quite comfortably, within a pantheon of black defiance.

Uncertainty creeps in, however, when I later suggest carving out a space for writers and thinkers as varied as Phillis Wheatley, Lucy Terry, or Victoria Earle Matthews in conversation and community with the likes of Sojourner Truth. Uncomfortable glares steadily supplant the confidence and poise of previous weeks. Recognition gives way to reluctance, if not a marked decline in participation and enthusiasm. Similarly, mandatory end-of-semester course evaluations consistently praise the inclusion of Truth's speech, or Ida B. Wells's strident anti-lynching advocacy, while complaining with increasing force about apparently more subdued assigned readings from Anna Julia Cooper's *A Voice from the South* (1892). Despite my own abiding passion for the field, alternate pedagogical approaches, and disparate classroom composition, outcomes rarely change. My students' reactions expose a very particular set of expectations about African-Americans' struggle for justice, but they are not alone. Comparable responses emerge outside the walls of academia.

Armed with more questions than answers regarding patterns of reverence and remembrance, I sought out Tina Allen's twelve-foot-tall bronze statue of Sojourner Truth in downtown Battle Creek, Michigan, a locale wherein the anti-slavery and women's rights advocate resided from 1857 until her death in 1883. Standing astride the stunning monument, directly across the street from city hall on the corner of Division and Michigan Avenues, I (as anyone might) felt immediately dwarfed in comparison. At once invisible and hypervisible—that is, largely obscured from street view, and yet rapidly increasing in size upon approach by foot—Truth occupies center-stage of a small amphitheater in the corner of Battle Creek Monument Park. Three placards appear to the rear

Figure 1. Sojourner Truth monument by Tina Allen. Monument Park, Battle Creek, Michigan, by Heritage Battle Creek and the Sojourner Truth Institute of Battle Creek. Courtesy of Mary Butler, archivist.

of a conservatively adorned Truth, one reading: "Lord, I have done my duty and I have told the truth and kept nothing back." A second panel contains a copy of the activist's only known signature. A third sign states, succinctly, "and Truth shall be my abiding name." As if only for a moment, Truth's right hand rests atop a closed bible. Opposite the waist-high podium on which the bible sits, her left hand is outstretched behind her.

Scorching summer temperatures notwithstanding, multiple visitors passed through the venue during my time there. With prior student feedback never far from my mind, I wondered: What prompted their respective trips that day? Was it, as it was for me, their first sojourn to Allen's creative rendering of Sojourner? What did they notice initially upon arrival at the site, and what would they take away from the experience? In their view, was it important to have a statue of Truth in Battle Creek (or anywhere, for that matter)? What makes someone statue-worthy? And what other historic figures merit attention in this way? Non-verbal cues displayed by guests included lingering, taking pictures, and leaning against Truth's substantial frame, indicating a palpable level of respect.

Still, I asked a few attendees to share their thoughts. Never having seen the massive carving before, two African-American women expressed relief that Truth was rendered "respectably." Each seemed aware of the capacity for women of color, then and now, to be characterized in exaggerated, stereotypical ways. Truth's floor-length frock and shawl, in a sense, signaled her fitness and appropriateness for the space, according to these observers. One of the women similarly praised the statue's incorporation in such a "nice area," demonstrating a parallel protectiveness of Truth's legacy. However, spectators' high regard soon manifested as a seeming collapse of Truth into Allen's artistic representation: "as a person, she was monumental," a woman remarked of the ex-bondwoman's far-reaching influence. And in accord with previous sentiments, one gentleman saw little need to query Truth's contributions or the terms of belonging enacted in and by her name. It's simple, he intimated, in earnest. "She *is* freedom."

Admittedly, the sculpture gave me pause. I was especially struck by just how solitary Truth appears on the large concrete platform. Lulls in pedestrian traffic and tourist attention amplify this impression. Though one plaque makes mention of Truth's husband and children, and another gestures toward her alluring charisma and song, the overall layout and design produce an aura of isolation. Quite literally unparalleled in stature, Truth is impressive and awe-inspiring, and at the same time, contained and remote. A younger African-American man evaluated the overall scene as an "uncommon" one. Truth is, from his perspective and that of many others, exceptional.

But then there's that left hand. It protrudes ever so slightly, without ceremony, but with purpose. Truth's subtle reach disrupts the plane of individuality, as she seeks contact through a deliberate act of retrieval, a summons. Truth invites witnesses into relation with her, and notably, several sightseers clasped their hands into hers as they snapped photographs. One might miss the motion, except that it mirrors that of Harriet Tubman's left hand in a bronze memorial to the Underground Railroad located about a half-mile away in Battle Creek's Kellogg House Park. Crafted by sculptor Ed Dwight, the fourteen-foot-tall, twenty-eight-foot-long tribute features Tubman alongside fellow rebels Erastus and Sarah Hussey, and runaways left unnamed. Truth and Tubman, often extricated from broader swaths of black contemplative, community-building endeavor, in fact, extend their hands outward and beyond their most immediate spheres of meaning and circumstance. They grasp at

Figure 2. Underground Railroad monument by sculptor Ed Dwight. Kellogg House Park, Battle Creek, Michigan. Courtesy of Ed Dwight.

expressions of awareness, discernment, and experience distinct from their own. They touch others in shared pursuit of mobilizing difference and generating meaningful change—if only we would let them.

To be sure, reticence to engage black knowledge production in its myriad forms provokes pivotal questions regarding a politics of representation. More than matters of individual taste or of general apathy, the examples above reveal a telling anxiety. What must a historical black thought leader look like, and why? What modes of black being and political consciousness are immediately legible? Does the nature of the opponent have an impact on the tangibility of resistance? And what needs determine either the narrowness or capaciousness of said boundaries? Indeed, pedagogical and popular cultural dynamics such as these point to a larger conundrum, including a devaluation of activists who not only target traditional modes of violence in palatable ways, but unsettle some of the most revered strains of progressivism of the day, in ways we'd much rather forget.

It's time to name, more adequately and adeptly, black women's ideology critique.

Introduction

Resistance and Legitimacy

In response to broader entanglements of misrepresentation and disregard, this book reads black women differently.[1] Detailing the story of nineteenth-century black authors' critical engagement with the fundamental disjunction between democratic promise and dispossession in the American nation-state, or what I term in the pages to follow the "liberal problematic," *Resistance Reimagined* departs from by-now-standardized depictions of resistance. Arguably, reimagining resistance, terrain too readily conceived as militant, vernacular, or masculine, can proffer fuller accounts of black humanity. Accordingly, this book unsettles evaluations of nineteenth-century African-American women's intellectual production—against the social action of a more tangibly formidable Sojourner Truth or Ida B. Wells, for instance—as bourgeois or accommodationist. Spotlighting literary critiques of liberalism, and the idiom of self-possession and volition by which the latter is reinforced, *Resistance Reimagined* positions black women's address of an insidious slippage between freedom and subjection as vital oppositional consciousness.

Indeed, despite research by Marilyn Richardson and Frances Smith Foster, Carla Peterson and Shirley Wilson Logan, John Ernest and Xiomara Santamarina, authors such as Harriet Wilson, Elizabeth Keckly, and Anna Julia Cooper (the subjects of the first three chapters of this book) seldom garner widespread recognition as incarnations of decisive black defiance. While distinct with respect to constraints of region and class throughout the course of their lives, Wilson's, Keckly's, and Cooper's analogous marginalization signifies reductive, if common, wisdom attending nineteenth-century black women's literary expression. Associated less with the formation of epistemology, or with advanced, mainstream systems of thought, pre-twentieth-century discourse by black women continually elicits indictments of unimaginative simplicity. Aesthetic and generic categorizations, including (but not limited to) "moral," "evangelical," and "domestic," often circulate as epithets in this context, whereas a perceived dearth of political, racial, or intersectional concerns implies conservatism and assimilation. To this end, some insist on reading texts such as *Our Nig* (1859), *Behind the Scenes* (1868), and *A Voice from the South* (1892) through a trajectory of what Elizabeth Higginbotham refers to as the "politics of black respectability," presenting disproportionate emphasis on such writers' apparent complicity and collusion. Thus, in contrast to Frederick Douglass or Harriet Tubman, figures like Charlotte Forten and Mary Church Terrell continue to provoke charges of indifference or elitism, passivity or acquiescence, vis-á-vis existing regimes of power. Equating conventional literary styles such as sentimentality with a capitulation to whiteness, or with pandering to gain majority sympathy and approval, others presuppose the obsolescence of black women's writing from the antebellum period through the post-Reconstruction era.

Apprehending this problem at the close of the nineteenth century, Anna Julia Cooper writes, "The thinker and the doer, the man who solves the problem by enriching his country with an invention worth thousands or by a thought inestimable and precious is given neither bread nor a stone. He is too often left to die in obscurity and neglect even if spared in his life the bitterness of fanatical jealousies and detraction" (136). In fact, a dichotomous relation between consciousness and activism, a privileging of radicalism and public forms of protest, and similarly circumscribing definitions of black struggle, haunt much resistance studies inquiry, past and present. The domain of resistive praxis subsequently takes on a proprietary cast, as an entity irretrievable beyond the bounds of outwardly incendiary transgression at the hands of embattled masses or of charismatic/celebrity male leadership via authorized avenues of dissent. This coincides with what Sianne Ngai identifies in *Ugly Feelings* as the "symbolic violence in the principle of commensurability itself," whereby "there is an underlying assumption that an appropriate emotional response to racist violence exists, and that the burden lies on the racialized subject to produce that appropriate response legibly, unambiguously, and immediately" (188). A strictly gendered and classed construct, "resistance" pivots upon racialized connotations of representativeness and narrowly quantifiable standards of credibility. Yet, as I consider here, meaningful black refusal can be as imbricated in contexts of combat and insurrection as intricate matrices of hierarchy, submission, and theory.

To be clear, the prevalence of relatively restrictive interpretations of African-American resistance, formally scholastic or lay in origin, does not denote complete abandonment. Landmark precursors, alongside an ever-expanding body of recovery work, complicate long-standing perspectives on the battles waged by a range of early black women thinkers. Investigating the subtleties of nineteenth-century black women's activism, these undertakings have drawn attention to the ways in which gender norms, exoticizing conditions of valor, and intra-racial conflict promote cherished icons of resistance at the expense of less-containable iterations of black literature, music, religion, and the erotic. The analysis advanced in this volume owes a debt to foundational works of this stripe, as it does to those considering literary critiques of power at the axes of gender, race, and class, and African-American public intellectuals' complex relationship to the uneven effects of liberal democracy. Scholars have also developed important studies tracing the function of contemporary neo-slave narrative in relation to prior black literary precedent (the subject of the fourth chapter of this book). As a result, interest in modes of witnessing and redress, as well as in surveying black agency, fostered by recent fictional turns to slave culture and antebellum racial politics, abounds. There could be no *Resistance Reimagined* without these formative critical endeavors.[2]

Consonant with a black feminist ethos of reclamation, then, this book examines nineteenth-century black women writers at times minimized as elitist, inauthentic, or otherwise inconsequential. In foregrounding these subjects as instigators of critical thought, the book expands perceptions of viable enactments of African-American resistance. Liberal ideology critique, an ever-nuanced enclave of contention, is one route among many by which black women historically intervened in reigning discourses of selfhood and universality. However, it is a site of enduring significance: it reflects persistent navigation of injunctions toward duty and intimacy buttressing the onset of Emancipation and sanctioning circuits of erasure in the wake of freedom. Hence, I offer not a complete story here, but seek to highlight the incompleteness of broader narratives of nineteenth-century black resistance that do not account for theorization of the limits of dominant notions of privilege and progress shoring up the liberal problematic.

Omission of the contributions of black women authors as practitioners of knowledge formation, moreover, marks a dangerous de-intellectualizing gesture. Via a contestation of liberal norms, the thinkers gathered in this book interpret and modify defining precepts of property and personhood. They undermine fonts of individualism and free will. And they confront, in unique ways, evocations of reason and autonomy that propagate disproportionate grief and racial turmoil. Additionally, in response to the liberal status quo, Wilson, Keckly, Cooper, and modern writer Sherley Anne Williams implement a series of critical literary strategies, from sarcasm to aurality. They leverage materiality and enforced embodiment to unmake cultural myths of advancement. And they activate opacity to counter presumptions of coherence and civility. Summoning fraught distinctions between complicity and subversion, these women demonstrate the utility and the peril of inhabiting the realm of the human.

Still, my investment in exploring black women authors' interrogation of the collision of market values and benevolent prescriptive to which liberalism aspires ventures further. One of the text's larger goals is to enrich a collective sense of the pretextual gamut brooking racial prejudice and subordination in the U.S. Nineteenth-century African-American thinkers fortunate enough to pass written records onto succeeding generations display crucial discernment regarding the manifestation of power. They anticipate contemporary black literary pursuits by reminding readers to be as attuned to the nadir of anti-black terror as to the ruse of tolerance. Reading Wilson's, Keckly's, Cooper's, and Williams's creative production differently requires one to access their vigilance against antagonisms acute and spectacular, alongside those exceedingly sly.

Rather than uncritically echoing sentiments of the governing sociopolitical order, the subjects of this study make visible alternate modes of being. They reveal other potentialities—and determinants—for social change. They raise questions not only about the forms resistance takes but also about the forces resistance targets, about various modes of subjugation permissible under the cover of reform, responsibility, even pleasure. Imperatively, their texts inquire: How does liberal intention condone and obscure violence? How do ethics of abstraction and rationality mediate processes of devaluation? How do protection and cultural mandates of self-help uphold order and control? Why must difference be theorized as a source of vision, not reducible to a tokenized otherness tethered to hegemonic whiteness? And how might opposition to conservative and ostensibly progressive nineteenth-century philosophies foster black empowerment? Configuring black women's intervention in the liberal problematic as legitimate resistance, *Resistance Reimagined* brings precisely such queries to the fore.

The Liberal Problematic

What I refer to throughout this book as the "liberal problematic" proposes that a bevy of contradiction, rather than certitudes of privilege or unity, underwrites what historically has been one of the central organizing provinces of politics and self-making in the U.S.: liberalism. Liberalism, as a practice and as an object of critique, takes many forms. As a mode of government, it ostensibly intervenes within and between states to curtail chaos. It locates self-determination as a product of discriminating repression, promoting education and the development of autonomous personhood. As economic domain, liberalism traditionally champions free enterprise. It affirms contract labor and the protection of private property. Simultaneously philosophical and cultural, liberalism also manifests in psychic, affective, and ethical terms.

Of especial relevance in this study are foundational tenets of liberalism that directly and indirectly facilitate disenfranchisement and racial otherness. According to David Theo Goldberg, and I quote at length:

> Liberalism is committed to *individualism* for it takes as basic the moral, political, and legal claims of the individual over and against those of the collective. It seeks *foundations* in *universal* principles applicable to all human beings or rational agents in virtue of their humanity or rationality . . . It is concerned with broad identities which it insists unite persons on moral grounds, rather than with those identities which divide politically, culturally, geographically, or temporally. The philosophical basis of this broad human identity, of an essentially human nature, is taken to lie in a common rational core within each individual, in the (potential) capacity to be moved by Reason. In keeping with

this commitment to the force of reason, liberalism presupposes that all social arrangements may be ameliorated by rational *reform*. Moral, political, economic and cultural *progress* is to be brought about by and reflected in carefully planned institutional improvement. The mark of progress is measured for liberals by the extent to which institutional improvement serves to extend people's liberty, to open up or extend spaces for free expression. Finally, and . . . perhaps most significantly, liberalism takes itself to be committed to *equality*. (5; emphasis in original)

Thus, in a democratic state, appropriate citizen-subjects exhibit rational and moral agency. By excising possible idiosyncrasies of character, model personhood circulates as universally accessible to all. Indeed, the very terms of humanity emerge as organic and self-evident. With freedom as its aim, liberalism tenders a distinct, if variously executed, theory of political purpose and communal order. A prominent rubric of citizenship, replete with requisite comprehensiveness and inclusion, it articulates conditions of mobility and remedy in the context of emancipatory vision.

However, liberal conceptions of humanity likewise rely on generalization and preferentiality to the detriment of the less propertied, urbane, white, or male. Despite associated emphases on civility and objectivity, among other aspects, liberalism delimits fraternity and worth along strict boundaries of gender, race, and class in order to project endemic similarity and accord. "As modernity's definitive doctrine of self and society, of morality and politics," Goldberg confirms further, "liberalism serves to legitimate ideologically and to rationalize politico-economically prevailing sets of racialized conditions and racist exclusions" (1). In particular, Enlightenment-refined discourses such as coherence codify a concerted expulsion of blackness, endorsing rationality, literacy, and language over opacity, materiality, and embodiment at all costs. Influencing modes of relation and usurping spaces of subjectivity, liberalism functions as sociality and as socializing agent—an ethos both pervasive and perverse.

Liberal ideology critique as resistance, on the other hand, exploits the vagueness and instability of customary rights provisions. That is, populations regarded as excess may engage, even appropriate societal forms never meant for their use. In the space of *Resistance Reimagined*, such groups lay liberalism bare as a site of yearning, as an enticing illusion of proportional humaneness and equity. In fact, "[T]he modern distinction between definitions of the human and those to whom such definitions do not extend is the condition of possibility for Western liberalism, and not its particular exception," as Lisa Lowe observes (3). An embedded nexus of identity and policy formation, liberalism lures via prospects of rational teleology and expansive community as individual and state attainments.[3] Nevertheless, as a number of nineteenth-century black thinkers reveal, normative political action and public discourse in this vein is too often conditional and contingent, dissimulating harrowing performances of tyranny and containment.

Arguing for the reconfiguration of prevailing ideologies of selfhood and consent as a significant, if underexamined, legacy of black feminist knowledge production, the concept of the liberal problematic forwarded in *Resistance Reimagined* underscores the semblant nature of sovereignty for many African-Americans in the nineteenth century and beyond. Without contravening what liberal custom might yet become, the liberal problematic situates democracy as an idealization, both of electoral standards and capitalist prerogative. Further, it signals a naturalization of mainstream, procedural iterations of equivalence. Contending with the liberal problematic, then, materializes the threat of purely nominal autonomy. Grappling with its paradoxes opens up possibilities for evaluating the effects, ideological and otherwise, of differential entitlement, especially for those left most vulnerable in its wake.

Importantly, black activists' disruptions of liberalism unmask logics of refusal underlying dominant notions of public culture and governmental practice—even when such efforts are partial, fleeting, or never fully outside the bounds of appeals for human recognition.[4] Traversing conventional disciplinary boundaries, African-American women often devised cogent analyses, ever mindful of precisely how prevailing ethics of individualism and rationality constrain black movement. That is, in a historical moment for which the slave narrative still frequently circulates as predominant signifier, figures such as Maria W. Stewart and Frances E.W. Harper leveraged genres from prose to memoir, fiction to poetry, to consider the ways in which politics of abstraction and decorum structure how black communities build relationships and encounter others.

Thus, the cadre of black scholars and theorists gathered in these pages crystallizes the duress of inhabiting Western jurisprudence, specifically for those perceived to embody, if not to epitomize, the limits of citizenship. Nineteenth-century black women writers, in particular, convey critical awareness about what it means to occupy the breach between the capacity and corporeal experience of liberty, between declarations of goodwill and routines of ruin. In this breach, I submit, resides knowledge of the productivity of difference. In this breach dwell tumults of black joy astride knowing instantiations of black anger. Lived realities of degraded labor, of stunning impoverishment and exploitation, populate this sphere, while tenuousness and uncertainty abound. It also houses perceptions of motherhood by way of sexual violation. The sound and spirit of a range of black material presences echo throughout. Suicide, too, limns the breach.

In representing this fissure, nineteenth-century black women writers contradict broader cultural propensities for binary, fixed logic. Their narrative acts of sarcasm, witnessing, and self-commodification undermine avowedly transcendental systems of value and exceptionalism. As liberal doctrine permeates literary and religious performance, black women attest to the hazards of engrained constructs of privacy and progress. Beyond this, Wilson, Keckly, Cooper, and Williams refract accepted discourses of virtue and intentionality according to specificities of gender and age. Seemingly commonsense notions of intimacy and empathy similarly give way under the weight of black women's textual manipulation of the opaque. Expectations of unequivocal volition yield to stirring renderings of black silence.

In drawing attention to the liberal problematic, I offer, these women contribute to a vital reservoir of African-American resistance, one with complex reverberations in our contemporary moment. As asymmetrical hierarchies of power are both retrenched and made invisible in the twenty-first century, it becomes even more necessary to probe how prior conventions of exclusion issuing from processes of sovereignty and individual rights are reconstituted in the present. Undoubtedly, oppression must be extricated from abiding frameworks of reasonableness. Violence must be unyoked from historic precedents of sentiment and economic determinism that obscure erasure. Coercion must be severed from protocol enacted in the name of emancipation. Returning to the past in this way enriches notions of the diverse means by which black people have (and will continue) to assert perspective and place in the world.

Returning to the past in this way acknowledges a necessary multiplicity of black presence.

Becoming Together

Notably, this book centralizes a cluster of writings from the period 1859–1892, in conjunction with late twentieth-century neo-slave narrative, by a collection of authors never before assembled in a single book-length study. However, its repercussions necessarily precede and exceed those boundaries. More specifically, *Resistance Reimagined* reveals a "becoming together" of black feminist intellectualism, a transitory association that produces cognizance of the intersectional and circumscribing effects of the liberal mandate.[5] As opposed to belonging together—thereby signaling occupation of a finite literary canon or stable tradition—Wilson, Keckly, Cooper, and Williams comprise a unique conclave surpassing conventional spatial and temporal markers.

My suggestion, that these figures become together, ultimately affirms their kindred literary commitment to challenging explicit and insidious practices of black dehumanization perpetuated in the guise of liberty, even as I acknowledge important differences among the figures themselves. As Saidiya Hartman observes in a related context, becoming together

> is not fixed but a fleeting, intermittent, and dispersed network of relations. The relations can neither be reduced to domination nor explained outside it. They exceed the parameters of resistance in creating alternate visions and experiences of subjectivity, though they do indeed challenge the dominant construction of blackness. This shared set of identifications and affiliations is enacted in instances of struggle, shared pleasures, transient forms of solidarity, and nomadic, oftentimes illegal, forms of association. (61)

Predicated less on the myriad hindrances to black connection insinuated in the course of enslavement and its aftermath, becoming together emphasizes abundant black attachment and the potential rooted in interim association. It speaks to unanticipated configurations of black correlation amid perpetual threats to black life. It captures the subversive quality of black convergence, of temporary bridges of minds and bodies, unauthorized and unbound.

To this end, the becoming together of African-American artists imagined in this project does not stipulate a literal encounter. Instead, it proposes dialogic reciprocity. Indeed, becoming together in this instance evokes heterogeneity intrinsic to black feminist realization and consistent with the mutability of historic patterns of violence and exclusion. Conjuring a context of possibility, of conceptual exchange among black women riven by the precise circumstances of their milieu yet plagued by an unceasing reconstitution of conditions of disenfranchisement from the antebellum period forward, *Resistance Reimagined* disputes taken-for-granted definitions of industry and autonomy.

Put another way, the chronological arrangement of this volume crafts a confrontation between pieces of literature that locate nineteenth-century black women as makers of theory, and as authors of liberal ideology critique, in particular. Intentionally selective, rather than exhaustive, it mobilizes genres from novelization to memoir to showcase black women's status as knowledge-producers and the complexity of their interventions into governing relations of property, development, and citizenship. Resisting firm strictures of periodicity, the becoming together staged herein fosters incongruity, but no more so than it foments creativity. It hinges together diverse thinkers subject to inattention in broader cultural registers of African-American opposition, resituating the latter as expansive enough to account for both conflict and engagement with liberal authority as valid means of black empowerment.

Hence, Wilson, Keckly, Cooper, and Williams are bonded by intellectualism, a critical consciousness not reducible to academic credentials or middle-class identity. They are linked by textual interventions that are innately epistemological, for in their respective ways, they make crucial literary claims about power and meaning-making subtending the liberal problematic. Indeed, each extends a competing framework of "truth" about race and freedom. By exposing liberal ways of knowing, including civility and choice, as vehicles of oppression, they trouble legal precedent and ideological justification by which asymmetrical control is sustained. In seeking access to mobility, and in questioning impediments to self-possession, these activists likewise unsettle ostensibly progressive grounds for maintaining unity as well as future prospects of tokenization-as-inclusion.

In sum, the black women at the heart of this study do not conform to normative standards of authentic black resistance. These thinkers are not emblematic, at least not cohesively so. Still, when studied collectively,

they reflect subjectivity astutely attuned to the ambiguity of liberal as-
surance. And in their very inauthenticity, they are true—true to various
black feminist conceptions of embodiment, reason, and community.

Methodology

Primarily, *Resistance Reimagined* is a work of African-Americanist literary criticism, one bearing significant cultural and historical resonances.
That is, while details germane to black women writers' lived experiences
anchor textual interpretation, biography is generally de-emphasized in
favor of close reading informed by black feminist theoretical perspectives and other interdisciplinary frameworks of analysis. Given that
nineteenth-century black women are so often relegated to the realms
of the cultural or sociological, or viewed as immediately and empirically
evident, rather than as subtle, savvy, or theoretically oriented, I opt for
a vein of inquiry that prioritizes unique mechanisms of understanding
and worldview ushered forth in the literary domain.

Black activists have long exceeded the confines of normative institutional reform to trouble a mythic social good and purported sameness fortifying the liberal project. They have long understood logic and
decorum as instruments of marginalization. Theorizing the way power
and authority are accrued via an abjection of black bodies, they have
long challenged practices of tolerance. Refusing to minimize difference
to uphold idealized norms, they have long called for an acknowledgment
of spectrums of black value and experience, and for substantive, rather
than solely administrative, political redress. Literature constitutes one
important arena in which this deliberation, as well as associated invention of black selfhood and epistemology, has taken place.

The archives of nineteenth-century black women's writing, in particular, signal that literature is ideological. Works by Amelia Johnson and
Linda Brent/Harriet Jacobs advance pastoral understandings of blackness at the same time as they imagine unforeseen ways of knowing. Ever
diverse, early black literature by Alice Dunbar-Nelson and Pauline Hopkins mediates relationships. On other occasions, it promotes spiritual
healing and joy. At times a recuperative space, African-American letters
by Phillis Wheatley and Victoria Earle Matthews memorialize and remember, establishing insurgent ground for resolving contradiction and
believing otherwise.

Moreover, African-American narrative houses political strivings and stages conversations about the relationship between resistance and discursivity—about the plethora of ways in which black refusal is lived, felt, and expressed. It activates contemplative language to assess dynamics of leadership and privilege imbuing liberal society. And as *Resistance Reimagined* indicates, African-American fiction and autobiography, among other genres, pose queries at once heretical and benign regarding the most basic terms of U.S. citizenship and belonging. Wilson's, Keckly's, Cooper's, and Williams's literary works, I argue, ponder the question of who can, in fact, inhabit the space of the human and the universal. Significantly, such authors also cultivate enduring strategies for countering entrenched codes of civility and coherence.

Accordingly, the reading and interpretive practice articulated in this volume, an accounting for black women's becoming together, rejects standard arguments that fix the figure of the black woman outside of or as metaphor for theory, as mere inspiration for its development. Instead, this book positions critical thought as survival, reclaiming black women's intellectual representation of labor and justice against the grain of liberal alibi. Of moment are Wilson's, Keckly's, Cooper's, and Williams's insights into collusion, but also their telling depictions of leading epistemologies of race and gender, via a distinctly literary politicization of memory, materiality, and difference.

Respecting both the specificity and the limits of various disciplinary borders, then, *Resistance Reimagined* invokes canonical nineteenth-century American literary studies, paradigms of black women's resistance, post-1960s histories of enslavement and black politics, ethnic studies, and rhetorical theory in order to apprehend irruptions into institutions of disembodied knowledge and value undergirding the liberal problematic. Deploying the scholarship of Lindon Barrett, Audre Lorde, and bell hooks, alongside interventions by Patricia Hill Collins, Lauren Berlant, and Hazel Carby, I analyze the ways in which black women's displays of musicality and wit contest received expectations of comportment and political subjectivity. Attending to the rhetorical effects of nineteenth-century activisms that exceed the spheres of pandering or mimesis, I augment research spearheaded by Elizabeth Alexander, Nell Painter, P. Gabrielle Foreman, and Kevin K. Gaines to interrogate nineteenth-century black women's engagement with fundamental liberal and Enlightenment precepts, an archive encompassing many, though certainly not all, black women writers publishing between 1859 and 1892.

Further, by the narrative's end, I mine intersections between early black published discourse and late twentieth-century novels that re-imagine antebellum America. Using the work of Barbara Christian and Roderick Ferguson, Arlene Keizer and Hortense Spillers, I explore how modern African-American art such as Sherley Anne Williams's 1986 novel *Dessa Rose* becomes together with Wilson's, Keckly's, and Cooper's writing in significant ways. Hence, *Resistance Reimagined* concludes by investigating the nuances of claims staked in the eras of enslavement and Emancipation by contemporary writers in a neoliberal age.

Contents

The major thematic concern of this book—nineteenth-century black women writers' performance of liberal ideology critique—pivots upon four distinct textual sites. One such touchstone is featured in each chap-ter of *Resistance Reimagined*. The first chapter in this volume, "'They Won't Believe What I Say': Theorizing Freedom as an Economy of Vio-lence," analyzes Harriet Wilson's *Our Nig* (1859), in which Wilson ex-poses the coerciveness of imbricated discourses of sentimentality and economic determinism sustaining the liberal problematic. In particular, Wilson offers a dense engagement with questions of labor, poverty, and the figure of the tragic mulatta, citing materiality as a critical register of political meaning and experience. Embodiment, though typically rendered antithetical to notions of logic or sense, bears theoretical im-plications and effects. Accordingly, Wilson implicates abstract rational-ism in hierarchizing, socially constructed processes of investment and exchange. Further, Wilson reimagines dominant ideologies of self-help and self-determination in the context of working class and underclass exploitation in the antebellum North, just as she revises governing per-ceptions of interracial altruism and charity.

In terms of the latter, Wilson catalyzes literature as a vehicle for un-covering the collusion of liberal empathy, Christianity, and capital in per-formances I refer to as "postures of abettal." Indeed, Wilson condemns goodwill as alibi throughout her text, critiquing characters such as Mr. Bellmont, Aunt Abby, daughter Jane, and sons James and Jack's pur-portedly unknowing reproduction of the conditions of Frado, the young, black protagonist's, dehumanization. Of the techniques by which the autobiographical novel's most ostensibly compassionate characters par-ticipate in Frado's abuse, Wilson theorizes many, as the well-meaning Bellmont cohort's alternate displays of covert refuge, reassuring humor, tokens of accommodation, and promises of spiritual salvation, finally do little more than sanction Frado's subjection. This account of the Bellmonts' advocacy for their orphaned black charge as merely a screen behind which they safeguard their property rights and economic standing typifies Wilson's intervention into liberalism as at once a political economy and a ritualized affective performance.

Conjointly, Wilson invokes blackness and associated figurations of opacity in *Our Nig* in order to challenge Western liberal dictates toward ocularcentrism. Through representations of swamp iconography and other dark courses to which Frado flees as an indentured black youth, Wilson problematizes Enlightenment-bound discourses of transparency and order. In dialogue with contemporary scholarship by Stephanie M. H. Camp and Daphne A. Brooks, Wilson subverts perspectives of blackness as threatening or lack. By appropriating obscurity as a symbol of revolt and a conflicting code of intelligibility, she supplants broader patterns of privileging fixed meaning and rational subjectivity. Articulating opacity in excess of abject difference, Wilson even frames her narrative as a whole with an insurgent preamble situating blackness as a source of healing and defiance.

Finally, Wilson also manipulates tropes of childhood and liberal assumptions of innocence in provocative ways. Conjuring a picaninny figure animated by, in the words of Lindon Barrett, a "politics of joy," Wilson politicizes the familiar nineteenth-century literary persona of "the disorderly girl." In Wilson's formation, Frado-as-picaninny functions to critique socio-political and economic norms, including Christianity and domesticity. Moreover, displaying contrariness to a liberal construal of black anger as fundamentally unlicensed, even criminal, Frado's politics of joy marks a euphoric consciousness inextricable from productive enactments of black fury. Distinct from Nathaniel Hawthorne's Pearl, Wilson's characterization warrants a critical reassessment of the chastity and of the vulnerabilities associated with youthfulness, and of the latter's utility in circumventing practices of discipline, management, and exclusion buttressing the liberal problematic.

Chapter 2, "The Production of 'Emancipation': Race, Ritual, and the Reconstitution of the Antebellum Order," likewise attests to nineteenth-century black women activists' complex contestation of the liberal problematic through a focus on Elizabeth Keckly's memoir, *Behind the Scenes* (1868). In this text outlining the author's years as a seamstress and laborer for the Lincoln White House, Keckly dislodges hegemonic models of individual sovereignty and progress. Underscoring the disturbing conditions facing the formerly enslaved at the onset of Emancipation, she depicts a state of epidemic black homelessness, starvation, and poverty, thereby disrupting prevailing mythologies of the postbellum North as quintessential racial asylum. Moreover, Keckly's theorization of suicide as an expression of black political consciousness, via a description of her uncle's death by hanging in the antebellum South, troubles logics of bodily, bounded integrity while foregrounding the precariousness of black freedom. Her politicized acts of witnessing and mediation, as well as her selective self-commodification, make visible insidious modes of social and economic control and disrupt conventional modes of fetishizing and Othering black women's bodies.

The second chapter also situates black women's textile production as a form of resistance. Producing meaningful critical and aesthetic effects throughout the memoir, Keckly's performances of material design complicate Western philosophical notions of order and abstract reason. Activating cultural histories of nineteenth-century black women's patchwork as an archive of communal memory, the representation of dressmaking in Keckly's text ascribes political meaning to an embodied practice which exceeds the purposes of utility or adornment. Further, this chapter confronts liberal tenets of exceptionalism by linking Keckly to widely recognized slave narrator and activist, Harriet Jacobs; for both women, embroidery and other needlework facilitate black reciprocity and function as acts of survival.

Keckly's subsequent articulation of counter-memory also casts doubt on teleological, "up from slavery" narratives. In fact, she consistently intervenes into racialized ideologies of development. Implementing processes of memorialization which acknowledge the lives and sacrifices of her ancestors—from her Aunt Charlotte to fellow laborers on the Garland plantation prior to her employment in Washington, D.C.—Keckly stages subversive performances of commemoration throughout *Behind the Scenes*, displacing pastoral images and plantation nostalgia with her own fragmented remembrances and problematizing state-sanctioned systems of knowledge production. Memory, in this instance, surpasses an ethic of precise recall or rational retrieval, as Keckly's selective reminiscences simultaneously embody practices of faith and of worldview. Via counter-memory I term "anti-pastoral reach," Keckly produces meaning and value in her life not finally tethered to whiteness, but to a manner of feeling and sense of creation that implicate tacit mechanisms of power and privilege.

What's more, Keckly as readily unmasks tropes of normative intimacy in her writing. Indeed, Keckly's literary representation of mid-nineteenth-century, interracial patron-client relationships exposes precisely how notions of the "Mammy" figure and of integrated friendships, in particular, entail oblique modes of compulsion. Routinized displays of fondness and familiarity, Keckly makes plain, extract docility and compliance: they do not affirm mutual respect. Hence, Keckly continually restages scenarios in which she counters employers' assertions of apparent confidence or care with a calm, self-imposed quietness. Such withdrawals from dominant performances of favor and esteem unsettle rigid power dynamics, foregrounding the ambivalence and artifice of intimacy as an institution. Juxtaposed with Keckly's non-rational articulation of motherhood, the affective contours of liberal rituals of servitude emerge as key objects of nineteenth-century black women's ideology critique.

In chapter 3, "'Wondering under Which Head I Come': Sounding Anna Julia Cooper's Fin-de-Siècle Song," I illustrate how Anna Julia Cooper undermines the liberal problematic by exposing the drawbacks of solely conceptual modes of thought forged in the absence of substantive interaction. Crucially, in *A Voice from the South* (1892), Cooper condemns prevailing ideals of abstraction and universality within traditions of U.S. Constitutionalism and Episcopalianism. She lodges similar critiques of the literature of prominent mainstream writers of the era, including William Dean Howells, for reductive and caricatured, if benignly crafted representations of black and mixed-raced bodies. By foregrounding the value of difference—of the necessity of conflict and heterogeneity within communities—and countering cultural mandates toward binary logic and individualism, Cooper hinders commonsense claims to progressivism. Further, Cooper incriminates a (white) Women's Movement which advocates parity, at the same time as it wields liberal affect as a mode of cultural policing along the lines of race and class.

Such critiques must also be taken together with Cooper's persistent invocation of music throughout the volume. From an aural organizational structure, to the use of the metaphors of harmony and of the Singing Something, Cooper's marshaling of sound defies Western models of reason and comprehensibility, many of which remain rooted in visuality. That is, Cooper's composition blends both literal and phonic embodied meaning in order to recuperate the subjectivities of black women, men, and commensurate groups subject to oppression in the U.S. Performatively demonstrating an inability of sense to transcend spirit, or of the mind to supersede material presence, Cooper recovers the body through song.

Paramount in Cooper's analysis of the liberal problematic, I explore further, is her reconceptualization of dominant tenets of civility and freedom as public pedagogy, a framework I am calling "critical regard." Cooper usurps established definitions of etiquette and appropriateness associated with liberal notions of uplift or self-help, remaining particularly attuned to the constraints of volition and sovereignty within the context of lived black realities. Indeed, her call for virtues of mutuality and respect produces conditions of sociopolitical awareness and possibilities for widespread change. A formulation positing accountability at the core of civil subjectivity, "critical regard" significantly alters governing tropes of citizenship and expectations of political responsibility. In prioritizing egalitarian ethics ever cognizant of gender, racial, and class difference, Cooper challenges prevailing assumptions of black resistance and agency.

Finally, I argue, Cooper's subtle and overt sarcasm broadens contemporary perceptions of humor and rationality. Expanding upon the work of Lawrence Levine and Mel Watkins, "'Wondering under Which Head I Come'" concludes with a reading of Cooper's wry intervention into the domain of black performativity. Cooper's departure from apparently "feminine" modes of public address, predicated upon purposeful word play, annuls standards of blackness as unconsciously ironic and derides patterns of state-sanctioned violence and exclusion. Via defiant displays of multi-vocality and feigned reserve, among other means, Cooper denaturalizes cultural myths and consequences of male and racial privilege and authority.

In the final chapter, "'Mammy Ain't Nobody Name': Power, Privilege and the Bodying Forth of Resistance," I locate *Our Nig*, *Behind the Scenes*, and *A Voice from the South* as pivotal intertexts for Sherley Anne Williams's novel *Dessa Rose* (1986). As I explore Williams's becoming together with previous legacies of resistance, I especially draw attention to her disruption of what one might gesture toward as a "neoliberal problematic" via her distinct problematization of abstraction and coherence. Usefully, Williams challenges representations of the mind-body split and associated tropes of antebellum mediation such as the interracial "as-told-to" dynamic. She theorizes the ways in which disembodied, conceptual jargon obfuscates power, and the ways in which rationality disavows black subjection as intractable difference.

As Harriet Wilson's *Our Nig* confronts circumstances of imposed materiality by recuperating the black body for the purposes of critique and redress, Williams's fiction exhibits a comparable attentiveness to situating blackness beyond conventional registers of containment. Therefore, I maintain that embodiment in Williams's novel continually intervenes in Enlightenment-era discourses of ocularcentrism and contained selfhood. Further, just as Wilson summons the rhetorical construct of Frado-as-picaninny in her autobiographical novel in order to counter reductionist readings of racialized anger as inherently groundless, Williams interrogates the indecipherability of black rage within both inter-racial and intra-racial liberal matrices of control. Arguably, only through this singular wrath and intensity, a decidedly Wilsonian restoration of black antagonism, can Williams's protagonist ascribe meaning to blackness apart from popular ideological formations.

Williams channels Keckly, on the other hand, through a destabilization of the "Mammy" figure. Rather than an infinitely exploitable site of sustenance and support, according to these authors, the "Mammy" construct consolidates white advantage under the guise of reciprocity. Thus, Williams undercuts liberal models of interracial friendship in significant ways. In contrast to effectively sensation-driven or strictly private modes of expression, Williams's concept of being "enveloped in caring," alternately termed sweetness, reflects a level of affirmation and regard posing a challenge to normative configurations of intimacy. Through the characterization of a bondwoman named Chloe and literary representations of an ethic of selective self-commodification, Williams likewise imports Keckly's articulation of the complexity of American liberalism as a ritualized, embodied performance and politico-economic apparatus.

Lastly, not unlike Cooper, Williams cultivates an insurgent politics of sound as she invokes black spirituals, love songs, call-and-response rhythms, and cries of mourning. Manipulating overriding systems of language and signification, Williams mobilizes a framework that refuses liberal bounds of intelligibility. Indeed, Cooper's and Williams's aurality establishes habits of meaning-making that de-emphasize visuality and its associated constraints, thereby fostering endurance and survival. Yet Williams simultaneously extends Cooper's paradigm as the former imagines routine tasks such as hair-braiding as embodied processes through which to build knowledge and community. For Williams, plaiting circulates as a conduit of black storytelling and memory-building, calling into question worn discourses of comprehension and belonging.

The Sojourn Ahead

Arguably, student dissatisfaction and popular cultural trends can become springboards for developing more expansive reading practices and interpretive methodologies. The closer reading outlined above and advanced in the subsequent pages of *Resistance Reimagined* is critical in order to correct the continued failure to understand black women's departure from the dictates of liberalism—rather than just their complicities with it—a failure that ultimately diminishes contemporary perspectives of nineteenth-century black women's epistemologies. Now is the time to cultivate even more robust theories of how black women activists fought and struggled, rather than presupposing how they ought to have done so.

1

"They Won't Believe What I Say"

Theorizing Freedom as an Economy of Violence

Much of what literary critics, cultural studies scholars, and historians currently know about the life and writing of Harriet Wilson, generally regarded as the first African-American woman to publish a novel in the United States, contradicts conventional notions of labor, of womanhood, and of blackness in the antebellum period. One of the earliest and most significant articulations of the "contrariness" that Barbara Christian theorizes as "the core of so much of Afro-American women's literature," Wilson's 1859 autobiographical novel *Our Nig, Or Sketches from the Life of a Free Black*, and its servant protagonist, Frado, extend a compelling lens through which Western standards of self-making and knowledge production might be problematized.[1]

It is precisely such contrariness, for instance, that James, one of the adult sons of the white family for whom Frado toils, artfully deflects in a scene following one of Frado's savage beatings at the hands of his mother, Mrs. Bellmont. As James entreats the victim of his mother's habitual, unprovoked rage simply to "try to be a good girl," the narrator relates: "'If I do, I get whipped,' sobbed the child. 'They won't believe what I say'" (Wilson 28). Indeed, what Frado says troubles the established order. As a consequence, her words must be contained and disavowed.

Yet, after initially appearing to concede to James's counsel to modify her attitude and behavior, Frado subsequently adds,

"Oh, I wish I had my mother back; then I should not be kicked and whipped so. Who made me so?"

"God," answered James.

"Did God make you?"

"Yes."

"Who made Aunt Abby?"

"God."

"Who made your mother?"

"God."

"Did the same God that made her make me?"

"Yes."

"Well, then, I don't like him."

"Why not?"

"Because he made her white, and me black. Why didn't he make us BOTH white?"

"I don't know; try to go to sleep, and you will feel better in the morning," was all the reply he could make to her knotty queries. (Wilson 28)

Frado's contrariness surfaces here in order to puncture the ostensible universality of Christian charity and compassion. Narrativized as "knotty queries," her inquiry reflects a crucial facet of what I locate as the novel's broader critique of liberal ideology and its attendant affective formations, one aspect of what I am calling the liberal problematic. In fact, the exchange crystallizes a slippage between a spirit of goodwill and black difference, of benevolent faith and racial prejudice. That is, though James is depicted as perhaps one of Frado's greatest allies during her indenture, he feigns ignorance in this scenario as Frado casts doubt on a sense of spiritual uplift strictly policed along the lines of race. While James attempts to avert Frado's attention with paternalistic, pathologizing discourse, the narrator's subsequent note that "a number of days [passed] before James felt in a mood to visit and entertain old associates and friends" (Wilson 28) alludes to black women's contrariness as a site of rupture.[2]

This chapter engages precisely such moments of rupture, expanding upon how the contrariness of writers and activists like Wilson theorizes an even more specific understanding of the limitations of liberal thought. In conversation with scholars including Hazel Carby and Carla Peterson, P. Gabrielle Foreman and Xiomara Santamarina, I suggest that

Figure 3. Harriet Wilson monument by sculptor Fern Cunningham, photograph by Cynthia Weber Stave. Milford, New Hampshire. Courtesy of JerriAnne Boggis, Harriet Wilson Project.

Wilson, and later Elizabeth Keckly and Anna Julia Cooper, undermine narratives of liberalism as fundamentally emancipatory. The primary idiom of such narratives includes equivalence, autonomy, reason, individualism, decorum, duty, and volition, all of which work in unique ways to constrain black being. By engaging with the liberal problematic, I maintain, Wilson exposes a critical aperture embedded within larger philosophical and cultural norms, a break within those mythologies manifest in founding documents and government policy, encoded in venerable frameworks of nation and belonging, and veiled in networks of property and exchange. In drawing attention to this dimension of Wilson's literary intervention in greater detail, I seek to demonstrate the complexity of nineteenth-century black women's intellectualism and the import of their resistive capacities.

Indeed, *Our Nig* discloses liberalism's coercive underside as a site of trauma while simultaneously offering witness to black defiance. In particular, *Our Nig* thinks with contemporary texts such as *The History of Mary Prince, A West Indian Slave* (1831), as Wilson invokes materiality as a valid, necessary source of meaning and worldview. Embodiment, for Wilson and for Prince, bears theoretical presence and substantive rhetorical effects, thereby revealing abstract rationalism as a self-interested performance. As the scene above intimates, Wilson likewise mobilizes her novel as a vehicle to lay bare the collusion of liberal empathy, Christianity, and capital. In this way, Wilson re-conceptualizes dominant definitions of asylum and altruism, occupying intellectual terrain reserved for presumably more radical or militant black women activists of the era such as Sojourner Truth and Ida B. Wells. Logics of intentionality, self-help, and self-possession, too, emerge as central objects of critique in *Our Nig*.

Moreover, Wilson marshals opacity as a means of countering ocular-centrism and associated liberal dictates toward order and coherence, all while drawing upon the trope of childhood to distinctly subversive ends. Specifically, Wilson appropriates the common nineteenth-century literary figure of "the disorderly girl" to issue biting social commentary and to imagine, as I will argue, a politicized picaninny animated by a "politics of joy." A consciousness informed not by indiscriminate euphoria, but by contrariness to a liberal prescriptiveness that always already delegitimates black anger, Frado's politics of joy exceeds the resistive register of Nathaniel Hawthorne's Pearl to foster a critical reassessment of contemporary notions of black innocence and of what it means to be human. By believing what Frado says, then, one can more effectively displace readings of nineteenth-century black women's writing as inauthentic or as purely sociological, situating liberal ideology critique as a significant, ongoing expression of black women's intellectual labor.

Embodied Consciousness

Though the place of the autobiographical remains a point of contention in Wilson scholarship, certain parallels between Wilson's history and that of the protagonist of *Our Nig*, Frado, are clear.[3] Wilson was born

March 15, 1825 in Milford, New Hampshire to a Margaret Ann Smith and Joshua Green. In the novel, Frado's white, indigent, and seemingly apathetic mother, Mag Smith, deposits her at the home of an unwitting, more financially secure family in the wake of the death of Frado's black father, Jim, and Mag's marriage to another man, Seth Shipley. The fictional Bellmont clan, in fact, refers to a prominent New England family for whom Wilson likely worked, the Haywards, who had close ties to the famed abolitionist group the Hutchinson Family Singers. Upon coming of age and obtaining release from indenture, Wilson—like Frado—endured chronic poverty and underemployment, frequently relying on public assistance. Accordingly, "Deserted by kindred, disabled by failing health," declares Wilson in the Preface to *Our Nig*, "I am forced to some experiment which shall aid me in maintaining myself and child without extinguishing this feeble life" (4).

And just as Frado (like her own mother, Mag, prior to the latter's marriage to Jim) is seduced and later forsaken to raise a child alone, Wilson, too, was a single mother. Toward the end of *Our Nig*, Frado is abandoned by her husband, Samuel, one of the "professed fugitives from slavery" (Wilson 64) making rounds in New England and who confesses upon his final departure that "his illiterate harangues were [mere] humbugs for hungry abolitionists" (65). Memorably, Wilson also issues an "appeal to my colored brethren universally for patronage" in the Preface in order to spur book sales to provide for her son, George Mason Wilson, following the dissolution of her marriage to Thomas Wilson (4). Upon George's death on February 15, 1860, less than six months after the publication of *Our Nig*, Wilson was forced into other experiments, such as the peddling of handmade straw hats and hair care products, and later made a name for herself in spiritualist circles. Wilson died on June 28, 1900.[4]

While archival inroads continue to be made surrounding Wilson's life post-indenture, it remains that the bulk of *Our Nig* attends to Frado's corporeality and to her violent tenure in the Bellmont household. All but three chapters and the appendix address a libidinal investment in Frado's sadistic violation and the consequences of these early experiences for her body. As a result, suffering and distress imbue many pages of the novel, suturing Wilson's aforementioned critique of liberal ideology to an increasingly important claim: materiality functions as a vital reservoir of sociopolitical awareness. Mrs. Bellmont's common use of a block of wood to prop open Frado's mouth during beatings, to take just one example, signals both a dissimulation of terror under enslavement and a hysteric form of silencing by one ever threatened by that which the black body might tell.

In the nineteenth-century U.S. landscape in which Wilson resided, popular representations of black women's form emphasized lack of mental or emotional depth and concomitant anatomization poised to maximize profit. Valuations of excess and primitiveness likewise obtained, as black adults were commonly associated with infantile stages of perception and maturity. In essence, African-American being marked a digression from fixed patterns of civility, order, and moral authority. At the same time, black women of varying regional and occupational stripes often marked the bounds of gendered discourses of cult ideology—as too "masculine" for traditional categories of the "feminine," for example— yet circulated as ever promiscuous and available for white predation and consumption. Embodiment, in Wilson's view, must be understood beyond the sphere of abject difference. The body must be foregrounded as a source of consciousness and dissent, thereby problematizing liberal discourses of objectivity.[5]

To this end, in *The Problem of Embodiment in African American Narrative*, Katherine Fishburn productively positions nineteenth-century black writing by the likes of Frederick Douglass and Harriet Wilson as contrary to discourses of reason predicated upon an ethics of abstraction. Thematizing the "quotidian experience of black bodies" in her project, Fishburn provocatively contends that "the slave narrative offered one of the most effective, if heretofore overlooked, pre-Heideggerian critiques of humanism and metaphysics ever attempted in the West" (1–2). Thus, "[W]e do not give [*Our Nig*] the reading it deserves unless we understand it as a book about the body-self," she later observes, citing Wilson's "insistence on the centrality of embodiment to the human condition and its revelation that the wealth of the bourgeoisie depends upon and is produced by the bodily effort of the working poor" (Fishburn 106). For Fishburn, performances of hegemonic rationality undergirding humanism are predicated upon disinterest and neutrality. Such disembodiment, however, covers over difference, perpetuates violence, and reinforces privilege.

Nevertheless, as opposed to a reading of Wilson's novel that focuses on her engagement with the liberal problematic, Fishburn recuperates liberal notions of universality—a reconstitution marked by her call for "our [collective] interrelatedness with other body-selves" (114). Hence, even as she emphasizes Wilson's discerning portrayal of the "deeply felt and unremittingly physical experience of poverty" (Fishburn 103), and the everyday experiences of black, laboring bodies as antithetical to Western philosophical underpinnings, an abiding optimism in the transformative capacity of interracial compassion anchors her inquiry. She cannot finally relinquish the prospect that Wilson "employ[s liberal rationality's] democratic ideals in order to define [herself] as equal to—if not indistinguishable from—white subjects" (Fishburn 1–2). I argue, on the other hand, that Wilson does not primarily seek to garner empathic appeal or to effect coalition across racial lines. Rather, she asserts a distinct mode of embodiment with intersectional effects. Ultimately, *Our Nig* clarifies the brutalization of working black women and girls and its interpenetration with illusory notions of freedom.[6]

Accordingly, Frado's young body, I submit, speaks not to Fishburn's view of the inextricability of blackness from whiteness and their respective definitions of liberty, but to the interminable chasm that separates them in the national imaginary. "From early dawn until after all were retired, was [Frado] toiling, overworked, disheartened, longing for relief," notes the narrator on one occasion (Wilson 35). Furthermore, "exposure from heat to cold, or the reverse, often destroyed her health for short intervals. She wore no shoes until after frost, and snow even, appeared; and bared her feet again before the last vestige of winter disappeared" (ibid.). As she performs never-ending, ungendering duties as maid, cook, nurse, farmhand, and driver—the completion of which are never deemed satisfactory by Mrs. Bellmont—Frado's swollen face and boxed ears bear out the speciousness of the Protestant work ethic and other mainstream liberal discourses of progress and self-possession at the Bellmont homestead.[7] Her weary limbs and increasingly stooped stature render pastoral images of antebellum New England suspect, extending an incisive critique of the ways in which racial and class dominance are inscribed onto laboring bodies.

As Frado's sensory experience attests, liberal autonomy is tethered to acquisition and ownership, while circulating as readily accessible to all. Indeed, "Frado's bodily testimony forcefully exposes the underside of . . . Jeffersonian discourse," as R. J. Ellis corroborates. "[She] is drained of strength by the Bellmonts' extraction of profit and then subjected to the rigors of public charity, in a grim economics that, whilst rooted in the particular racist constructions of American life, portrays the ways in which American freedom is constructed around class, property and value" (Ellis 156). Thus, as liberalism and Western rationalization affect objectivity and impartiality, in fact, the very prospect of Jeffersonian (among other Lockean-derived) reason necessitates disciplining, managing, and often erasing "unreasonable" bodies. Put differently, class mobility and liberty rely on the elision of the material conditions that sustain such positions in the first place.[8]

Wilson, by contrast, consistently mobilizes Frado's battered, pained body as a site of rupture and of competing truth. Nowhere is this more palpable, perhaps, than in the novel's utmost moment of black contrariness and refusal: Wilson's dramatic revision of Frederick Douglass's and Mr. Covey's legendary brawl. In a crucial shift from Douglass's 1845 *Narrative*, Frado overcomes her mistress by retracting her labor rather than resorting to combat. Upon Mr. Bellmont's advice—"when she was SURE she did not deserve a whipping, to avoid it if she could"—the young girl subsequently stops her mistress from shattering a piece of lumber over her head (Wilson 54; emphasis in original). "You cannot endure beating as you once could," Mr. Bellmont had warned (54). Thus, standing "like one who feels the stirring of free and independent thoughts," Frado vehemently asserts, "Stop! Strike me, and I'll never work a mite more for you" (ibid.). Specifically, Frado marshals her bodily knowledge to disrupt the order of things. Cognizant, in corporeal terms, of her status within prevailing processes of capital accumulation, Frado destabilizes her mistress's perpetual disavowal of black value and black difference. Mrs. Bellmont's compliance in this moment, though fleeting, signals the force of Frado's objection to ostensibly abstract logics of nation and belonging rooted in power and property.[9]

In this sense, *Our Nig* becomes together with texts such as *The History of Mary Prince, A West Indian Slave* (1831). Penning, with amanuensis Susanna (Strickland) Moodie, the first narrative by a black woman published in Britain, Mary Prince similarly invokes embodiment as a politicized site of discernment and recognition. As Prince narrates her exploits at the hands of brutal owners in Bermuda, Turks Island, Antigua, and London in *The History of Mary Prince*, distinctions between indenture and enslavement, region and temporality collapse as Wilson and Prince tender strikingly consonant and graphic knowledge claims. Of one of her mistresses, Prince reveals, "She taught me to do all sorts of household work; to wash and bake, pick cotton and wool, and wash floors, and cook. And she taught me (how can I ever forget it!) more things than these" (14). To the generic domestic catalogue, Prince thereafter concludes, "she caused me to know the exact difference between the smart of the rope, the cart-whip, and the cow-skin, when applied to my naked body by her own cruel hand" (ibid.). Prince's own excessively violent and traumatic experiences are also compounded by those of others forced to endure similar fates, or worse, such as pregnant Aunt Hetty and old, lame Daniel, whose ruthless beatings were, in Prince's words, "always present to my mind for many a day" (16). Indeed, "In telling my own sorrows, I cannot pass by those of my fellow-slaves—for when I think of my own griefs, I remember theirs," declares Prince (22).[10] Stylized representations of infected and infested wounds, bloodied and bruised flesh, boils and pinched necks and arms, articulate Prince's consciousness of the expendability of blackness as well as its capacity for subversive telling.

Ultimately, Prince—as would Wilson—contests perceived lack of sentience and enforced materiality by locating the body as a means to sound a critique of black abjection. With and through the body, Prince targets the instrumentality of racial and class dominance, insisting on black meaning in excess of the constraints of chattel. In a flicker of resistance especially resonant with Frado's aforementioned stand against Mrs. Bellmont, the narrator details a bold proclamation by Prince to her master, Capt. I——: "I then took courage and said that I could stand the floggings no longer; that I was weary of my life, and therefore I had run away to my mother" (18). Here, in a remarkable assertion of black materiality and black maternity, Prince shifts prevailing standards of knowledge formation; her body and experience theorize a sense of black humanity and kinship consistently demeaned or made invisible.

Reading Wilson and Prince in concert, then, facilitates a denaturalization of liberal imperative toward universal moral and political subjectivity. In truth, mainstream iterations of democratic promise and normative reason fail to account for Wilson and Prince's respective realities. Propelling lived and felt meaning as a source of insight, *Our Nig* positions the problematization of abstract rationality as a prominent intervention of nineteenth-century black women's prose.

A Sense of Fellow Feeling

Significantly, ruptures of contrariness attuned to the degrading effects of the liberal problematic are also evident in *Our Nig* through a demystification of the trope of good intentions. Notably, throughout the bulk of the novel, Wilson condemns kindheartedness, consigning superficial concern to the realm of alibi.[11] As Vorris Nunley argues in a modern context, "While individual intention matters, rationalities mediate intentionality, operating on the level of power, categories, and framing . . . who gets to speak as a citizen and how, and what behaviors, rhetorics, knowledges, and identities are deemed legitimate, acceptable, normative, and natural within the American imaginary as citizenship" (12). In fact, what shifts if and when we read Wilson's novel principally as an indictment of liberal humanist compassion? In what ways does the text enable us to understand the latter as a performance with meager returns for black laboring bodies? What does it mean to take seriously the ways in which an apparent sense of fellow feeling does not diminish, but rather colludes with Christianity and capital to exacerbate Frado's pain? And how might we inquire into what Wilson is after, without taking the ameliorative thrust of liberal consideration and care for granted?[12]

As foils to Mrs. Bellmont and her filial protégé, Mary, Mr. Bellmont, Aunt Abby, daughter Jane, and sons James and Jack immediately elicit readerly identification. Unencumbered by the repellent, racist pleasure structuring the domineering Bellmont women's relation to their servant, these characters ostensibly shelter Frado from the women's violent machinations. However, as the introduction to this chapter makes plain, it is precisely through the characterization of figures such as James Bellmont that Wilson mounts her attack on the well-intentioned. As a collective, the Bellmont men and other sympathizers condone Frado's dehumanization by adopting what I refer to as "postures of abettal." Through these largely guilt-inspired, faith-derived acts, they simultaneously mask and sanction sedimented hierarchies of power and privilege.

James achieves this not only by dismissing Frado's "knotty queries" as they relate to race and religion, but by countenancing her near self-immolation in the weeks leading up to his death. On this subject, Wilson's narrator reveals that "[w]ith all his bodily suffering, all his anxiety for his family, whom he might not live to protect, [James] did not forget Frado. He shielded her from many beatings, and every day imparted religious instructions" (40). However, Wilson deftly juxtaposes this with the narrator's subsequent statement that "[n]o one, but his wife, could move him [in and out of bed] so easily as Frado; so that in addition to her daily toil she was often deprived of her rest at night" (ibid.). James "is fixated on the state of Frado's soul," as one critic observes: "he cannot see that his own selfish need for Frado's ministrations is wearing her out and ruining her health. . . . *Even this caring and compassionate man* has the power—and apparently the will—while he is on his deathbed to work Frado until she no longer has the strength to stand" (Fishburn 112; emphasis added). Part and parcel of James's implicitly sexualized posture of abettal, then, are tokens of charity and accommodation that hold out to Frado the promise of spiritual salvation without threatening the Bellmonts' personal and economic standing.

Moreover, Frado "*insisted* on being called [by James]," the narrator explains; "she wished to show her *love* for one who had been such a friend to her" (Wilson 41; emphasis added). Ultimately, James's paternalistic compassion signals tacit approval of Frado's subjection, while transforming any deviance on her part from her ever more diversified workload into the appearance of thanklessness or into a source of profound personal guilt. James relies on liberal and Christian discourses of sanctuary and asylum to cover over the Bellmonts' mutual investment in extorting Frado's use-value at all costs.[13]

Much of this also coincides with an earlier conversation between James and Aunt Abby in which the former recalls overhearing Frado sobbing in despair in the family barn. James proceeds to ventriloquize Frado's bitter, suicidal rant before, in an abrupt shift, he informs his aunt that "I took the *opportunity* to combat the notions she *seemed to entertain* respecting the loneliness of her condition and want of sympathizing friends" (Wilson 40; emphasis added). During the course of the remembered conversation, James positions the cruelty of his mother as the exception rather than the rule in the North, and declares that Frado surely "might hope for better things in the future" (ibid.). In *Scenes of Subjection*, Saidiya Hartman usefully critiques precisely such processes of empathetic identification, the slippery politics of which reinscribes an unequal set of power relations along racial lines. According to Hartman, empathy installs a dynamic predicated upon a "phantasmic vehicle of identification," a substitution contingent upon the disappearing, or invisibility, of the racialized object. Put another way, interracial empathy "requires that the white body be positioned in the place of the black body in order to make this suffering visible and intelligible" (Hartman 19). Within the space of Wilson's novel, Frado's striking claim that "No one cares for me[,] only to get my work" (Wilson 40) only accrues meaning via its displacement by James's subsequent mediation and opportunistic shoring up of white liberal subjectivity.

When James later discloses that, "Having spoken these words of comfort, I rose with the resolution that if I recovered my health I would take her home with me," one indeed wonders, comfort for whom? In fact, Frado remains voiceless for the entire interlude. Her understanding of (black) death as a site of resistive possibility—"Why can't I die? Oh, what have I to live for?" she cries out in the Bellmonts' barn—is reduced by James to juvenile ignorance.[14] Making visible the "facile intimacy" enabled by the empathy about which Hartman theorizes, James's relationship with Frado demonstrates how black captive bodies persistently serve as fungible commodities for white economies, material and ideological.[15]

Aunt Abby's response to James's anecdote in this scene is likewise symptomatic: "I don't know what your mother would do without her; still, I wish she was away" (Wilson 40). Throughout the narrative, Aunt Abby's posture of abettal merges covert acts of refuge with glimmers of apparent defiance. That is, in the wake of Mrs. Bellmont's brutal rages, Aunt Abby secretly supplies Frado with pastries and other provisions. Moreover, she emboldens the young girl's spiritual yearnings, and intercedes with her own male relatives (if futilely) on Frado's behalf. "I think I should rule my own house, John," Abby quietly scolds her brother on one occasion, urging him to stand up to his wife and protect the servant girl (Wilson 25).[16] Yet Aunt Abby extends considerate gestures only insofar as they do not bring down Mrs. Bellmont's "reserved wrath on *her* defenceless head" (Wilson 25; emphasis added). Mrs. Bellmont already views Abby's entitlement to a portion of the family homestead as theft from her husband, the rightful heir, and Aunt Abby risks little in Frado's name that might imperil her tenuous property rights. Another Bellmont daughter, the "apparently uninterested" Jane (Wilson 15), renders her own posture of abettal in similar terms. Jane could not "brave the iron will of her mother": "Kind words and affectionate glances were the only expressions of sympathy she could safely indulge in," discloses the narrator (Wilson 21).

Moreover, Aunt Abby's attempts to convert Frado are buttressed by a disciplinary tolerance tethered to the dictates of capital. Hence, the girl's occasional outbursts of anger are generally met with Aunt Abby's pious alarm followed by an immediate injunction to get back to work (Wilson 43). Further complicating P. Gabrielle Foreman's interrogation of Abby's "analogous disenfranchisement" with Frado within the confines of the Bellmont home (*Activist Sentiments* 53), I argue that Abby's intercession rarely exceeds the register of tepid protest. Her plight exists in hierarchical relation to the experiences of her young charge, obscures Abby's implication in Frado's struggles, and, poignantly, displays the drawbacks of a liberal ambit of alliance.

Mr. Bellmont, in addition, perhaps epitomizes the effects of what Ellis aptly characterizes as the novel's "quietly savage portraits of the male family members' persistent failure to intervene effectively on Frado's behalf" (110). For Ellis, the conditions that Wilson depicts provisionally upset conventional gender formations in the (white) domestic sphere, as male characters cede, for all intents and purposes, free reign to a vengeful matriarch. Indeed, Ellis concludes, at least within the chapters focused on Frado's indenture, Mr. Bellmont's "intermittent assumptions of patriarchal power are precarious" (111). Mr. Bellmont's admission that "Women rule the earth and all in it," in the oft-cited conversation with his sister briefly alluded to above, reinforces such an interpretation. In a gesture of self-interest akin to that displayed by Aunt Abby, Mr. Bellmont justifies his complacency by referencing the hellish conditions to which he would likely be subject if he openly opposed his wife's demands, before finally "saunter[ing] out to the barn to await the quieting of the storm" (Wilson 25).

However, Wilson's recurrent choice to cast Mrs. Bellmont's violence against Frado's body as tempests during which Mr. Bellmont casually disappears at will indexes not the ambiguity of patriarchal prerogative, but rather its fulfillment. The privilege that structures and sustains patriarchy, in fact, authorizes mobility and absence as apposite expressions of maleness. Mr. Bellmont "was a man who seldom decided controversies at home," corroborates the narrator, yet "the word once spoken admitted of no appeal" (Wilson 18). Mr. Bellmont's posture of abettal, then, hinges precisely on his capacity to retreat or reassert dominance arbitrarily and with impunity.

Following one of Frado's displays of "sauciness," or purported affronts to her employers' delicate sensibilities, Mrs. Bellmont viciously kicks Frado until those rushing in to inquire about the noise grant an opportunity for escape. Significantly, Frado's disappearance lasts far longer than anticipated in this instance, extending beyond the dinner hour and James's arrival on the night coach. "I'll not leave much of her beauty to be seen, if she comes in sight," Mrs. Bellmont warns amid others' growing panic (Wilson 26).

Having by now returned from his jaunt, Mr. Bellmont subsequently intervenes. "Mr. Bellmont raised his calm, determined eye full upon

[Mrs. Bellmont], and said, in a decisive manner," the narrator observes, "'You shall not strike, or scald, or skin her, as you call it, if she comes back again. Remember!' and he brought his hand down upon the table" (Wilson 26). Mr. Bellmont's mandate starkly shifts the dynamic of control in the scene; an organized search for Frado commences right away. Yet his ongoing absent presence affirms his manhood at Frado's expense. That is, his vacillation between neglect and advocacy at whim solidifies his masculinity without regard for Frado's continuing fight for basic survival.

In a later scenario, Mrs. Bellmont again seeks retaliation against Frado, this time for divulging to James that his mother had forbidden Aunt Abby to attend to him on his deathbed. Familiar accoutrements of chattel slavery, including the raw-hide and a block of wood between the teeth of the victim, adorn Mrs. Bellmont's spectacle of supremacy. However, as readers ultimately learn, "Frado was thus tortured when Mr. Bellmont came in . . . and seeing her situation, quickly removed the instrument of torture, and sought his wife. Their conversation we will omit; suffice it to say, a storm raged which required many days to exhaust its strength" (Wilson 49). Again, Mr. Bellmont turns up and seizes control of the situation. Presumably, he "sought his wife" for disciplinary action and to reinstate his authority over and above all bodies in the Bellmont domain. But here, the novel's abiding metaphor of the "storm"— earlier termed "a whirlwind charged with fire, daggers and spikes" (Wilson 15)—as representative of a distinctly feminine chaos also collapses in on itself. It remains unclear which Bellmont spouse entirely drives this eruption, each perhaps absorbing the other, as Frado is basically abandoned to seek any semblance of calm. Ultimately, Mr. Bellmont's manifestation of white, patriarchal privilege crystallizes, rather than inverts, traditional gender roles, as Mrs. Bellmont's sadism and Mr. Bellmont's well-intentioned mediation work in conjunction to maintain the status quo.

Lastly, son Jack Bellmont's posture of abettal also encompasses other family members' aura of earnest concern, though it appears marked by a distinct joviality and playfulness. Indeed, Jack's overflowing laughter permeates the kitchen in a notable scene in which Mrs. Bellmont prevents Frado from using a clean dinner plate for her meal. In response to James's recent insistence that "our Nig" dine at the table with the rest of the family, Mrs. Bellmont compels Frado to eat from the former's soiled dinner plate. "To eat after James, his wife or Jack, would have been pleasant; but to be commanded to do what was disagreeable by her mistress BECAUSE it was disagreeable, was trying," relates the narrator (Wilson 38; emphasis in original). Thus, Frado lets her dog, Fido, lick the plate clean before carrying on with her dinner. Following the incident, Jack retrieved "a bright, silver half-dollar from his pocket, [and] threw it at Nig, saying, 'There, take that; 'twas worth paying for'" (ibid.).

Here, Jack cheapens Frado's pointed critique of her dehumanized status in the Bellmont homestead. His patronizing gesture empties Nig's performance of its sarcastic intent, effectively reducing her to an object of personal amusement worthy of minstrel fare. Further, while Frado expressly cites Jack's presence as the source of her bravery, crediting him for a lack of retribution by Mrs. Bellmont in this moment, Jack thoroughly relishes the event without taking into account the consequences for its creator. According to the narrator, after this particular insult, Mrs. Bellmont, "only smothered her resentment until a convenient opportunity offered. The first time she was left alone with Nig, she gave her a thorough beating, to bring up arrearages" (Wilson 38). Throughout the novel, Jack mocks Frado's experiences, uncovering humor in the material conditions from which his race, gender, and class exempt him.

On the whole, Jack's posture of abettal oscillates between lightheartedness and apparent pity. On a separate occasion, finding Nig with "her mouth wedged apart, her face swollen, and full of pain" after a confrontation with his sister, Mary, and his mother, Jack promptly "relieved her jaws, brought her some supper, took her to her room, comforted her as well as he knew how, sat by her till she fell asleep, and then left the sitting room" (Wilson 20). In passing by his mother, he exclaims, "If that was the way Frado was to be treated, he hoped she would never wake again!" (ibid.). Excessive and unwarranted, the menacing effects of the Bellmont women surpass the bounds of morality, even mortality, in Jack's estimation.

Yet the limits of such a sentimental perspective, as Valerie Smith establishes in relation to Harriet Jacobs's 1861 narrative *Incidents in the Life of a Slave Girl*, are glaring. Jack's "self-indulgent mythicization of death," not unlike that of Miss Fanny on behalf of Linda Brent, patently prioritizes his own emotional well-being and sense of personal comfort (Smith 43). The prospect of Frado's demise supersedes any sustained desire for racial or class justice, and before long, Jack's inevitably cheerful demeanor returns. Though, in and of itself, the interracial dimension of the Bellmonts' relationship with Frado does not preclude shared understanding, attentiveness to the nuances of subjection and control in the context of antebellum progressivism—as well as to the intricacies of early black women writers' intellectual responses to it—must not be minimized.

Jack's liberal compassion, informed by his seeming delight in Frado's pain, also engages the specter of sexual abuse pervading the novel. During the family's initial conversation about the possibility of keeping the girl after Mag abandons her at their front door, Jack offers, "Keep her . . . she's real handsome and bright, and not very black, either" (Wilson 16). And in a subsequent exchange with Frado following Mrs. Bellmont's shaving of the former's signature "glossy ringlets," Jack replies, "Thought you were getting handsome, did she? Same old story, is it; knocks and bumps? Better times coming; never fear, Nig" (Wilson 38). Indeed, Jack good-naturedly sanitizes both Frado's blackness and his mother's savagery, frequently calling attention to the attractiveness of Frado's mixed-raced body in the process.

A range of critics, including Carla Peterson, Johnnie Stover, and Ronna C. Johnson, extend similar claims regarding the Bellmont men.[17] "The Bellmont sons' repeated references to Frado's beauty and their frequent presence in her sleeping quarters as well as her presence in their own are particularly sexually suggestive," adds Claudia Tate (48). Other readings point to Mrs. Bellmont as Frado's likeliest sexual tormenter.[18] As Nell Painter asserts in relation to Northern-born and -bred Sojourner Truth's sexual abuse by her mistress Sally Dumont, only implicitly addressed in Truth's *Narrative*, "Then, as now, the sexual abuse of young women by men is deplored but recognized as common. Less easily acknowledged, then and now, is the fact that there are women who violate children" (16). Without diminishing the significance of Frado's exploitation at the hands of multiple perpetrators, it remains that Jack's sexualized reproduction of exoticized tragic mulatta iconography powerfully underwrites her subjection. Jack's relation to "Our Nig"—"How different this appellative sounded from him; he said it in such a tone, with such a rogueish look!" observes the narrator (Wilson 38)—in the end, signals an all-too-familiar, if mirthful, iteration of uneven power and possession, put on display by almost all of Frado's ostensible allies.

Finally, Jack's acquisitive motivations, a willingness to condone Frado's maltreatment as long as it contributes to his own welfare or to the economic stability of the Bellmont family as a whole, likewise surface following his own marriage. Despite Mrs. Bellmont's stern warnings to all of her offspring against choosing a partner from a lower class, Jack marries a poor, orphaned woman named Jenny. As Jack travels to seek employment to support his new family, Mrs. Bellmont fabricates tales of Jack's and Jenny's respective infidelities, diverts their attempted correspondence to one another, and subjects Jenny to public shaming. Though it is Frado who eventually eludes Mrs. Bellmont's trap and expedites Jack's homecoming, he returns solely to free his wife. Frado—the family's sole laborer—remains, despite far worse handling.

Taken together, Jack, James, Abby, Jane, and Mr. Bellmont enact postures of abettal that do not counter Mary and Mrs. Bellmont's overtly racist, denigrating conduct, but rather contribute to Frado's manipulation and misuse. Thus, Wilson deploys characterization in her novel in order to problematize dominant discourses of altruism and goodwill. By clarifying a spectrum of violent effects attending liberal notions of compassion, Wilson makes visible affective constraints and hierarchical economic primacy embedded in American liberalism. By first mobilizing a politics of embodiment, and later detailing the collusion of empathy, Christianity, and capital reinforcing the liberal problematic, Wilson intervenes in self-perpetuating origin stories of majority communities in the antebellum North. New England emerges not as a terrain of unqualified opportunity and choice, but as one of consistent unfreedom. Enriching existing perspectives on nineteenth-century women's literary resistance, Wilson positions the reconceptualization of liberal ideologies of selfhood, privilege, and consent as a significant legacy of black feminist knowledge production.

Black Matters

Just as Wilson's novel contests prevailing principles of disembodied rationalism and well-meaning benevolence, *Our Nig* further evokes figurations of blackness and of escape to problematize an Enlightenment-refined ethos of comprehensibility. In many contexts of Western liberal humanism, rational formation is hinged to objective reality, to that which can be accessed or seen without obstruction. Transparency, in essence, begets veracity. The search for this eternal, graspable truth—attainable by way of apparently unencumbered reason—yields freedom and moral command. Forgoing the constitutive definition, precision, and clarity underlying the liberal problematic, however, Wilson's youthful and indentured Frado calls up a tradition of insurgency predicated on deliberate obscurity. She constructs abstruseness at odds with established frameworks of universality and individual progress, representing diverse modes of black female experience and alternate processes of making meaning.

Indeed, at the very outset of the novel, Frado's mother foreshadows her daughter's subsequent disappearance into a dim and gloomy unknown. "Frado is such a wild, frolicky thing," Mag suggests, "and means to do jest as she's a mind to" (Wilson 12). When Mag and her partner, Seth, later approach the young girl about moving to a new home, Frado immediately flees. Thereafter, "All effort proved unavailing," declares the narrator, as neither nightfall nor a small search party produces the outlier (ibid.). Finally, both Frado and a second missing "little colored girl" resurface:

> [A]nd from them and their attendant [Mag and Seth] learned that they went to walk, and not minding the direction soon found themselves lost. They had climbed fences and walls, passed through thickets and marshes, and when night approached selected a thick cluster of shrubbery as a covert for the night. They were discovered by the person who now restored them, chatting of their prospects, Frado attempting to banish the childish fears of her companion. As they were miles from home, they were kindly cared for until morning. (Wilson 12–13)

Though Frado's playmate appears panic-stricken and fearful during their predicament, Frado consciously pursues a dark and wooded course. Rather than haphazard meandering, Frado's lengthy nocturnal trek and careful selection of a "thick cluster of shrubbery" signal a purposeful activation of the coverture of blackness. Moreover, among all those portrayed by Wilson as relieved by the girls' reemergence, Frado's name is conspicuously absent. Following one critic's call that "[w]e might, then, examine the potential for swamp iconography to signify on the politics of representing black resistance efforts in antebellum popular culture" (Brooks 105), I maintain that Wilson's account of black elusiveness in this instance, if fleeting, installs a province of black political expression that is in conflict with dominant standards of knowledge production and to which Frado must necessarily return.

Usefully, historian Stephanie M. H. Camp addresses intersections between spatiality and power that coincide with Wilson's critical engagement with opacity in Northern antebellum terrain. Though Camp's study, *Closer to Freedom*, focuses on the context of enslavement in particular, she extrapolates from various iterations of nineteenth-century black autobiography and far-reaching expanses of colonialism to consider the interplay between complicity and resistance.[19] According to Camp, women may erect "rival geographies" amid conditions of internment. While such arenas "did not threaten to overthrow American slavery, nor . . . provide slaves with autonomous spaces," they effectively disrupted panoptic surveillance and developed other epistemologies for harnessing the plantation sphere (7). Truancy and absenteeism, as well as harboring communities of outlying slaves, further typify black women's resistant cartographies in this regard. Though Frado's actions do not instigate widespread insurrection, or influence Mag's and Seth's intentions to dispose of her, I argue that they do serve a vestibular function. This preliminary rival geography leverages darkness to facilitate unauthorized black shelter, privacy, even intimacy, anticipating Frado's future manipulation of liberal protocol at the Bellmont homestead.

In fact, often during the course of her indenture with the Bellmonts, Frado seeks release from torment in liminal spaces, including the woods, as well as in outdoor locales like the family barn. On one occasion, referenced briefly in the discussion of Mr. Bellmont's posture of abettal, Mrs. Bellmont's characteristic violence prompts Frado's swift retreat from the domestic realm. All but Mary and Mrs. Bellmont display trepidation and alarm when Frado still cannot be found after dusk. Then, in a scene resonating with the sprightly romp spotlighted above, the narrator observes, "Jack started, the dog followed, and soon capered on before, far, far into the fields, over walls and through fences, *into a piece of swampy land*" in order to locate the absent girl-servant (Wilson 27; emphasis added). Finding sanctuary in the doubly dark veil of night and Northern everglades, Frado mobilizes "spectacular opacity" in order to dispute the terms of her containment.[20]

In this literary adaptation of spectacular opacity, Wilson undermines persistent notions of blackness as criminal, as threatening, as lack. Contrary to Western imperatives of fixed meaning and coherent subjectivity, spectacular opacity positions darkness as a potential site of "narrative insurgency, discursive survival, and epistemological resistance" (Brooks 108). In the same vein, swamp imagery functions as an especially powerful signifier through which blackness is re-embodied and re-conceptualized. Harkening back to the 1831 rebellion of Nat Turner, among others, maroonage and separatism in shaded bayous and other wetlands represent a striking revision of spatio-temporal authority and control while operating as distinct symbols of opposition (Brooks 104). Thus, by appropriating obscurity as a competing code of intelligibility, artists articulate blackness in excess of difference. Here, in the context of antebellum New England, Wilson draws upon analogous imagery to carve out a space for black solitude and healing, as well as for Northern black female defiance.

As opposed to a mutually agreed-upon homecoming for Wilson's protagonist, then, the narrator makes known that "Jack followed close and soon appeared to James, who was quite in the rear, *coaxing and forcing* Frado along with him" (Wilson 27; emphasis added). As Foreman aptly observes, "Transmogrifying into metaphorical slave catchers in this scene, her allies return her to what they call 'safety,' but to what the text, as does Mrs. Bellmont, might call her 'rightful place'" (*Activist Sentiments* 56). Ultimately, Frado consciously substitutes the cipher of obscurity for the ineptness of liberal humanist intentionality and compassion. In this way, she thwarts mainstream ideals of lucidity and logic, those yoked to specifications of capital that reduce her to little more than property or a naïve, domestic charge in need of salvation. For Wilson, opacity does not provoke disorder. Instead, it calls reigning modes of racial and class privilege into question.

Such a reading perhaps gains even more traction if one situates the entire preface to *Our Nig* as a willfully opaque theoretical framework. As would Linda Brent/Harriet Jacobs in her wake, Wilson confesses, "I do not pretend to divulge every transaction in my own life, which the unprejudiced would declare unfavorable in comparison with treatment of legal bondmen; I have purposely omitted what would most provoke shame in our good anti-slavery friends at home" (4). This gesture— alongside feminine expressions of authorial deference—registers black women writers' particular vulnerabilities in light of the tenuousness of antebellum freedom.

However, given a similar refrain in the penultimate paragraph of the novel's final chapter, I suggest that this passage also functions as a refusal of implicitly gendered and ethnocentric Enlightenment touchstones, including transparency and coherence, and thus constitutes an act of resistance. "Refuse not, because some part of her history is unknown, save by the Omniscient God. Enough has been unrolled to demand your sympathy and aid," the narrator concludes (Wilson 66). Indeed, Wilson's oblique words depose a traditional abolitionist preamble, by the likes of

Frederick Douglass or Lydia Maria Child, or a supplemental portfolio. Contrarily, she crafts her own palpably dense prelude, bookended with yet another striking claim to indistinctness. By opting for opacity as a valid means of not just concealing but of articulating embodied truths of black escape and black being, Wilson reimagines Western patterns of knowability.

Child's Play

In addition to forwarding opacity as a means of engaging the liberal problematic, a manipulation of the trope of childhood in the novel merits sustained attention as a legitimate mode of black women's literary resistance. While considerable liberal ideology aspires to moral humanness accessible to all, perhaps no figure embodies said goodness and virtue more than a child. Simple and unknowing, the young occasion the utmost honor and protection. Still, as Robin Bernstein reminds us, "[t] he connection between childhood and innocence is not essential but is instead historically located" (4). Beginning in the late eighteenth and early nineteenth centuries, "sentimental childlike innocence manifested through the performed transcendence of social categories of class, gender, and . . . race" (Bernstein 6). Epitomizing liberal notions of purity and innocence, as well as the unmitigated capacity for liberty and rights, children encompass an ideal source of tenderness and affection.

In fact, various episodes in *Our Nig* work to theorize youth as a fraught construct, both romanticizing Frado's modesty and naivety and casting the sanctity of childhood into unrelieved crisis. For instance, when Mrs. Bellmont begrudgingly allows a seven-year-old Frado to attend school for the first time alongside her daughter, Mary, their teacher, Miss Marsh, immediately attempts to recuperate Frado's juvenility. That is, of Miss Marsh's charge to her class as it relates to their new classmate, the narrator explains, she "reminded them of their duties to the poor and friendless; their cowardice in attacking a young innocent child; referred them to one who looks not on outward appearances, but on the heart" (Wilson 18). Further, the narrator characterizes as "the most agreeable sound which ever meets the ear of sorrowing, grieving childhood" Miss Marsh's subsequent claim to her students that, "She looks like a good girl; I think I shall love her, so lay aside all prejudice, and vie with each other in shewing kindness and good-will to one who seems different from you" (ibid.).

Apparently, the intervention works, temporarily positioning Mary— rather than Nig—as social outcast at the school. Miss Marsh, likely based on educator Abby A. Kent (1802–1857), delivers a lecture fixing childhood as inherently moral. She reinforces ideologies of the sacredness of the family and of motherhood (and of maternal surrogates, including teachers) as bastions against base, worldly influences in the lives of youth. Inquiring, in effect, "What would Jesus do?," Miss Marsh centers her critique of petty bigotry and intolerance in a duty to preserve the chaste character of childhood.

However, fractures embedded in the same scene crystallize the aforementioned instability of the category "child," exposing the racial and class privilege underlying Miss Marsh's formulation. Violent, if familiar, racial slurs and other rituals of public shaming announce Frado's arrival on the premises of the schoolhouse in the third chapter of the text. She is depicted "with scanty clothing and bared feet" and looking "chagrined and grieved," her experiences inciting a slippage from the controlling iconography of youthfulness in liberal humanist discourse. Even Miss Marsh's qualified act of reclaiming leaves something to be desired. Though the schoolteacher asserts that every child deserves early years free of turmoil, this inviolable right endures precisely through a neutralization of Frado's difference.

That is, while Eva Allegra Raimon writes that "Miss Marsh is perhaps Frado's most effective ally" (Boggis, Raimon, and White 172), one might also align Miss Marsh's tepid performance with that of the Bellmont clan, or think of it as yet another illumination of the detrimental effects of the liberal problematic. Based on a leader in the common school movement in 1830s New England, Miss Marsh likely sought to construct a "community that offers a model of a republican government founded on principles of genuine equality" (Boggis, Raimon, and White 178), yet Wilson arguably condemns, rather than exalts, such lofty ethics. Miss Marsh flattens out Frado's cultural variance, I suggest, in the name of shallow schoolroom amity. In effect, students benefit not from heightened sociopolitical awareness of the black girl-servant in their midst, but from the prospect of a hollowed-out sameness.

If, as Raimon concludes, "this scene [on Frado's first day of school] goes as far as is possible in the context of its production explicitly to advocate for racial equity" (Boggis, Raimon, and White 173), Wilson implicitly positions this fact as far more disconcerting than celebratory. Mrs. Bellmont, too, self-interestedly acknowledges Frado's racialized-cum-moral, if finally assimilable, distinction from other young girls, particularly from previous child-servants in her employ, maintaining that she "felt that she could not well spare one who could so well adapt herself to all departments—man, boy, housekeeper, etc." (Wilson 59). Lower-class children and children of color, then, were not deemed fundamentally virtuous or vulnerable, but excessive and exploitable.

Picaninny Pleasure

Wilson likewise disturbs ostensibly progressive stereotypes of childhood by borrowing from mainstream literary convention. Locating Frado's characterization in *Our Nig* as an arrogation of the popular literary figure of "the disorderly girl," scholar Lisa E. Green cites overlap between Wilson's text and novels by the likes of Susan Warner, Maria Cummins, and Nathaniel Hawthorne. "Frado-as-picaninny," a theory I articulate below, extends beyond the terrain of liberal custom, however, to underscore additional affinities between enslavement and Northern class exploitation, while simultaneously foregrounding Wilson's critique of capital. Moreover, the notion of Frado-as-picaninny reflects a consciousness validating black rage—a sentiment demeaned within the context of normative liberal comportment—at the same time as it advances, in the words of Lindon Barrett, a "politics of joy."

In their respective bestsellers *The Wide, Wide World* (1850) and *The Lamplighter* (1854), Warner's and Cummins's wayward young heroines Ellen Montgomery and Gerty appear willful and full of rage. Though "in both novels the heroine's fury is justified by the mistreatment that provokes it," Warner and Cummins both marshal their wildly successful sentimental novels "to impose a sense of order on a changing and unstable society by instilling self control and religious faith in 'disorderly' young girls" (Boggis, Raimon, and White 143). Additionally, Green joins Claudia Tate in tracing coincidences between the corporeal and affective attributes of Frado and Pearl, daughter of Hawthorne's Hester Prynne in *The Scarlet Letter*, also published in 1850. Strikingly beautiful, as signified by shining eyes and flowing hair, and demonstrating a corresponding spiritedness, Frado and Pearl execute unruly resistance that incisively troubles institutionalized religion, circumscribing social customs, and gender norms.[21] Though for Green, Hawthorne's, Warner's, and Cummins's novels reflect different objectives, each finally contains the radicalism of girl heroines via dominant discourses of Christianity and domesticity (144).

Yet Wilson mobilizes familiar symbols of childhood in the landscape of mainstream nineteenth-century American fiction and pushes them in new directions. Even as Wilson includes a generic "disorderly girl" in *Our Nig*, Frado departs from Ellen's, Gerty's, and Pearl's eventual processes of maturation and womanly development, visions projected by mainstream authors for whom Frado's racialized body constituted the bounds of femininity. Instead, I argue here, she approximates the form of the "picaninny," an expression descending from a form of nineteenth-century American currency: the picayune.[22] Ever cognizant of collapsing the terror of Southern bondage with the tenuousness of black freedom in the North, Wilson nevertheless imports the figure of the picaninny in order to emphasize the manipulation and objectification of Frado's body. Indeed, Frado's sometimes-mirthful, sometimes-irate antics problematize the terms of her containment, unsettling existing logics of value, productivity, and exchange. Through Frado, Wilson theorizes the distinct epistemological import of black childhood, particularly its capacity to defy the liberal problematic.

In contrast to the stagnant "happy darkie" image, Frado-as-picaninny displays a nearly unfathomable, ecstatic sense of delight that disrupts ordinary measures of order and control. In readers' initial introduction to Frado in chapter two, the narrator declares, "Frado, as they called one of Mag's children, was a beautiful mulatto, with long, curly black hair, and handsome, roguish eyes, sparkling with an exuberance of spirit almost beyond restraint" (Wilson 11). Thus, from the very beginning—in addition to exotic features commonly associated with "tragic mulatta"-types—the narrator calls attention to Frado's energy. Inextricable from a palpable slyness on her part, signaled here by her "roguish eyes," Frado's dynamism unsettles the borders of strictly raced spheres of biological difference and pathology.[23] Instead, she activates a profound, non-rational mode of relation.

"Her jollity was not to be quenched by whipping or scolding," the narrator adds tellingly, and "in the kitchen, and among her schoolmates, the pent up fires burst forth" (Wilson 21). Though narrativized in the national imaginary as excessive emotion, Frado's "pent up fires" emerge, in fact, as a form of self-expression that obscures normative opposition between joy and fury, and flouts dominant registers of coherence and restraint, including whipping and scolding. To be sure, "[s]he would venture far beyond propriety," the narrator affirms, alluding to sundry types of mischief perpetuated by Frado, from "infantile pranks" (Wilson 10) with her sibling before arriving at the Bellmonts to simulating fire by puffing cigar smoke into an unsuspecting teacher's desk drawer (21). Crucially, however, Frado's conduct amounts to more than cheap thrills and immature tricks; she gestures to an elsewhere space of creativity and imaginative fulfillment. According to the narrator, "When she had none of the family around to be merry with, she would amuse herself with the animals," cavorting in the Bellmont barn and teaching lessons to stubborn sheep (Wilson 30). Simply put, while her gleeful demeanor often invites an audience, it does not require one. "Strange, one spark of playfulness could remain amid such constant toil," offers the narrator, "but her natural temperament was in a high degree mirthful" (ibid.). Frado cultivates, in many respects, a self-sustaining pleasure that opens up alternate possibilities of being.

Frado's singing likewise personifies her politics of joy. Not long after Aunt Abby permits Frado to begin accompanying her to church, the latter "had all their sacred songs at command, and enlivened her toil by accompanying it with this melody" (Wilson 37). Her "clear voice" and "joyous notes" often ring throughout the Bellmont compound (43). While Lindon Barrett does not formally delineate a politics of joy in his published writings, in his foundational 1999 volume *Blackness and Value* he asserts that "The singing voice stands as one very important sign of the value of . . . voices situated in the dark . . . it provides a primary means by which African Americans may exchange an expended, valueless self in the New World for a productive, recognized self" (57). Moreover, "It provides one important means of formalizing and celebrating an existence otherwise proposed as negative and negligible" (ibid.).[24]

When Alice Walker remarks in "In Search of Our Mothers' Gardens" to a "sickly little black girl" that "It is not so much what you sang, as that you kept alive, in so many of our ancestors, *the notion of song*," the black child (Phillis Wheatley, in Walker's case) could easily be Frado (237; emphasis in original). In essence, singing marks a deeply embodied act, one that relies upon an unquantifiable and unquenchable sense of spirit. Alongside the aforementioned manifestations of Frado's joy, song sounds Wilson's critique of a system of abstract rationality that privileges knowledge formation severed from particularized histories, experiences, and bodies. By appropriating the "picaninny" trope, Wilson engages dimensions of racial politics and class privilege—of power—that many of her contemporaries integrating the generic "disorderly girl" figure into their fiction could afford to overlook. Significantly, Wilson mobilizes childhood as a platform from which to interrogate processes of capital accumulation and liberal authority and to uphold the value of black pleasure.

Just Anger

Another conceptual limitation of "the disorderly girl" within the context of *Our Nig* pertains to Green's assertion that "the heroine's fury is justified by the mistreatment that provokes it" (Boggis, Raimon, and White 143). The wrath of Mary, and of adults Mag and Mrs. Bellmont, too, circulates as relatively appropriate and unrestrained, if not inevitable, throughout the course of the narrative.[25] By contrast, in her characterization of Frado-as-picaninny, Wilson demonstrates a keen awareness of leading perceptions of racialized anger, in particular, as unjustified and threatening. In this regard, she counters Western standards of civility that deny black sentience. She also stages a literary critique of liberalism's inadmissibility of livid blackness as a font of meaning.[26]

For example, in one angry exchange between Frado and Aunt Abby, following the departure of Frado's nemesis, Mary, for Baltimore, the narrator relates Frado's at-once happy and furious exclamations. "She's gone, Aunt Abby, she's gone, fairly gone" and "I hope she'll never come back again," Frado declares (Wilson 43). When Aunt Abby tries to remind the girl that Mary is James's sister, the flesh and blood of one to whom Frado is especially attached, Frado retorts that Mary is no better than the Bellmonts' stubborn sheep that Frado recently "ducked" in the river. "I'd like to try my hand at curing HER too," Frado reveals, much to Aunt Abby's dismay (ibid.).

Later, upon the occasion of Mary's unexpected death, Frado heatedly if wittily proclaims to Aunt Abby, "She got into the RIVER again, Aunt Abby, didn't she; the Jordan is a big one to tumble into, any how. S'posen she goes to hell, she'll be as black as I am. Wouldn't mistress be mad to see her a nigger!" (Wilson 55).[27] According to the narrator, such statements were "not at all acceptable to the pious, sympathetic dame; but [Aunt Abby] could not evade them" (ibid.). As Aunt Abby endeavors, with varying degrees of success, either to channel the girl's anger into her chores or deny it altogether—a manifestation of her posture of abettal—readers glimpse both a concerted effort to suppress Frado's rage and a sense, though fleeting, of the perceptiveness of black anger as a vehicle to contest conditions of subjection.

Subtly, Wilson confronts liberal renditions of black anger as unavailing or dysfunctional. She posits a self-aware and conscious fury in excess of reason that can harness the insight and creativity of outrage in order to trouble the status quo. By engaging black anger on its own terms, rather than as the pathological site broader cultural mythologies purport it to be, Wilson's readers—then and now—might uncover a previously neglected agent of growth and survival.

In another remarkable passage later in the text, one seldom referenced in critical scholarship, the narrator observes that Frado crossly "contemplated administering poison to her mistress, to rid herself and the house of so detestable a plague" (Wilson 56). In this instance, an incensed Frado displays a powerfully resistive, homicidal impulse, one not necessarily uncommon within the context of nineteenth-century indenture. She is eventually "restrained by an overruling Providence" without bringing her plan to fruition (ibid.). Nevertheless, Wilson carefully crafts scenarios throughout her text in which black anger circulates as illicit. She simultaneously complicates readings of order-as-antidote to "the disorderly girl" by evoking the striking power of Frado's ireful ruptures.[28]

Black feminist critics today continue to articulate and combat the effects of popular representations of black women's anger in ways that intersect with Wilson's theoretical claims. In *All the Women are White, All the Blacks are Men, But Some of Us are Brave*, Michele Wallace explains that "Being a black woman means frequent spells of impotent, self-consuming rage" (11). In *Black Feminist Thought*, Patricia Hill Collins attends to precisely how sedimented notions of black female antagonism, among other factors, sanction the perpetuation of images such as the matriarch, "overly aggressive, unfeminine women" credited with the disintegration of normative black kinship structures (83). As Collins clarifies, distortions of black women's indignation, as with related biases regarding their sexuality or class status, deflect accountability for systemic oppression and inequality (84). And in "Eye to Eye: Women, Hatred, and Anger," Audre Lorde likewise states that "Every black woman in America lives her life somewhere along a wide curve of ancient and unexpressed angers" (145). In productive dialogue with Collins, Lorde juxtaposes her own personal enmity—"a molten pond at the core of me, my most fiercely guarded secret"—with hatred, or institutionalized practices of discrimination and violence consistently leveraged against disempowered groups without reprisal (Lorde 145). More than a century earlier, Wilson utilizes literature as a platform on which to theorize an equally forceful mode of anger.

Through her politicized picaninny figure, Frado, Wilson opens up the possibility of positioning black rage outside the scope of liberal prescriptive, thereby participating in a black feminist discourse relevant far beyond her historical moment. Bypassing narrow readings of black fury as a space of danger, Wilson establishes anger as an epistemological formation. In her project, black irritation elucidates ever more insidious modes of social control in the antebellum era. By accounting for black exasperation in conjunction with a politics of joy, Wilson extricates the former from the terrain of unwarranted bitterness, and recuperates truly diverse childhood feeling and embodiment.

Quite Contrary

Wilson's narrative, in the end, compellingly reinforces the contrariness of black women writers about which Barbara Christian theorizes. According to Wilson's narrator, "They won't believe what [Frado] says." As readers, we can, and must, do exactly that.

By reading *Our Nig* differently, readers glean a sense of Wilson's willingness to confront violent, if taken-for-granted, assumptions regarding Enlightenment and humanist thought. Contrary to liberal norms, what Frado says undercuts dominant discourses of progress, objectivity, and rationality. Indeed, by assembling disparate notions of embodiment, Wilson foregrounds the necessity of distinct meaning and experience. As had Mary Prince before her, she invokes conditions of materiality in order to counter systems of belief relying predominantly, if not exclusively, on pretexts of abstraction.

Moreover, she exposes liberal postures of abettal as tactics by which to cover over the collusion of empathy, Christianity, and capital. She likewise conjures opacity in order to interrogate dictates regarding transparency and coherence that fortify the liberal problematic. Through the figure of the politicized picaninny, too, Wilson refuses to sever emotional and intellectual production, expanding upon the trope of "the disorderly girl" to envision the mutuality of black anger and of a politics of joy. Only by acknowledging black women writers' long-standing interventions into such hegemonic codes of intelligibility can we ordain more thoroughly capacious and sustainable habits of black being.

2

The Production of "Emancipation"

Race, Ritual, and the Reconstitution of the Antebellum Order

With few exceptions, black women appear sparingly in Steven Spielberg's 2012 award-winning motion picture *Lincoln*. On occasion, glimpses of a black female servant's hands (or alternate appendage) populate the screen, her visage cropped from view. Women also figure among the number of black slaves in the daguerreotypes scoured by an inquisitive, young Tad Lincoln in the opening scenes, as they do in the audience of sundry public orations dispensed by the title character, and in the gallery of the House of Representatives during the January 1865 vote on the Thirteenth Amendment, the film's ostensible climax. One brief exemption from this peripheralization is Lydia Smith (played by S. Epatha Merkerson), black housekeeper and lover to Radical Republican leader Thaddeus Stevens (played by Tommy Lee Jones). She, as the film's logic would have it, partially motivates Stevens's decades-long crusade for the abolition of slavery: he brings home the original copy of the constitutional provision, in the immediate wake of its passage, as a "gift" to her. The other arguable exception to the ornamental status of black women, if one still restricted in representational scope, is black author, activist, and seamstress to the Lincoln White House, Elizabeth Keckly (played by Gloria Reuben).[1] By the end of *Lincoln*, its namesake emerges as a paragon of governance due to a shrewd capacity for disarming Democratic opposition, convincing them to "see the here and now" in the context of heated congressional deliberation. Notably, a conversation with Keckly

Figure 4. Photograph of Elizabeth Hobbs Keckly by Nicholas H. Shepherd on original cabinet card of the Jefferson Fine Art Gallery, Richmond, Virginia. From the Lincoln Financial Foundation Collection, courtesy of the Allen County Public Library and Indiana State Museum.

on the White House steps precipitates Lincoln's pivotal tactical adjustment, securing his enduring sociocultural and diplomatic legacy.

Tethering Keckly's identity so narrowly to the storied ascent of white masculine prowess, however, eclipses a meaningful accounting of her foundational pedagogy, entrepreneurship, and community organizing. Evidently pensive and aware in the film, Keckly nevertheless lacks the complex characterization readily attending her white counterparts (stifled ambition à la Robert Lincoln, raging grief à la Mary Todd Lincoln, etc.). Tentative smiles and incipient tears, in turn, project an air of fragility, while exceedingly close physical proximity to her employer, Mary Todd Lincoln, connotes seeming dependence. In response to Keckly's pressing question to the president in her very first appearance, Lincoln does not deign to reply, further voiding any sense of tangible authority on her part. Subsequent ambiguity only amplifies a persistent omission of black female interiority.[2] In the end, Spielberg reduces her—like Lydia Smith—to little more than a plot point.

Alternate scholarly and popular cultural representations of Keckly are equally unsettling, as contemporary critics across disciplines have minimized her literary and political significance. For instance, Jennifer Fleischner, author of the only full-length history of the relationship between Mary Todd Lincoln and Keckly, writes that "Lizzy's presence in [Abraham Lincoln's] family circle also likely contributed to his evolving comprehension of black life in America" (263). She particularly invokes Keckly's "quiet relationship with the President," noting that "while combing his hair or sewing in the sitting room when he happened to enter, they sometimes fell into conversation" (ibid.). While such interactions certainly leave open possibilities for a measure of influence on the part of the seamstress, Fleischner typically casts such contact as altogether constructive, namely as a vehicle for Lincoln's enhanced civility and ethics, while retreating from a fuller interrogation of Keckly's silence in this necessarily uneven power dynamic. Here, as elsewhere, the Lincolns' integrity is inflated in inverse relation to Keckly's humanity.

What's more, in the oft-cited *Mary Todd Lincoln: A Biography*, Jean H. Baker positions Keckly's book *Behind the Scenes; Or Thirty Years a Slave, and Four Years in the White House* as a "ghostwritten exposé" whose "testimony is suspicious," inexplicably claiming its initial circulation as a "novel" (212–13). Further, Baker emphasizes the orientation of the memoir as fundamentally vengeful, retaliatory, and aggressive (280). Samuel A. Schreiner Jr. resuscitates the Baker school of thought almost ten years later by attributing her work to "two enterprising New York newspapermen," despite multiple authoritative studies linking the project to Keckly and the editorship of James Redpath (69). Nearly seamless integration of Keckly's insights in *Behind the Scenes* into modern historiographical accounts as fact—at times without acknowledgment—only compounds the offense.[3] This constitutes an elision of Keckly's subjectivity, ultimately covering over her critical consciousness regarding the drawbacks of liberalism as the dominant political rationality of the period.

Instead of contributing to an intensifying re-mythologization of Lincoln-as-Great-Emancipator, this chapter analyzes critical challenges posed to the liberal problematic by Elizabeth Keckly's life and writing. Theorizing both the overt and covert ways in which she makes visible the constraints of American liberalism as political economy and affective performance, I undercut gestures of de-authorization within present-day scholarship in which Keckly's presence is enlisted exclusively in the service of verifying Mary and/or Abraham Lincoln's humanist impulses.[4] Of all of Keckly's purported motives for penning her autobiographical piece—clearing Mary Lincoln's name regarding the "Old Clothes Scandal," alleviating her own poverty, even procuring revenge—I argue that her interrogation of precisely how liberal ideology informs juridical practice, processes of citizenship, and bodily rituals of duty remains undertheorized.[5]

More specifically, this chapter expands upon the scholarship of Fleischner, Frances Smith Foster, and Sheila Smith McKoy to interpret even more precisely the strategic means by which Keckly undermines prevailing conceptions of individual sovereignty and progress. I contend that her description of her father's letters and of her uncle's hanging in the antebellum South frames Keckly's understanding of later postbellum conditions of pain and of possibility. By prompting a reading of death as a mode of sovereignty, and of suicide in particular as an expression of black political consciousness, Keckly foregrounds the fraught and nuanced terms of black resistance and freedom. Additionally, *Behind the Scenes* depicts the harrowing conditions facing the previously enslaved at the onset of Emancipation, including homelessness and poverty. In this way, Keckly disrupts common perceptions that the majority of communities in the U.S. North were quintessential racial asylums.

Associated with such critiques, moreover, is an articulation of counter-memory that I term "anti-pastoral reach," a force by which Keckly at once stakes provocative claims for herself in the inhumane institution and contests teleological "up from slavery" narratives. Taken together with politicized acts of witnessing and mediation, Keckly's subsequent engagement in processes of selective self-commodification further problematizes conventional modes of fetishizing and Othering black women's bodies. My reading of black women's textile production as a form of resistance troubles liberal practices of tokenization, too, by directly linking Keckly to widely recognized slave narrator and activist Harriet Jacobs. In concluding with an analysis of the violence of white privilege and maternalism, and of the tropic function of friendship, intimacy, and the "mammy" figure, I allow these critiques of liberalism to emerge as crucial facets of nineteenth-century black feminist knowledge production.

Progress Unmade

Buying her freedom from slavery in 1855, Elizabeth Keckly published her famed narrative in 1868, almost ten years after Wilson's release of *Our Nig*. Two mixed-raced, working women with links to Spiritualism, Wilson and Keckly nevertheless experienced racial, class, and gender stratification in unique ways. Using her sewing expertise to gather the twelve-hundred-dollar purchase price required by her master to buy her freedom before eventually relocating to the U.S. North, Keckly became far more solidly literate and middle-class than Wilson, her indentured counterpart. Over time, Keckly established ties to a widespread black abolitionist and activist community base, including Frederick Douglass and Henry Highland Garnet, due in large part to her extensive philanthropy in the nation's capitol before and after the Civil War. She also maintained a lasting affiliation with the elite Fifteenth Street Presbyterian Church in Washington, D.C. Still, as Wilson and Keckly's literary becoming together in this volume seeks to highlight, vital commonalities exist between the two authors' autobiographical renderings. Distinctively marginalized, these relatively powerless thinkers engage liberal authority in their writing in powerful ways.

Keckly, formerly Elizabeth Hobbs, was born in Dinwiddie County, Virginia, in February 1818 to a bondswoman named Agnes Hobbs. "Mammy Aggy," as she was often called on the plantation, served as nurse and seamstress in the household of Armistead and Mary Burwell. Despite Colonel Burwell's status as Elizabeth's biological father, a slave man named George Hobbs dutifully performed the roles of husband and father until the family's permanent dispersal during Elizabeth's child-hood. As a slave, Elizabeth dispensed her labor primarily within the inner sanctums of relatively well-to-do families such as the Burwells. Fleischner speculates that Agnes imparted the skills of stitching, spin-ning, and weaving to Elizabeth when the latter was three, during occa-sional reprieves from their respective tasks (39).

Not insignificantly, in a text notorious for epistolary display, specifi-cally the written exchanges between Keckly and Mary Lincoln reproduced in the appendix, the love letters from Keckly's father, George Hobbs, to his wife and child are often overlooked as a site through which Keckly begins to unmake liberal standards of progress. In fact, in the months and weeks leading up to its publication, *Behind the Scenes* was persis-tently hawked by the periodical press as the next big sensation, a veri-table "must-read," given the revelatory bent of the Lincoln dispatches. By April 1868, however, major mainstream editorials pilloried the book's os-tensible indecency and confrontational style. As opposed to a free black entrepreneur and widely sought-after mantua maker,[6] Keckly instead surfaces in an April 18, 1868 *New York Citizen* article as "an angry negro servant." For the white reading public, her words in *Behind the Scenes* did not register a distinct epistemological standpoint or worldview. Rather, her disclosure of private details reflected an act of betrayal against an influential white benefactor. Whereas considerable interest attends the representation of interracial relationships in the memoir's supplemen-tary correspondence, other meaningful, often familial connections are given only brief mention, despite the fact that George Hobbs's writing surfaces in the opening chapter.

Indeed, Keckly deliberately harnesses George's words, a source of per-sonal strength and wisdom, to commence the narrative. Her perspective on slavery and postbellum life in the United States, I argue, is filtered precisely through her slave father's abiding spirituality, as well as the acute sense of sorrow and deprivation expressed in the memoir's lesser-known missives. Notably, George's letters relay his struggle to reunite with his kin following his mandated move to Shelbyville; futility and disempowerment pervade his words. As he expresses fear over instilling feelings of abandonment in his daughter, he posits black improvement as tenuous at best. In fact, George never sees his family again.

On the other hand, George stresses that Elizabeth must "learn her book" in his absence (Keckly 25). Thus, he promotes traditional literacy, while encouraging her to cultivate a life of the mind and spirit apart from the forces that bind her. "I want Elizabeth to be a good girl and not to thinke that because I am bound so fare that gods not abble to open the way," he explains in one letter (27). Keckly thereby accents an indefatigable hope and cheerfulness on the part of her father. Instead of relying on conditional or uncertain patience, he manifests faith, which, in his view, presupposes liberation. Keckly's mobilization of her father's messages in this way suggests appreciation and formative influence, particularly as it relates to her subsequent capacity to identify and navigate unequal hierarchies of power.

Tactically, Keckly concludes the same chapter featuring George's letters with the story of "an incident . . . which my mother afterward impressed more strongly on my mind" (30). In the wake of the theft of the second pair of plough-lines loaned to him by Colonel Burwell, Agnes's brother commits suicide. As Keckly relates, "My mother went to the spring in the morning for a pail of water, and on looking up into the willow tree which shaded the bubbling crystal stream, she discovered the lifeless form of her brother suspended beneath one of the strong branches" (ibid.). In a manner regarded by critic James Olney in his introduction to the Schomburg Library edition of the text as "surprising and taciturn," Keckly continues in the chapter's concluding lines, "Rather than be punished the way Colonel Burwell punished his servants, he took his own life. Slavery had its dark as well as its bright side" (ibid.).[7] Forgoing Olney's stance—one tied to a broader, more deferential approach to Frederick Douglass's 1845 *Narrative* as touchstone for all slave narrative—I position Keckly's ambiguity as purposeful, her reticence as rhetorical.

That is, the reserve embedded in Keckly's reaction connotes not emotional detachment or aloofness. It strikes at the heart of liberal ideologies of contained selfhood. Pivoting upon the likelihood of death as, in fact, the "bright side" of slavery for those in bondage, Keckly challenges the concept of bounded, bodily integrity central to Western individualism. Individual ascendancy, she demonstrates, does not conform to singular modes of logic or economic imperative.

Moreover, her uncle's predicament, not unlike her father's words, belies notions of equitable access. It undercuts the feasibility of institutional reform in the context of enslavement. And, as Rafia Zafar notes in *We Wear the Mask*, "coming where it does in the chapter [the suicide] serves as a profound full stop" (175). Keckly prompts readers to adopt an expanded view of reason, of how it might be alternately expressed or channeled for legitimate claims to black life, within the confines of servitude.

Put another way, contrary to governing perceptions of discrete personhood and property rights, Keckly inserts a striking black radical ethos into her narrative. By reconfiguring slave mortality as freedom, Keckly summons diverse African epistemologies of collective resistance alongside sacred rituals of kinship, life, and death. Per Cedric Robinson in *Black Marxism*, maroonage, theft, Obeah (magic), and suicide signal the contours of a distinct political consciousness informed by, though not reducible to, Western imperialism, extending an irruptive force into conventional modes of power and liberty. Keckly's depiction likewise disturbs normative notions of democracy and autonomy by dislodging the individual subject as universally constitutive of sovereignty and of "authentic" political meaning and experience.[8]

Keckly, then, displays a keen, subtle understanding of death as an ever-fraught yet substantive terrain of release. Given Keckly's tendency to "pass rapidly over the stirring events of [her] early life," this effort to remember her uncle's suicide certainly bears significance (Keckly 31). In my reading, constraints of liberalism emerge here as through-lines by which Keckly binds her history under enslavement to its insidious reconstitution under purportedly progressive postbellum terms of order. Keckly's representation of black death signals possibilities for productive contestation.

Keckly also specifically calls attention to continuities between bondage and the fiction of Emancipation via a portrayal of mid-century conditions in the U.S. North. In 1860, Keckly separates from her intemperate husband and moves from St. Louis to Baltimore, and eventually to Washington, D.C. Extreme poverty and business failure plague Keckly upon arrival. For instance, blatantly racially discriminatory laws of the period extract inordinate sums of money from freedmen and -women for the right to occupy public space (Keckly 65). Thus, her living conditions prior to becoming the personal modiste of Mrs. Jefferson Davis, and later of Mary Lincoln, closely mirror the deleterious circumstances faced by black denizens in the North after the Civil War, a conflict in which, in Keckly's words, the "people [of the North] would fight for the flag that they pretended to venerate so highly" (72). Such shallow patriotism, for Keckly, signals an outward expression of the limitations of liberal tolerance and non-racism. As this book argues throughout, racial difference is rendered arbitrary or irrelevant in much liberal doctrine, facilitating notions of blanket equity. Given the desperate conditions to which she and others are subject, such non-racism does not, however, equate with anti-racism.[9]

Accordingly, observes Keckly, "Fresh from the bonds of slavery, fresh from the benighted regions of the plantation, [freedmen and -women] came to the Capitol looking for liberty, and many of them not knowing it when they found it. Many good friends reached forth kind hands, but the North is not warm and impulsive" (111). "For one kind word spoken, two harsh ones were uttered," she adds (ibid.). Here, Keckly collapses enduring mythologies of liberal philanthropy and benevolence, introducing instead the realities of white Northern hostility, epidemic black homelessness, and starvation. Intervening in persistent ideological displacement of racism to the South, Keckly confronts illusory notions of teleological racial progress.[10]

In a later, comparable scene in which Keckly accompanies her employers, the Lincolns, on a trip to Petersburg, Virginia following the fall of the Confederate capitol, Keckly recounts the approach of a "little ragged negro boy" to President Lincoln's convoy (167). The young boy proceeds to ask whether he might "tote" their luggage. In the confusion that ensues as the president and an accompanying senator attempt to decipher the boy's meaning, black dialect emerges as fundamentally "colloquial" or as "not elegant, certainly"—in essence, as Other (Keckly 168). "For myself, I should prefer a better word," notes the senator, "but since it has been established by usage, I cannot refuse to recognize it" (168–69).

Not unlike her portrayal of her uncle's suicide, Keckly brings the scene to an abrupt close with a single, off-set line: "Thus the conversation proceeded in pleasant style" (169). Indeed, in depicting the stark contrast between executive pleasantries and black poverty, and the apparent unsuitability of black language to the white ear, Keckly slyly articulates the ways in which nineteenth-century Republican practice often hinged upon notions of the illegibility of blackness. As with the emaciated rather than emancipated bodies of the "contraband of war," this misapprehension of blackness as excess renders liberal discourses of recovery and reconciliation, regardless of formal political party affiliation, as fallacies. The fact that *Behind the Scenes* ends with the image of an utterly impoverished Keckly—sewing and writing in a "garret-like" space to make ends meet—further establishes the contingency and privilege (as opposed to the universality) of the leading progressive ethos.

In *Written by Herself: Literary Production by African American Women,*

1746–1892, Frances Smith Foster cites the transformative influence of *Behind the Scenes* on the genre of the postbellum slave narrative, an effect comparable to the impact of *Incidents in the Life of a Slave Girl* on narratives of the antebellum period. Examining the fundamentally political nature of Reconstruction-era accounts, especially scenes of reunion between former slaves and owners, Foster delves into later tales' themes of transcendence and achievement in contrast to the abjection known to have spurred earlier abolitionist activity. While Foster's analysis of the explicitly raced and gendered dimensions of postbellum depictions of slave culture proves invaluable, the examples above indicate Keckly's palpable concern with progress yet to be made under the aegis of American liberalism. Though, in fact, tracking Keckly from the nadir of enslavement to the pinnacle of Western affairs of state, *Behind the Scenes'* premise exceeds liberal prospects of growth and linear advancement. Proffering, instead, discernment and awareness of an expansion of conditions of violence and brutality under slavery, Keckly rejects a superficial sense of "how far we've come," alternately revealing how far we have left to go.

Anti-Pastoral Reach

In addition to racialized ideologies of progress, Keckly confronts pastoral processes of memorialization.[11] Passed down to Elizabeth from her mother, Agnes, and to her from earlier generations of Burwell slaves from both the West African coast and the Niger Delta, memory functions for Keckly as a mode of survival. Indeed, as scholars such as Foster, Hartman, and William Andrews suggest, bondsmen and -women, as well as recently emancipated slaves, often asserted insurgent nostalgia despite the agonies of captivity.[12] Relatedly, I maintain that Keckly engages in subversive performances of cultural memory, called anti-pastoral reach, throughout *Behind the Scenes* in ways that problematize conventionally archivable, state-sanctioned systems of knowledge production. In particular, Keckly activates a keen sense of personal belonging and place in her memoir via recollections that, even when coincident with dominant transcripts, cannot finally be reduced to the instrumental designs of the slaveholding regime.

For instance, in response to Northern suspicion of her curiosity regarding her former owners in the wake of the Civil War, Keckly replies, "You forget the past is dear to everyone, for the past belongs [to] that golden period, the days of childhood. The past is a mirror that reflects the chief incidents of my life" (241). Continuing on, she writes, "To surrender it is to surrender the greatest part of my existence—early impressions, friends, and the graves of my father, my mother, and my son. These people are associated with everything that memory holds dear, and so long as memory holds dear, and so long as memory proves faithful, it is but natural that I should sigh to see them once more" (241–42). Memory, in Keckly's formulation, exceeds the Western domain of rational retrieval. Instead, her incarnate reminiscences move in the realm of faith. In a distinct shift to first person, she selectively recalls "the chief incidents of my life" as a means of forging her own worldview, while never finally submitting the full details of "the greatest part of my existence" for public consumption. Hence, to take into account those directly culpable for her enslavement does not mark a concession to the conditions of subjection, but registers an attempt to create meaning and purpose apart from violent circumstances. Such a gesture resonates with Keckly's commentary in the preface that Southerners "were not so much responsible for the curse under which I was born, as [were] . . . the fathers who framed the Constitution of the United States" (xii). That is, Keckly refuses to privatize racism, seeking instead to expose its juridical sanction and naturalization as law. For her, anti-black terror functions institutionally, rather than on the level of the individual. Anti-pastoral reach allows retention that fortifies without traumatizing.

However, just as Keckly foregrounds anti-pastoral reach as a vehicle through which to access her own truths, she also does so specifically to launch a broad-based critique of liberal sentimentality. Specifically, she spotlights emotionality, including gestures of reconciliation, redemption, domestic affiliation, even distress, that aspire to democratization and meaningful relation, yet more often than not amount to futile custom. Therefore, readings that associate the significance of Keckly's July 1866 reunion with the Garlands, the family of a former master, in Rude's Hill, Virginia, with a capacity to bolster Keckly's self-esteem, affirm her humanity, or, more generally, assuage white fears of black resentment curtail Keckly's insight into the underside of liberal affective economies.[13]

An example of precisely how such analyses fall short relates to Keckly's literary depiction of the aforementioned postwar visit to the home of her former owners, at least one of whom concludes a letter to Keckly about her impending visit with the conspicuous imperative, "Come; I will not take no for an answer" (246). After an elated chorus of "It is Lizzie! It is Lizzie!" at the sight of their former slave, the Garlands "carr[y her] to the house in triumph" (250). Yet, amid the euphoric fanfare, the voice of the Garlands' nameless black cook notably intervenes: "I declar, I nebber did see people carry on so. Wonder if I should go off and stay two or three years, if all ob you wud hug and kiss me so when I cum back?" (252). Aside from the notable shift into dialect, the passage produces a crucial slippage. Indeed, the cook's testimony—"I nebber did see people carry on so"—positions the celebratory response as far from common practice in this household. Though both are ostensibly free women at the point of this exchange, Keckly and the anonymous cook garner starkly divergent treatment. Other servants, too, "looked on in amazement" (250).

I argue that this critical difference, the gap between placation and servitude, renders the Garlands' sycophancy as a thinly veiled expression of a liberal discourse of exception, or a species of individualism in which singular ascent supersedes collective justice. By remembering the words of the cook in this way, via anti-pastoral reach, Keckly authors a performance in which the "faithful slave returned to the homestead" cannot be severed from the postbellum "faithful servant." Put differently, it is precisely the exploitation of the unidentified laborer that makes the excessive praise of Keckly possible in the first place; they constitute flip sides of the same dehumanizing coin.

Discourses of exception of this ilk exist, in Keckly's narrative, in implicit binary relation to those of racial representativeness. As evident in an early passage, liberal bias may perpetuate the value of private attainment and sanction communal disadvantage in one breath. In *Behind the Scenes*' memorable "a-p-e" incident, a young Tad Lincoln, under the tutelage of his mother at Hyde Park, performs poorly on a spelling lesson, mistaking the word "ape" for "monkey" in light of the appearance of the wood-cut used to illustrate the term. Not to be deterred from his initial response by Mary or Elizabeth, Tad only reluctantly concedes his error (to his older brother) after repeated explanation. "Whenever I think of this incident I am tempted to laugh" Keckly suggests, "and then it occurs to me that had Tad been a negro boy, not the son of a President, and so difficult to instruct, he would have been called thick-skulled, and would have been held up as an example of the race" (219). Using racially inflected primate imagery, Keckly reveals the limits of frames of mind that cannot reconcile the fact that "if a whole race is judged by a single example of apparent dullness, another race should be judged by a similar example" (220).

Keckly also deploys anti-pastoral reach to make visible the coerciveness of liberal affect as she and Mrs. Garland muse over the exploits of a perhaps less celebrated, though no less important, antebellum aunt than Frederick Douglass's Aunt Hester, Agnes's sister, Charlotte. "A maid in the old time meant something different from what we understand by a maid at the present day," observes the Southern matriarch, nostalgically (Keckly 255). "My mother was severe with her slaves in some respects, but then her heart was full of kindness," she adds, reinforcing the by-now-stagnant trope of the "feeling plantation slave mistress." I reproduce Mrs. Garland's story at length below:

> [My mother] had your aunt punished one day, and not liking her sorrowful look, she made two extravagant promises in order to effect a reconciliation, both of which were accepted. On condition that her maid would look cheerful, and be good and friendly with her, the mistress told her she might go to church the following Sunday, and that she would give her a silk dress to wear on the occasion. Now my mother had but one silk dress in the world . . . and yet she gave this dress to her maid to make friends with her. Two weeks afterward mother was sent for to spend the day at a neighbor's house, and on inspecting her wardrobe, discovered that she had no dress fit to wear in company. She had but one alternative, and that was to appeal to the generosity of your aunt Charlotte. Charlotte was summoned, and enlightened in regard to the situation; the maid proffered to loan the silk dress to her mistress for the occasion, and the mistress was only too glad to accept. She made her appearance at the social gathering, duly arrayed in the silk that her maid had worn to church on the preceding Sunday. (255–56)

Though the two women proceed to laugh together, and even to chide those doubting their loyalty to one another, the sincerity of these acts is undercut by the arresting anti-pastoral reach toward Aunt Charlotte.

Amid the recuperation of Charlotte's body as testament to white female compassion and generosity, Keckly subversively recalls the extortive means by which her aunt's pleasure is extracted, a feat that Mrs. Garland seemingly seeks to reproduce in the postbellum present. As with Frado in the face of James Bellmont's posture of abettal detailed in chapter one, Charlotte is voiceless in this recollection: accordingly, "the narrative's silence . . . underscores that the sympathetic exchanges envisioned here are dictated by the mistress's desire, and constitute a species of narcissism" (Merish 249). Given the scene's strategic placement in the memoir—on a continuum with Keckly's depiction of her own silencing by multiple patrons, from Mrs. McClean to Varina Davis to Mary Todd Lincoln—I contend that Keckly memorializes Charlotte by elucidating a liberal production of compulsory black acquiescence.[14]

In fact, when her former mistress poses the final query "Do you always feel kindly towards me, Lizzie?," Keckly declines to give the emphatically affirmative answer Mrs. Garland craves (257). Though Joanne Braxton claims that "the bond between freedom and literacy" constitutes "a theme noticeably absent from Keckley's *Behind the Scenes*," in this moment, Keckly rejects the posture of docility expected of her, forgoing complicity, specifically by challenging the Garlands' suppression of her access to formal education (Braxton 44). "To tell you candidly, Miss Ann, I have but one unkind thought, and that is, that you did not give me the advantages of a good education. What I have learned has been the study of after years," Keckly admits, if euphemistically (257). Demonstrating precisely the unintended irony in Mrs. Garland's claim that "a maid in the old time meant something different from what we understand by a maid at the present day," Keckly goes off-script in a way in which Charlotte most likely could not have done. Mrs. Garland's desire to recapitulate and renew her mother's liberal generosity subsequently rings hollow, as Keckly calls up anti-pastoral reach to denaturalize interracial dynamics of domination and control.

In-Between-ness

Throughout *Behind the Scenes*, Keckly also mobilizes her mix-raced body to trouble politics of race and national belonging subtending the liberal problematic. Through its constitutive disregard for difference, liberalism propagates and preserves racial exclusion. Accordingly, critics have long established the ways in which mulatta figures—the antithesis, in certain respects, of uniformity or sameness—yield particular tropic effects within nineteenth-century literature and public discourse. Extrapolating from Frances E. W. Harper's 1892 novel *Iola Leroy*, Hazel Carby writes, "As a mediating device the mulatto had two narrative functions: it enabled an exploration of the social relations between the races, relations that were increasingly proscribed by Jim Crow laws, and it enabled an expression of the sexual relations between the races, since the mulatto was a product not only of proscribed consensual relations but of white sexual domination" (xxi). Carby historicizes the in-between-ness of the mixed-raced body in this instance, politicizing processes of mediation in a mode deeply resonant with Keckly's project.

Notably, Keckly actively manipulated broader cultural investments in her intercessory potential to her own advantage. Most famously, she facilitated the October 1864 visit between Abraham Lincoln and spiritual leader, abolitionist, and women's rights activist Sojourner Truth at the White House. Though Nell Painter rightly observes that "Keckley's autobiography said much about the Lincolns but nothing about Sojourner Truth," as compared to repeated references in the memoir to male figures including Douglass and Garnet, Painter expressly underscores Keckly's "keen sense of relative power" and enthusiastic participation in brokering the historic meeting (204). Keckly also intervened on behalf of the lesser-known Maria W. Stewart of Boston, the first African-American rhetor to speak in public before a mixed-gender assembly. Stewart's memoir piece, "Suffering during the War," reflects sincere gratitude for Keckly's personal and financial support upon her arrival in Washington, D.C. in 1861; Stewart credits the arrangements, associations, and contacts of her "ardent friend" with the development and eventual success of her school (Richardson 102; Forbes 68). Ultimately, Keckly's re-appropriation of the role of mediator imbues her writing in *Behind the Scenes* as well, locating her as a discreet, watchful witness.

For instance, as a laborer in the Washington, D.C. household of Varina and Jefferson Davis, soon-to-be First Family of the Confederacy, Keckly personifies her intermediary status precisely by marshaling at once legitimate and unauthorized channels of knowledge in order to process the impending fracture of civil war. "The prospects of war were freely discussed in my presence by Mr. and Mrs. [Jefferson] Davis and their friends," Keckly claims (67). Moreover, "Almost every night, *as I learned from the servants and other members of the family*, secret meetings were held at the house; and some of these meetings were protracted to a very late hour" (66–67; emphasis added). In this scenario, gossip and rumor are syntactically hinged to more open, casual dialogue. Ever invisible and hypervisible as a mulatta woman worker, Keckly binds together the intelligence gleaned from both sites to assess the consequences of the ensuing conflict for black denizens and to determine her own future

course of action. Acts of tact, restraint, and unobtrusiveness comple-
ment Keckly's expert sewing skills, granting her access to uncensored
whiteness and to widespread liberal protocol in need of critique.

However, when Mrs. Davis proposes the possibility of Keckly traveling South with her to avoid alleged retaliatory measures, deeds to be
instigated by Northerners incensed by the prospect of imminent seces-
sion, Keckly feigns ignorance. To Mrs. Davis's query, "You know there
is going to be war, Lizzie?," Keckly supplies an emphatic "No!" Further
prodding on Mrs. Davis's part meets with equally false incredulity: "Who
will go to war?"; "And which do you think will whip?"; "But, Mrs. Davis,
are you certain that there will be war?" offers Keckly (70–71). She counters Mrs. Davis's display of liberal trepidation for Keckly's safety, actually
motivated by the fact that Mrs. Davis deems Keckly a "so very handy"
employee, with a show of bewilderment and surprise. Slyly capitalizing
upon her standing as an ostensibly neutral onlooker, Keckly accumulates
vital insight and issues subtle commentary on white self-interest.

In a similar fashion, Keckly's access to the inner sanctum of the Lincoln White House yields insurgent discursive effects throughout *Behind
the Scenes*. As modiste, nurse, hairdresser, and caregiver to the Lincoln
brood, among other miscellaneous duties, Keckly dispenses myriad services; each role permits unique contact with the president and his family. One such instance, just prior to Lincoln's assassination, results from
Keckly's fleeting, unsolicited glimpse "through the half-open door" of
the room of the Commander-in-Chief. "Seated by a desk was the President," Keckly reports, "looking over his notes and muttering to himself"
(175). Yet, proceeding to thicken her initially straightforward account,
she adds, "His face was thoughtful, his manner abstracted, and I knew
as I paused a moment to watch him, that he was rehearsing the part that
he was to play in the great drama soon to commence" (ibid.). Though the
scene effectively conveys the preparation and anticipation surrounding
Lincoln's first public speech following his second inauguration, it simultaneously marks Keckly's usurpation of a panoptic gaze and strategic
insertion of self into the strictly raced and gendered sphere of citizenship. Keckly's deliberate lingering just beyond Lincoln's half-open door
punctures the abstractness of the American body politic that the president envisions in that moment, thrusting her onto the plane of history.
As witness to the man at the helm, silent spectator to the leader of a fal-
tering country, Keckly's presence—in her particularity as a mixed-race

woman—contests the state's avowedly disembodied prescriptive of national belonging. Further, she implicitly challenges Lincoln's Emancipation policy, an opportunistic political agenda finally founded upon the abjection of difference.[15]

I would add that Keckly's capacity to leverage her proximity to her employers achieves rhetorical effect not only in the register of formal politics, but in the realm of spirituality. As illustrated by an 1863 vignette in *Behind the Scenes*, one set in times the author characterizes as "sad, anxious days to Mr. Lincoln" and in which she says, "those who saw the man in privacy only could tell how much he suffered," Keckly again uses her "privileged" position as witness. As Keckly pins a dress to Mary's frame, Mr. Lincoln enters, dark and despondent over the most recent news from the war front. Keckly observes:

> He reached forth one of his long arms, and took a small Bible from a stand near the head of the sofa, opened the pages of the holy book, and soon was absorbed in reading them. A quarter of an hour passed, and on glancing at the sofa the face of the President seemed more cheerful. The dejected look was gone, and the countenance was lighted up with new resolution and hope. The change was so marked that I could not but wonder at it, and wonder led to the desire to know what book of the Bible afforded so much comfort to the reader. Making the search for a missing article an excuse, I walked gently around the sofa, and looking into the open book, I discovered that Mr. Lincoln was reading that divine comforter, Job. . . . What a sublime picture was this! A ruler of a mighty nation going to the pages of the Bible with simple Christian earnestness for comfort and courage, and finding both in the darkest hours of a nation's calamity. (119–20)

Here, Keckly foregrounds the select cohort to which she belongs, the exclusiveness of the group with access to the president at his most vulnerable. Yet, her laboring, raced body in a white space compels inconspicuousness nonetheless. In other words, freedom of movement—for a free black or mulatta woman—always entails an alibi.

Nevertheless, via tactful performances both as attendant and as author, Keckly simultaneously illustrates the value of black faith. Indeed, Keckly's reference to the Book of Job, in its appeal to the downtrodden and outcast, would have especially resonated with nineteenth-century African-American readers (Foster 119). In his "simple Christian earnestness," Lincoln closely resembles bondsmen and -women in their turn to Word and spirit, rather than to the abstract sphere of Western rationality sustaining the liberal problematic, for "comfort and courage" in times of trial.

Finally, her surveillance in this moment harnesses the presence of her mulatta body, antebellum blacks' penchant for Old Testament verse, even Job's own status as intercessor, in order to dislodge Lincoln and install God as the "Great Emancipator" from all suffering. In the end, she artfully collapses the distance between Lincoln's authorized reprieve from worldly sorrows and blacks' purportedly illicit spiritual practices, an appropriation of religious doctrine that opens up alternative epistemological possibilities. As with her aforementioned exchange with Mrs. Jefferson Davis, Keckly's politicized mediation and witnessing—her in-between-ness—within the space of the White House enable forceful social critique of the dominant meanings of race and nation.

Selective Self-Commodification

Attuned to commercial dimensions of *Behind the Scenes*, literary critics have also taken into account a host of consequences produced by Keckly's seemingly market-oriented concerns. For instance, Susan S. Williams situates Keckly's memoir as evidence of "a pivotal moment in women's understanding of authorship as a business as well as an aesthetic practice" (126). Xiomara Santamarina, too, in her focus on literary representations of women's labor, cites "the way in which [Keckly's] coerced labor performance could provide a form of self-production that countered mechanisms of racial and gender inferiority and dependence" (148).[16] Building upon these discussions, I argue that accompanying Keckly's aforementioned deconstruction of liberal tenets of progress and individualism, her assertion of anti-pastoral reach and politicized witnessing, is an ethic of selective self-commodification. Keckly's strategic representation of self in this regard exceeds broader aims of federal reconciliation or narratives of uninterrogated complicity with the dictates of Northern capital. The latter interpretations work to contain the theoretical scope of Keckly's project, especially as it pertains to the ways in which self-commodification, as an analytic, makes visible the interpenetration of liberal notions of freedom and property. Keckly's relegation to sporadic sewing engagements in her last years, and eventual consignment to the National Home for Destitute Colored Women and Children—not unlike

Harriet Wilson's recourse to pushing handmade hats and copies of *Our Nig* in the 1850s in order to survive—no doubt acutely underscores the necessity of attempting alternative systems of value.

Above all, selective self-commodification reflects a mobile mode of self-determination. It demonstrates a simultaneous awareness and wariness of widespread normalization of capital accumulation, a process with starkly divergent racial consequences. Conscious of mainstream, liberal preoccupation with contractual obligation and purportedly ordered distribution of material goods, self-commodification makes visible an embeddedness of market-driven reason in moral, social, and political life. Ever-tactical, self-commodified subjects remain cognizant of given circumstances, and accordingly, itinerant within prevailing systems of economic power.

Selective self-commodification thereby crystallizes the liberal problematic. As liberalism idealizes capitalist privilege—covering over the breach between progressive ambition and lived, black realities of subordination—self-commodification pinpoints subjugation as part and parcel of standard elaborations of wealth management and free enterprise. As Saidiya Hartman reminds us, cultural alliances between independence and ownership attest to the convergence of American liberalism with Lockean economic philosophy, the latter advancing "an ideal of liberty founded in the sanctity of property, and the vision of liberty forwarded in the originary narrative of the Constitution, which wed slavery and freedom in the founding of the nation and the engendering of 'we the people'" (122). While some critics engage the tradition of liberalism by theorizing Keckly's reconfiguration of conventional contract theory and rights discourse in relation to authorship, I draw specific attention to the non-conciliatory ends of her confrontation with racialized market ideology.

Remarkably, Keckly's skill in the art of textile production generates an opportunity for her to purchase her own (nominal) liberty as well as that of her son. Surveying her business prospects upon moving to St. Louis with the Garlands, she notes that "when my reputation [as a seamstress] was once established I never lacked for orders" (Keckly 45). In fact, "With my needle I kept bread in the mouths of seventeen persons for two years and five months," Keckly maintains, before scoffing at those whites who dared deem her "not worth her salt" (45–46). Thus, as the chapter title "How I Gained my Freedom" intimates, Keckly manages to attain independence precisely by developing quality product, brokering profitable exchange rates, and carefully maneuvering relationships with high-status clientele. Yet just as her performance in the rational marketplace stimulates near surplus demand for her services, it also productively problematizes her condition as chattel. Indeed, the shrewdness she exhibits in an economic terrain in which she circulates as flesh and as supplier of a specialized, embodied form of labor—and later as disenfranchised freedwoman and as public author—flouts traditional modes of valuation during the period. Keckly's unmediated projection of self into the sphere of capital signals resistance to her object status.

This is akin to slave narrator Olaudah Equiano (Gustavas Vassa)'s success in the arena of small trade. As Houston A. Baker observes in *Blues, Ideology, and Afro-American Literature*, Gustavas Vassa's autobiography of spiritual awakening extends an insightful critique of "commercial deportation" and the "economics of slavery," two governing tropes in African-American discourse according to Baker's foundational paradigm. "*The Life of Olaudah Equiano* can be ideologically considered as a work whose protagonist masters the rudiments of economics that condition his very life," asserts Baker. "It can also be interpreted as a narrative whose author creates a text that inscribes these economics as a sign of its 'social grounding'" (33). For Baker, the double-voiced mode of address in the 1789 narrative reflects a "self-conscious, mercantile, self-evaluation" (34), evincing Vassa's realization "that only the acquisition of property will enable him to alter his designated status *as property*" (35; emphasis in original). That is, Vassa's path to freedom is marked by a mutual fluency, or bilingualism, in Anglicanism and the ethics of capitalism, in Christian piety and laissez-faire sensibility. His spiritual strivings and quest for literacy as means to secure manumission cannot be understood outside of his savvy rhetorical manipulation of the commercial landscape. Keckly demonstrates a comparable astuteness to that of her literary forebear, I suggest, if one also decidedly influenced by her gender difference.

Keckly's subsequent rebuttal of her master's claim that she intends to run away, as well as her refusal of another suspicious white male patron's assistance in raising the twelve hundred dollars required for her emancipation, further demonstrate this point. Vexed by Keckly's continued broaching of the subject of manumission, Mr. Garland offers her a quarter, encouraging her to take a ferry to the nearest free state if she desires liberty so keenly. "No, master, I do not wish to be free in such a manner. If such had been my wish, I should never have troubled you about obtaining your consent to my purchasing myself," Keckly replies

(48). A later conversation with Mr. Farrow, from whom Keckly needs a signature verifying that she will return to the Garland home following a trip North to raise funds to meet her purchase price, evokes an analogous response from Keckly. Aiming to diminish Mr. Farrow's skepticism about her return, Keckly declares, "But I assure you, Mr. Farrow, you are mistaken. I not only *mean* to come back but *will* come back, and pay every cent of the twelve hundred dollars for myself and child" (52; emphasis in original). As with her adept entrée into the free market economy as a dressmaker, Keckly's rejection of truancy asserts a self-commodifying stance that discomfits the contemporary socioeconomic order.

Indeed, in the scenarios outlined above, Keckly displays pecuniary eloquence and agility. By slyly leveraging her knowledge of dominant patterns of acquisition in this way, Keckly accrues white favor. Nevertheless, her engagement with (white) faith in the principles of the market outstrips the purposes of concession or accommodation. Rather, her acquaintance with the fiscal lexicon of the day reorganizes her relationship to the conditions of labor and bondage structuring her world, thereby initiating possibilities of defiance and release. To be sure, Keckly's self-commodification does not bespeak radicalism. It does not raze the institution of slavery or ravage its long-standing effects. Still, single-minded attention to militancy misses how her resistance undercuts processes of dehumanization by exposing the tenuousness of freedom, making legible a troublesome nexus of autonomy and property within the liberal state.

By Design

Keckly's artisanship extends a critique hinged on more than an intrinsic, hierarchical investment in property, however. I contend that, in addition, textile work functions critically and aesthetically throughout *Behind the Scenes* in order to contest an overt privileging of order and abstract reason within the Western philosophical tradition. Indeed, rather than emphasizing the exclusively utilitarian objectives of black cultural production, Keckly's memoir taps into the ways in which embodied practices such as quilting often granted African-American women a space from which to improvise their subjectivities within and against systemic white hegemony. Thus, I argue that the process of dressmaking recurs in the narrative less as an articulation of style or facile adornment than as an affirmation of a nascent black feminist politics. Keckly demonstrates

understanding of weaving and material design as inherently epistemological, as non-empirical modes of intellectual production and awareness, and as enactments of worldview.

More specifically, the construction and exhibition of white fashion
enabled seamstresses such as Keckly to imagine freedom. It also allowed
them to develop alternate systems of meaning-making and to mete out
penetrating critiques of the liberal status quo. Ascending to the exclusive
rank of mantua-maker, a position to which even the most talented seldom rose, Keckly consistently impressed elite patrons with her intricate
design and ability to pin to form. Yet she just as routinely surpassed conventional dress codes, elaborately bedecking the First Lady while in her
employ. "[T]he mourning dresses Lizzy Keckly made for Mary assumed
a highly luxurious quality, and mourning jewelry—often crafted of then
popular tightly woven hair—decorated the first lady's fingers, wrists,
neck, and ears," observes one historian.[17] Even Jean H. Baker concedes
Keckly's remarkable overhaul of styles, those initially inspired by the
wardrobe of French Empress Eugenie, yet transformed into masterful,
previously unimaginable costumes. In fact, many of Keckly's garments
boasted over twenty-five feet of material, ultramodern angles, and bold
hues. The often-duplicated 1861 Mathew Brady portrait of Mary Lincoln,
in particular, showcases Keckly's productively manipulative techniques:
sixty velvet bows and as many black dots embellish the otherwise relatively plain silk frock for which Lincoln's widow is now widely known
(Baker 193, 195).

In her own words, Keckly modestly allows for only a measure of el-
egance in her designs—of the gown she creates for Mrs. Captain Lee of
Washington, for example, she says little, though she makes sure to note
that it "attracted great attention at the [Prince of Wales's] dinner-party"
(78). Likewise, in the narrative, it is one of the stunning "chintz wrap-
pers" that Keckly fashions for Mrs. Davis, just prior to the pre-war Confederate exodus from the capitol, that Jefferson Davis reportedly sports
at his moment of capture by Union forces. A wax figurine of Davis at a
charity fair, outfitted in Keckly's unique creation, still inspires awe in
crowds years later (74–75).

In this respect, Keckly effectively shifts established conventions of
dress; she modifies the relation between traditional aesthetic bench-
marks of ostentation and originality, uniformity and multiplicity. As
Stephanie M. H. Camp summarizes in a related context, "At least since

Figure 5. An 1861 photograph of Mary Todd Lincoln by Mathew Brady. Courtesy of National Archives, photo number 111-B-5864.

the eighteenth century, with roots in African visual arts, black style had distinctively stressed the dynamic interplay of color and texture over the harmonies of similar elements, and surprise, movement, and argument over predictable patterns and order" (84). In essence, Keckly's introduction of geometry and play offers a striking reinterpretation of governing models of liberal coherence and decorum.

On the other hand, the worth of black women's sartorial production is not finally contingent upon recognition by majority culture, but remains steeped in imaginative and resistive potentialities with interracial and intra-racial effects. "The origin, manufacture, cost, color, cut, and display of clothing were all significant features of black women's self-representation," corroborates Elizabeth Young, "as constituted both in opposition to white ex-masters and in affirmative relation to communities of free African-Americans" (127).[18] Keckly strategically activates embedded cultural histories in which nineteenth-century black women's handicraft frequently contributed to vital intergenerational contact. As Keckly teaches and employs other black seamstresses in the region, her patchwork serves to undermine slavery's patterns of dispersal, promoting a performative archive of communal memory.

Though *Behind the Scenes* primarily features instances of Keckly sewing for white benefactors, rather than for herself or the surrounding black community, cutting, fitting, and spinning remain skills imparted to her by her mother. Agnes Hobbs instills in young Elizabeth the value of textile work as a collective, felt performance of witnessing and survival, not unlike Harriet Jacobs's grandmother, "Aunt Marthy," also a seamstress, had done for her own descendants. As Jacobs (Linda Brent, as she is called in the narrative) recalls in her 1861 *Incidents in the Life of a Slave Girl*, embroidery yielded bodily and spiritual salvation during her containment in the garret (265). Like Keckly in her postbellum slave narrative, Jacobs/Brent positions needlework as hermeneutic; in particular, she grapples with questions of ontology and liberation through its distinct lens.

Furthermore, both writers import this ancestral, kinesthetic practice into their later relief work. In addition to fundraising and other philanthropic pursuits, Keckly and Jacobs instituted sewing circles among newly freed bondsmen and -women in post-Emancipation Washington, D.C. (Forbes 72). In this way, the activists mitigated anti-black prejudice reconstituted in the wake of Jubilee (that is, Emancipation) through the assembly of clothing and medical supplies, while simultaneously cultivating complex philosophies of reciprocity and belonging. Moving beyond individualistic, liberal indignation predicated upon self-seeking intervention rather than social justice, Keckly's and Jacobs's stitching produces public pedagogy. They reconceptualize meanings of black freedom, and following Jacobs in the preface to *Incidents*, seek not "to excite sympathy for [personal] sufferings," but to "arouse . . . a *realizing sense* of the condition of two millions of women at the South, still in bondage" (126; emphasis added). Theorizing a becoming together of Keckly's and Jacobs's narrative representations of textile labor, then, undoes the logic of exceptionalism typically cohering around each writer, heralding their participation in a far more expansive culture of nineteenth-century black women's embodied, intellectual practice.

Lastly, the memoir on the whole reflects tangible texture, with theoretical implications for black women's engagement with the liberal problematic. As Susan S. Williams rightly discerns, *Behind the Scenes* "is thematically held together by accounts of [Keckly] sewing, which foreground the material means of its production as well as the metaphor of narrative threads" (129). Evidencing a quasi-vignette, if predominantly chronological structure, Keckly's narrative features one chapter pieced to the next via the thread of a memory or a relationship, the full meaning of which only becomes legible when a subsequent piece brings the larger arrangement into view. Striking in its layering, *Behind the Scenes* laces and plaits together flashbacks and reveries, with bits of omniscient narration and foreshadowing. Incidents from the past are ever emerging in the narrative present, and vice versa, and the weaving in of reluctance and omission, shifts in point of view, and other strategies of subversion yields an arresting pattern of political import.

In one particularly important strand, one that pertains directly to textile production, Keckly discloses the grievances of a "good, old, simple-minded woman, fresh from a life of servitude," and I quote:

> "Why, Missus Keckley," said she to me one day, "I is been here eight months, and Missus Lingom an't even give me one shife [shift]. Bliss God, childen, if I had ar know dat de Government, and Mister and Missus Government, was going to do dat ar way, I neber would'ave comed here in God's wurld. My old missus us't gib me two shifes eber year." (141)

Ascertaining that the woman "thought the wife of the President of the United States very mean for overlooking this established custom of the plantation" (142), Keckly confesses that she "could not restrain a laugh at the grave manner in which this good old woman entered her protest" (141). Though mocking and ridicule are detectible in Keckly's representation of the exchange, I am drawn to other latent rhetorical effects within the passage, and to its placement within the chapter titled "Behind the Scenes."[19] Resonating with the stifled voices of the Garland family cook as well as that of Aunt Charlotte, the "protest" of the newly emancipated bondswoman marks an irruption. I argue that the "pith of the joke," which Keckly later suggests "Northern readers may not fully recognize" (142), in fact pivots as much upon the notion of clothing as a means to induce pliancy as upon its aforementioned propensity for manipulation toward alternative ends. Thus, Keckly—as author—stages a performance that channels the improvisatory possibilities of black women's understandings of the relationship between autonomy and attire.

That is, the unidentified freedwoman does not merely install a nostalgic hierarchy wherein plantation-era coercion is exonerated. Rather, Keckly expands the context of racialized subjection to account for Northern complicity. White Northern readers' misrecognition of the apparently comedic scene makes visible a liberal self-aggrandizement by which racial brutality in the South remains discrete from similar, if less spectacular, practices in the North. In this scenario, however, the North and South alike emerge as sites of dispossession. While projected as accessible to all, sovereignty remains conditional and elusive at both sites.

Appositely, this narrative thread follows Keckly's depiction of blacks' "exaggerated ideas of liberty" in Washington, D.C., and the shattering of their "beautiful vision [of] a land of sunshine, rest, and glorious promise" in light of extreme deprivation (139). After Keckly recalls the ostensibly amusing scene, she details former bondmen's and -women's sincere efforts to restore a sense of humanity and of home in Freedmen's Village. Ultimately, the anecdote knits together antebellum conditions of repression in the South with landscapes of Northern deficiency, in order to begin conceptualizing avenues for substantive change. By specifically appropriating the image of the dress—a symbol of embodied knowledge in the lives of black women—Keckly issues a call for expanded freedom and accountability on the part of the liberal state.

Privilege and Pretense

Another central preoccupation of *Behind the Scenes* is the at-once ritualized and invisibilized performance of white privilege reinforcing the
liberal problematic. Keckly's literary representation of interracial patron-client relationships in the mid-nineteenth-century North exposes
maternalism, in particular, as an insidious mode of compulsion. Often
striking in its instrumentality, the maternal relation deploys fictive kinship ties, among other less-explicit filial logics, to extract docility and
submission.

Keckly dramatizes precisely such a dynamic when detailing an exchange with Mrs. General McClean, the daughter of General Sumner,
upon Keckly's initial arrival in Washington, D.C. Euphemistically referring to Mrs. McClean's ensuing conduct as her "emphatic way," Keckly
depicts the influential customer's urgent demand for a new frock. "I have
just purchased material, and you must commence work on it right away,"
commands McClean. To Keckly's response, indicating the unfeasibility
of such a project on such short notice, McClean retorts, "Pshaw! Nothing is impossible! I must have the dress made by Sunday." Not surpris-
ingly, Keckly's subsequent attempts to reiterate her position, as well as
to apologize, are met with irritation. "Now don't say no again. I tell you
that you must make the dress," interjects McClean imperatively (Keckly
79).

McClean thereafter offers Keckly a proposition to help her gain employment at the White House—as long as McClean's dress is complete
in time for Sunday's soiree. In the end, Keckly depletes significant re-
sources to meet the looming deadline. Yet, despite the narrative's characterization of this final incentive as "the best [inducement] that could
have been offered" (Keckly 80), it is arguably McClean's preliminary invocation of privilege that secures Keckly's consent. Under the belated
guise of a potential liaison between Keckly and Mary Lincoln, McClean
first forcefully asserts her race and class advantage over her black counterpart. As the script of white supremacy—even when cloaked in a liberal spirit of (commercial) collaboration—stipulates Keckly's categori-
cal assent, McClean wrests the requisite response from her interlocutor.
Brusquely, if smilingly, silencing the one whose services she so desper-
ately desires, McClean infantilizes Keckly by de-authorizing her speech.
As author, Keckly rhetorically stages an acquisition of fidelity rooted in

strictly hierarchized terms of order, an all-too-familiar and violent scenario of dominance.

A related instance features Keckly's interaction with one of her white patrons in St. Louis, the fittingly denominated Mrs. Le Bourgois. Following Mr. Farrow's disclosure of his belief that Keckly would likely fall prey to abolitionists' schemes during her trip up North to raise the money for her purchase price, Le Bourgois arrives unannounced at Keckly's door. "Lizzie, I hear that you are going to New York to beg for money to buy your freedom," she declares. "I have been thinking over the matter, and told Ma it would be a shame to allow you to go North to *beg* for what we should *give* you. You have many friends in St. Louis, and I am going to raise the twelve hundred dollars required among them" (Keckly 54; emphasis in original). In the wake of Le Bourgois's pronouncement, "the flowers no longer were withered, drooping" (55). "Again, they seemed to bud and grow in fragrance and beauty," observes a third-person narrator (ibid.).

Notably, tropes of brightness and sweetness scaffold the entire conversation between the two women: "Like a ray of sunshine [Mrs. Le Bourgois] came, and like a ray of sunshine she went away," relays Keckly (55). The overt logic of the passage, then, christens Le Bourgois as Keckly's savior. Seemingly impervious to the rigorously policed constructions of the social world to which her surname alludes, Le Bourgois accumulates redemptive capital in the eyes of readers by seeking to relieve Keckly and her son of the "bitter heart-struggle" of slavery (55). Romanticized and rhetorically commonplace, references to luster and radiance surface on at least twenty-one occasions in Keckly's volume, at times more than once on a single page.

However, given Keckly's earlier theorization of suicide as the "bright side of slavery," I maintain that the effects of light as a framing device exceed the affective register of unconditional gratitude and praise. As evidenced by Douglass's 1845 *Narrative*, "sunniness" indexes a black opacity at odds with Enlightenment-era injunctions regarding rationality and comprehensibility.[20] Nineteenth-century black women thinkers likewise manipulated obscurity, as outlined in chapter one, to subversive ends in their texts. "Alas! the sunny face of the slave is not always an indication of sunshine in the heart," confirms Keckly in the memoir's opening pages (29). Imbued with political meaning and experience, Keckly's sunbeams and blossoms, in fact, subtly conjure the saccharine nature, posture, and pretense of liberal racial sentimentality.

Thus, proposes Dana Luciano, "Lebourgois's offer reads alternately as expressing the 'human' kinship of sympathy, responding generously to another's display of grief, or, less sentimentally, as expressing a kind of genteel feminine modesty on behalf of Southern custom" (255). And yet Le Bourgois's unsolicited appearance at Keckly's residence, not to mention her ability casually to mull over "the matter" of Keckly's basic survival at her leisure, belie the sympathetic orientation of her pitch. Le Bourgois remains principally, if not exclusively, concerned with safeguarding the status of the local white community. The narrative act of "saving face," choreographed so carefully by Keckly in this instance, positions white etiquette as little more than an expression of privilege meant to instate a relation of long-standing indebtedness. Moreover, Keckly's literary performance illuminates the ease with which whites' face-saving often comes at the expense of any substantive engagement with black life.

A scathing parody appearing in 1868 under the copyright of "D. Ottolengul"—*Behind the Seams; by a Nigger Woman who took in work from Mrs. Lincoln and Mrs. Davis*—speaks, similarly, if inadvertently, to the aura of childlike dependence permeating this encounter. Simultaneously ventriloquizing and mutating Keckly's words, the burlesque's author writes of Mrs. Le Bourgois: "Heaven bless this good Southern Lady. I love her, and I love the South for her sake; and so I shall not be ungrateful, and I never shall write a book full of no-such-things about the Southern people . . ." (10). For the satirist, a perennially senseless, unsightly (yet sexually available), minstrelized Keckly violates the bounds of normative tolerance. Exceedingly arrogant, she fabricates white transgression, manipulating liberal munificence all the while.

Privilege also surfaces in *Behind the Scenes* through the projection of a staple of the white liberal imaginary: interracial intimacy. Modern historical scholarship and commercial publications alike constantly reproduce this falsehood when addressing Keckly's legacy, interring Keckly and Mary Todd Lincoln's dynamic in pastoral, wistful longing. Presumably mistaking physical proximity or a shared employment landscape for mutually sustaining emotional ties, biographers routinely spotlight Keckly and Lincoln's special acquaintance, their "genuine friendship" (Packard 29).[21] According to Fleischner, "It is easy to see why well-dressed women considered themselves almost intimates with their dressmakers," for "[t]he laborious dressmaking techniques of the day made close relationships between women and their dressmakers largely impossible to avoid" (133). Interestingly, despite Fleischner's initial suspicion in her monograph of a "too easy use of the word" friendship with respect to Keckly and Lincoln's entwined histories, she finally retreats from the asymmetry inherent in the relation, granting a unique "warmth, understanding, and intimacy" between the two given the nature and duration of their business together (5–6).

But, as Lauren Berlant argues, intimacy constitutes a kind of affective artifice. At once ideologically and materially violent, intimacy as normative institution fails to acknowledge its own intrinsic idealism and ambivalence, if not its virtual impossibility. "[I]ntimacy . . . involves an aspiration for a narrative about something shared, a story about both oneself and others that will turn out in a particular way" (281), Berlant corroborates in a twentieth-century, though not unrelated context: it "builds worlds; it creates spaces and usurps places meant for other kinds of relation. Its potential failure to stabilize closeness always haunts its persistent activity" (282). Further, as Berlant theorizes, the intimate remains tethered to the performative, trafficking in hollow iconography and gestures of deep feeling. Deemed natural, rites of intimacy imported across divergent terrain, in fact, cover over the acuteness and specificity of uneven contexts of subjection.

The artificiality of interracial intimacy emerges on multiple occasions in the memoir, especially in scenes in which Keckly is cast as a "mammy" figure. Though Keckly's relationship with the Garland daughters most readily prompts such a reading,[22] I contend that Keckly's association with Mrs. Lincoln likewise invokes the increasingly stale "mammy" image, a trope Patricia Hill Collins refers to as the quintessential "asexual woman, a surrogate mother in blackface" (80–81). Katherine Helm, niece of Mary Lincoln and author of *The True Story of Mary: Wife of Lincoln*, too, invites such an assessment, claiming that her aunt often "reverted to the impulse of her childhood, which had been to seek the love and help she had unfailingly found in her black mammy. . . . In the faithful, sympathetic colored woman, Elizabeth Keckley . . . , Mary saw the only available substitute, and to her she turned blindly for sympathy and advice" (266). In Helm's configuration, Lincoln collapses Sally, a black bondswoman employed by the Todd family during Mary's childhood, with Elizabeth, a free black entrepreneur in postbellum Washington, D.C. For Lincoln, "mammy" represents an anonymous yet ever-present reserve of black sustenance, while Helm, in her uncritical reproduction of the term "mammy" as an expression of endearment, renders Sally nameless, thereby extending her Aunt Mary's legacy.

In this vein, pictures of exploited labor—conceived by the dominant group in a matrix of motherly affection, autonomy, and consent—abound in *Behind the Scenes*. Indeed, as the extensive array of services for which Keckly is responsible in the Lincoln household increases, the institutionalized character of white privilege undergirding the liberal problematic enables this escalation to circulate as intensified care and nurturing shared between employer and employee. As Sau-ling C. Wong argues, "by conceding a certain amount of spiritual or even physical dependence on people of color—as helpers, healers, guardians, mediators, educators, or advisors—without ceding actual structural privilege, the care-receiver preserves the illusion of equality and reciprocity with the caregiver" (69). Following Wong, the fantasy of Keckly-as-mammy presumes black volition while precluding any significant access to power or authority. In the context of the prevailing political rationality of liberalism, Keckly's progressively more intensive, if diversified, meniality indexes not obligation or duress, but mutuality and shared investments in buttressing "the biopower of white comfort."[23]

Importantly, mythologies of superhuman black female strength remain central to the traction of the dehumanizing "mammy" stereotype and to the liberal production of interracial intimacy. Hence, Helm cites the ostensibly "unfailing" quality of Sally's support for Mary Lincoln. Likewise, in *The Spy, the Lady, the Captain, and the Colonel*, an illustrated biography for young adults featuring a section on Keckly, the historical tendency to de-emphasize black women's subjectivity in order to accentuate their physical potency asserts itself. While the text arguably offers relatively complex perspectives on Keckly's ambivalent relationship to Emancipation, as well as on her spiritual grounding and commitment to political activism, it appears unable to relinquish the worn trope of black women's unyielding fortitude. "She was the rock of strength on which Mary Lincoln leaned" (Stiller 58), notes the narrator in one prominent example. Evidently, her circumstances "never made her weak and afraid" (Stiller 48). Overall, Keckly's resilience coincides with little more than her apparent stamina in staving off Lincoln's mental and emotional collapse in the wake of her husband's assassination.

Usefully, bell hooks locates at least one of the problems inherent in such a move. As she traces continuities between the nineteenth- and twentieth-century Women's Movements in *Ain't I a Woman: Black Women and Feminism*, hooks maintains, "When feminists acknowledge in one breath that black women are victimized and in the same breath emphasize their strength, they imply that though black women are oppressed they manage to circumvent the damaging impact of oppression by being strong—and that is simply not the case" (6). As hooks clarifies, black endurance does not yield panacean social transformation. Instead, liberal stereotypes of extraordinary black female strength—relics of antebellum conditions of containment—facilitate a mode of white self-exoneration by which accountability for structural domination is elided.

Finally, alongside the "mammy" caricature, Keckly turns up quite often as the First Lady's dearest companion. Given their mutual status as grieving mothers and as ostensible outsider figures in mid-century D.C. polite society, the two are quick to be labeled comrades. Keckly is even identified as Mary Lincoln's "trusted friend and confidante" on Keckly's tombstone.[24] As interraciality alone does not prohibit alliance, it is necessary to acknowledge the feelings of interest, community, comfort, and pride likely vested in their ongoing connection. Nevertheless, liberalism, in its erasure of particularity, posits the effects of the affiliation as proportional, if not identical, for each woman. Instead, I argue, a nuanced spectrum of aggression characterizes patron-client interactions throughout much of the era.

As in many of the previous scenarios discussed here, acts of interracial respect and regard—of friendship—frequently obscure rigid power dynamics. For example, just prior to the president's assassination, Keckly requests permission from her "friend" to attend what would become Lincoln's final public speech. "Certainly, Lizabeth; if you take any interest in political speeches, come and listen in welcome," Mary replies. "Thank you, Mrs. Lincoln. May I trespass further on your kindness by asking permission to bring a friend with me?" continues Keckly. "Yes, bring your friend also," answers Lincoln, adding immediately thereafter, "By the way, come in time to dress me before the speaking commences" (175). Though hallmarks of intimate familiarity adorn the scene, from the use of a pet name to a general aura of hospitality, I suggest that competing rhetorical elements are simultaneously at play.

That is, Keckly strategically situates interracial friendship as a rapport rooted in tolerance, for Lincoln does not actually "welcome" Keckly to witness the lecture. Rather, she allows her to do so with the caveat that she must first dispense with her requisite domestic tasks.[25] Despite an ethos of seeming congeniality and acceptance, Keckly cannot acknowledge Lincoln's informality with equivalent signs of acquaintance. Indeed, she cannot refer to her employer by her first name, apply the term "friend" to their patron-client relationship in her employer's presence, or exceed her careful, deferential stance very much at all. Therefore, Lincoln, in fact, only reconstitutes the terms of forced intimacy inflicted by Keckly's past owners and patrons, from Mrs. Garland to Mrs. McClean to Mrs. Jefferson Davis, First Lady of the Confederacy.

Another moment in the memoir, involving the Lincoln family's move to Chicago following President Andrew Johnson's inauguration, especially resonates with these previous experiences with white privilege, but manifests itself through the trope of friendship in particular. According to Keckly, "When Mrs. Lincoln first suggested her plan [to take Keckly with her to Chicago], I strongly objected; but I had been with her so long, that she had acquired great power over me" (209). While the ambiguity of the passage leads some critics to attribute Keckly's hesitancy to a deep "emotional bond" between the two women,[26] the episode as readily provokes a reading of Keckly's muted critique of the coerciveness of interracial intimacy. As Keckly attempts to explain to her employer that she cannot possibly desert her own business and philanthropic pursuits in Washington, D.C., to travel to Illinois, Lincoln sternly interrupts: "Now don't say another word about it, if you do not wish to distress me. I have determined that you shall go to Chicago with me, and you *must* go" (209–10; emphasis in original). In an all-too-common gesture of silencing, construed by the figure of authority as an articulation of fondness and devotion, Lincoln compels Keckly's compliance.

It is on the first night in transit to Chicago, though, that Lincoln explicitly invokes the notion of friendship. As Keckly attends to the former First Lady's latest ailment, Lincoln announces, "Lizabeth, you are my best and kindest friend. I wish it were in my power to make you comfortable for the balance of your days. If Congress provides for me, depend upon it, I will provide for you" (210).[27] In another, off-script moment, however, Keckly supplies quite the telling response to Lincoln's declaration: silence. Countering Lincoln's routine suppression—both her allocation of erratic hours and wages and the continued stifling of Keckly's voice—with an abrupt, self-imposed quietness on her own terms, Keckly withdraws from her employer's performance of intimacy.

"The trip was devoid of interest," resumes the narrator unemphatically. "We arrived in Chicago without accident or delay" (Keckly 210). In place of the affirmation, gratitude, or approval prescribed by the hegemonic racial order, Keckly offers a resounding calm. Her refusal to speak back to Lincoln's assertion forces readers to linger, to borrow from Berlant again, with Lincoln's haunting "failure to stabilize closeness." As with her previous address of both suicide as the "bright side of slavery" and prevailing Republican notions of blackness as fundamentally illegible, Keckly enacts a rhetorical disjunction that at once exposes the racialized rites and rituals—as well as the slippages—at the heart of the project of liberalism.[28]

Non-Rational Praxis

In closing, however, it is important to signal the ways in which Keckly contrasts the intimacy driven by dominant ideological and fetishistic impulses with that motivated by non-rational forces. Of the latter, Berlant asserts, "in practice the drive toward [intimacy] is a kind of wild thing that is not necessarily organized [in a conventional] way, or any way" (284). Keckly's relationship with her son, to take just one example, epitomizes precisely such a dynamic. The apparently peripheral mention of George's life and death throughout the course of the memoir, not unlike details around her sexuality or her mother's continued residence in the South after Keckly's move North, confounds many critics. Yet the ostensibly tangential affiliation with her son not only concretizes her reduction to the status of "mammy," a role in which—by definition—her own family's needs must be overlooked, but re-conceptualizes black maternal affection. In fact, in admitting that "God knows that she did not wish to give him life," Keckly conveys a fierce connection to her offspring (39). She expresses an unruly closeness to her child, a love profound enough to encompass her labor for his freedom and formal education and her ambivalence and pain over the violent circumstances of his birth.[29] Keckly's passion for her son, then, is not effortless or inborn. It is not a space of privilege, but a site of struggle.

In this regard, Keckly's contestation of circumscribed understandings of family and intimacy coincide with the broader critiques of liberalism that this chapter outlines. Indeed, *Behind the Scenes* problematizes established discourses of sovereignty, progress, and individualism. In like mind with other subjects in this study, Keckly challenges entrenched ethics of tolerance and exceptionalism, privilege and decorum, universality and self-possession. By mobilizing her role as witness, as well as textile work as a way of knowing, even deploying practices of anti-pastoral reach and self-commodification, Keckly literally stages an intervention into the foremost political rationality of the day. Though conventional wisdom contains the significance of Keckly's life and writings, fixing her alternately as Mary Lincoln's arch nemesis or best friend, a closer reading reveals her insights into the inner workings of liberalism as political, economic, and affective machine. By century's end, educator and social reformer Anna Julia Cooper will pick up where Keckly leaves off, sounding a critique of the liberal problematic founded in similar discernment of the limits embedded in frameworks of objectivity and intention. Though typically cast beyond the pale of legitimate black resistance, Wilson, Keckly—and, later, Cooper—extend theories of power of enduring consequence today.

3

"Wondering Under Which Head I Come"

Sounding Anna Julia Cooper's Fin-de-Siècle Song

In September 1902, Anna Julia Cooper contests, with fervor devout and political, what I have referred to throughout this book as the liberal problematic. Imparting a speech titled "The Ethics of the Negro Question" to the General Conference of the Society of Friends in Asbury Park, New Jersey, Cooper renders a fundamental disjunction between democratic promise and dispossession in boldly accusatory terms. "It is no fault of the Negro that he stands in the United States of America today as the passive and silent rebuke to the Nation's Christianity, the great gulf between its professions and its practices, furnishing the chief ethical element in its politics," she avers (Lemert and Bhan 206). Perhaps none other than a black body—given the particular history and trauma it encompasses—could inveigh against this founding paradox quite so palpably, she maintains, "constantly pointing with dumb but inexorable fingers to those ideals of our civilization which embody the Nation's highest, truest, and best thought, its noblest and grandest purposes and aspirations" (ibid.). In a telling turn to the spectral, she concludes, "[t]he American conscience would like a rest from the black man's ghost" (209).

Without fully relinquishing appeals for national belonging here, Cooper nevertheless punctures procedural iterations of equivalence and progress. Those "[p]rofessing a religion of sublime altruism, a political faith in the inalienable rights of man as man . . . jugglers with reason and conscience" (207), in fact, perpetuate racism, lynching, greed, and

Figure 6. Portrait of Anna Julia Cooper in doctoral rega-
lia. Courtesy of the Moorland-Spingarn Research Center, Howard University Archives, Howard University,
Washington, DC.

economic devastation, under the guise of individualism, civility, and order, she reveals. Ultimately, Cooper posits Christian education as the
remedy to widespread racial acrimony, a first step in bridging the divide
between abstract notions of liberty and lived black experience.

Yet, Cooper's protest in "The Ethics of the Negro Question" does not
materialize without prelude or precedent. Rather, in my view, it signals a
persistent preoccupation with the liberal problematic evident in her earliest theoretical work. Arguably, her best-known monograph, published
ten years prior to the conveyance of "Ethics," constitutes not a precursor

to subsequent, more authentic radicalism, but an avenue of legitimate dissent in its own right. Accordingly, this chapter attends to Cooper's analysis of the limits of tenets of American liberalism, such as inclusion and autonomy, by way of a return to *A Voice from the South*, the interpretive possibilities of which have been previously explored, but not fully recognized.

More specifically, I augment inquiry among Cooper scholars vis-à-vis the ways in which her resistive potential is frequently rendered illegible as activism. Foregrounding Cooper's perceived class status, late-Victorian social standards, and intermittent Christian ethnocentrism as relevant, yet finally insufficient grounds for reducing her interventions solely to staunch conservatism, or to a facile mimetic impulse in relationship to whiteness, this project forwards another perspective.[1] That is, it shifts the critical register away from a narrowly historical or sociological bent toward a focus on precisely how Cooper dislodges prevailing liberal precepts enmeshed with Enlightenment discourses of what it means to be human. Put differently, I explore here Cooper's refusal and subsequent reconceptualization of dominant notions of civility, freedom, and equality, thereby complicating understandings of the relation between resistance and discursivity and deepening our sense of Cooper's engagement with contemporary discourses of black feminism.

Chief among Cooper's contributions in *A Voice* to be addressed herein is her condemnation of prevailing ideals of abstraction and universality within Western philosophical thought more broadly, but especially those ensuing from the traditions of U.S. Constitutionalism and of institutionalized religion under the auspices of the Episcopalian Church. In dialogue with other nineteenth-century black female public intellectuals, including Maria W. Stewart and Frances E. W. Harper, Cooper also extends a compelling indictment of the provinciality and elitism of the (white) Women's Movement, homing in on practices of white middle-class female discomfort as a mode of cultural policing still relevant today. An avowed embrace of difference and conflict likewise characterizes Cooper's prose. These facets of her analysis, in particular, problematize the preeminence of a fixed and self-contained transcendental subject. Additionally, her criticism of the maintenance of hierarchies of racial oppression, of reigning cultural mythologies of the U.S. North as fundamentally emancipatory, and of black male gender bias in the realm of higher education signal keen insight into the nuances of ostensibly progressive politics of the era. Finally, my turn in the chapter to subversive and still undertheorized dimensions of *A Voice*, including its framing via musical metaphor and irruptions of sarcastic wit, compels a radical re-evaluation of our ways of knowing and recognizing social change.

In the Abstract

Born Annie Julia Haywood in Raleigh, North Carolina in approximately 1858, Cooper was the daughter of a bondswoman named Hannah Stanley Haywood. Hannah imparted to her daughter an "outsider-within" critical consciousness informed by a twinned set of beliefs in the value of labor—both its import and its capacity to be exploited—as well as the significance of a formal education and the opportunities it enables.[2] Cooper's written account of the identity of her father, composed much later in life, states that "I owe him not a sou and she [her mother] was always too modest and & shamefaced ever to mention him," suggesting that paternity could be attributed to her mother's master, Dr. Fabius J. Haywood (Lemert and Bhan 331). In the wake of the Civil War, Hannah astutely steered nine-and-a-half-year-old Annie toward a scholarship to Dr. J. Brinton Smith's St. Augustine's Normal School and Collegiate Institute. Consistently challenging the institution's status quo, which then permitted only male students to partake in Greek language curricula, Anna independently and successfully organized for women's participation in the course at St. Augustine's in 1873. On July 27, 1881, she wrote to the president of Oberlin College for admission to the university, eventually ranking among the first African-American women awarded a Bachelor's degree in the United States. After three years of pedagogical development establishing her competency as a teacher at the university level, Oberlin granted Cooper a Master's degree in mathematics in 1887.

In September of 1887, Cooper began her pioneering role at M Street High School in Washington, D.C. This marked a formative experience in her life for a number of reasons, not the least of which was her ousting as principal in 1906 as a result of the joint machinations of whites on the D.C. Board of Education and other associates of Booker T. Washington's Tuskegee Machine. Cooper also pursued graduate studies at Columbia University and later at the Sorbonne. Successfully defending her doctoral thesis on the relation between Haitian slavery and the democratic ideals of the French Revolution in Paris in March 1925, she was the fourth African-American woman to earn a doctoral degree. Providing decades of material labor as an educator and intellectual until her death in 1964,

Cooper was also one of the only black females invited to speak at the American Negro Academy and to attend the first meeting of the Niagara Movement. Her foresight was likewise integral to the formation of the National Association of Colored Women's Clubs in 1896, and to the development of Frelinghuysen University, an institution dedicated to educational access for the black working poor and disabled in Washington.[3]

Notably, the becoming together of Cooper with earlier writers and thinkers such as Harriet Wilson and Elizabeth Keckly demonstrates striking parallels and divergences. Each offers crucial insight into the strictures of liberalism, a normative social good predicated upon tokenization, sexism, and racial and class exclusion. Each similarly debunks canards of American democracy and progress, producing alternate claims to autonomy and community. Still, Cooper's tome reflects a uniquely post–Civil War and post–failed Reconstruction vantage point. Her work, in certain respects, springs out of a tension between the onset of Jim Crow, and increasing, if relative, economic and professional opportunity for a number of blacks (especially in the industrialized North) at the turn of the twentieth century. As a result, Cooper's analyses necessarily depart from her forebears' portraits of power. Situated within an unprecedented flurry of black women's intellectual formation and secular movement, Cooper's scholarship, unlike that of Wilson or Keckly, prompted widespread readership and a measure of critical acclaim in her lifetime.

One critique central to Cooper's public thwarting of the liberal problematic regards dispelling pretenses toward unqualified abstraction and universality. Indeed, on several rhetorical occasions in *A Voice*, I argue, Cooper engages in liberal ideology critique by specifically attending to the limitations of broad-based theorization severed from the contexts and realities of black life. At precisely one such juncture in "Womanhood a Vital Element in the Regeneration and Progress of a Race," a speech delivered in Washington, D.C. in 1886 preceding the convocation of "colored" clergymen of the Protestant Episcopal Church, and later integrated as the first chapter of the opening section of *A Voice*, Cooper observes, "A conference of *earnest* Christian men have met at *regular* intervals for some years past to discuss the best methods of *promoting the welfare and development of colored people* in this country" (37; emphasis added). However, the earnestness and regularity of Christian ethics of promotion and uplift belie their actual impact. Accordingly, Cooper continues, "Yet, strange as it may seem, they have never invited a colored man or even intimated that one would be welcome to take part in their deliberations.

Their remedial contrivances are purely theoretical or empirical, therefore, and the whole machinery devoid of soul" (37).

Here, in the vein of Sojourner Truth before her, Cooper de-centers a logocentric approach founded in disinterestedness and detachment. She contests processes of empiricism that pivot upon static notions of "welfare and development," concepts vested with ostensibly all-encompassing applicability, yet that finally elide racial difference. Cooper's articulation of "soul," though not fully fleshed out in the volume, articulates a desire for less-facile, more-consequential terms of engagement; she understands, in the words of Patricia J. Williams, that "it is a liability as much as a luxury to live without interaction" (72). Soul, for Cooper, stands in stark contrast to a positivist politics of objectivity in which a disembodied and masculinist rhetorical tradition circulates as hegemonic.[4]

Later in the same essay, Cooper adds, "Men are not 'drawn' by abstractions. Only sympathy and love can draw, and until our Church in America realizes this and provides a clergy that can come in touch with our life and have a fellow feeling for our woes, . . . the good bishops are likely to continue 'perplexed' by the sparsity of colored Episcopalians" (41). While much contemporary scholarship draws attention to Cooper's tendencies in A Voice to value a Protestant ethos of containment and restraint over ecstatic, demonstrative forms of worship characteristic of other denominations, this passage marks Cooper's explicit advocacy of "sympathy" and "love" among church leadership. Cooper effects a call for "touch" across the borders of the rational self, for effusiveness attentive to black pain and black suffering. Further, her charge is to embrace resonance above the ruse of rationality.[5] Without accounting for "sympathy" and "love" as disciplinary, coercive constructs in Christian proselytizing and missionary efforts, Cooper nevertheless powerfully mobilizes the perplexity of "the good bishops," as she playfully dubs them, to illustrate the inevitable breakdown of exclusively theoretical modes of thought.[6] Cooper also constructs a related assessment of black male clergy's neglect of black women's privations and desires for intellectual and professional growth (Cooper 18).

Cooper extends this analysis of abstraction into the realm of the literary in a later essay in the collection, "One Phase of American Literature." Citing her own abundance of "respect for the autonomy of races"—or in more pious terms, "too much reverence for the collective view of God's handiwork to speak of any such condition, however general, as characterizing the race"—Cooper intervenes in misrepresentations of blackness in popular culture, especially among establishment writers of the day (204). "We meet it at every turn—this obtrusive and offensive vulgarity, this gratuitous sizing up of the Negro and conclusively writing down his equation," Cooper maintains, "sometimes even among his ardent friends and bravest defenders" (203).

Juxtaposed with what Cooper deems the politicized prose of Albion Tourgée, the "humility and love" imbuing the narratives of Harriet Beecher Stowe, and the "enlightened" self-critique present in the fiction of George Washington Cable, the writing of William Dean Howells conspicuously bears the brunt of Cooper's critique of stereotypical imagery (Cooper 186, 191).[7] Evaluating the reductionist effects of Howells's work, Cooper's "One Phase" locates problematic universalizing inclinations in journalism and mainstream fiction, including Howells's 1891 novel *An Imperative Duty*. Significant for its circumscribed treatment of mulatta protagonist Rhoda Aldgate, among other black figures, Howells's work prominently features "the frog-like countenances and cat-fish mouths, the musky exhalations and the 'bress de Lawd, Honey' of an uncultivated people" (Cooper 202–3), whom Howells all the same refers to as "the best [of] colored society" (202). To Cooper, such purported likenesses—of blacks as predictably repugnant, obsequious, or hypersexual, even naturally separatist (as opposed to being subject to institutionalized segregation)—are, in fact, propagandistic, rather than indicative of highly venerated, objective truth. This late-century literary effort by one of the most prolific and influential writers of the era functions as a prototypical cultural site immersed in precisely the raced and gendered relations of power and privilege that Cooper seeks to overturn.

On the other hand, from the beginning of her essay, Cooper establishes that depictions of blackness as fundamentally without fault, or a sort of inverse of existing dynamics, are myopic in scope: "Our grievance then is not that we are not painted as angels of light or as goody-goody Sunday-school developments," she clarifies (206). Instead, like Elizabeth Keckly before her, Cooper laments the burden of black representativeness preserved by disparaging caricature.[8] Continuing on, Cooper asserts, "[W]e do claim that a man whose acquaintanceship is so slight that he cannot even discern diversities of individuality has no right or authority to hawk 'the only true and authentic' pictures of a race of human beings" (206). Indeed, she bemoans the fact that one equipped with such a limited understanding of black folk, in her words "at long range and only in certain capacities," determines the very standards by which "authentic" blackness is to be consumed by the reading public. As gatekeeper, observes Cooper, Howells peddles black "Truth," manipulating its status as a commodity in the literary marketplace. Not unlike her subsequent close reading of Maurice Thompson's poem "A Voodoo Prophecy," published on January 21, 1892 in the New York Independent (Cooper 211–17), Cooper's interrogation of the interpenetration of race and narrative into the literary pursuits of majority culture—of the ways in which American (literary) identities are often forged against the bodies of racialized Others—remains especially important in a "post-racial" era.[9]

Finally aligning Howells not with vituperative racists, but with more conventionally liberal proponents, such as international attendees of the 1893 Columbian Exposition, Cooper condemns Howells's privileging of an abstract, inherently subservient blackness. Couched in complex, class-inflected terms that almost diametrically oppose black bootblacks and hotel waiters with more "quiet, self-respecting, dignified" blacks, Cooper's inquiry productively exposes the famed critic's acute misapprehension of black integrity. Anticipating Howells's major misreading of black anger as aesthetic lack and "bitterness" in his review of Charles W. Chesnutt's The Marrow of Tradition (1901), and of dialect use in Paul Laurence Dunbar's second volume of poetry, Majors and Minors (1896), Howells's archive emerges in Cooper's narrative as complicit in the trafficking of patronizing tropes of blackness. By propelling her critique of critical abstraction beyond the scope of religion to literature, Cooper's influence upon pivotal cultural landscapes, both in her day and beyond, becomes more readily apparent.

In addition to religion and literature, Cooper challenges the intangibility of legal precedent throughout A Voice from the South. While rarely relinquishing the possibility for reconciliation of the divergent originary interests embodying the liberal problematic, she problematizes the state's production of abstract citizenship at the expense of certain raced and gendered bodies, and of black women, in particular. Moreover, she unsettles the sedimented excess U.S. liberal imperative typically relegates to the realm of the private.

In fact, African-American rhetors' address of critical abstraction in formally juridical terrain—by explicitly citing the slippage among the Declaration of Independence, the Constitution, the Emancipation Proclamation, and lived black realities—gained quite a bit of traction in the wake of mid-nineteenth-century abolitionism (Waters and Conway 288). Cooper, though writing in the final decade of the period, was no exception. For instance, in the chapter titled "Has America a Race Problem; If So, How Can It Best Be Solved?," Cooper consistently figures universal freedom and development as potentialities. She signals liberal norms as unrealized ideals, attainable only through more expansive and thoroughgoing engagement with blackness (Cooper 160). In showcasing "liberality" among "conditions of the nation's birth" codified in its official documents, and as perhaps the only path to the perpetuity of the nation, Cooper points up its marked absence in her fin-de-siècle present (165). Thus, accentuating liberty as desired terminus rather than a current point of habitation, she writes, "I confess I can pray for no nobler destiny for my country than that it may be the stage, however far distant in the future, whereon these ideas and principles shall ultimately mature" (168). In lamenting fallow and uncultivated, if admirable, aims, Cooper thereby speaks in *A Voice* to the crux of the liberal problematic, to the hypocrisy embedded in a tradition of constitutionalism in which autonomy is inextricable from property, freedom yoked to repercussions of enslavement.[10]

Cooper's chapter "Woman Versus the Indian," too, foregrounds precisely this foundational slippage as it relates to formalized discourses of equity amid epidemic violence and brutality against blacks. Importantly, Cooper confronts the limits of a Lockean constitutional legacy by directly engaging the history of enslavement and the ongoing material conditions of its aftermath in the daily lives of black women. In addition to her attentiveness to cruelty to black women on railroad cars, Cooper especially focuses on black women's "forced association" with white men, an appropriation of a term commonly deployed by whites panicked by even the slightest prospect of equality between the races, in order to account for interracial rape (Cooper 111).

By the same token, Cooper attests later in the chapter that "if one intimates that some clauses of the Constitution are a dead letter at the South and that only the name and support of that pet institution [slavery] are changed, while the fact and essence, minus the expense and responsibility, remain, he is quickly told to mind his own business" (106). Here, Cooper usefully highlights a pervasive, state-sanctioned dissimulation of terror at the turn of the century. Even more provocatively, she theorizes the instrumentality of patriotism (that is, if one merely "intimates" dissent, dire consequences arise) and the finally mythic nature of substantive equality.[11] In the end, she pinpoints an institutionalized, liberal ethic of critical abstraction—from religion to literature to law—contingent upon the vehement repression of black difference.

Productive Dissonance

Notable continuities exist between two of Cooper's essays in *A Voice*, "Woman Versus the Indian" and "Has America a Race Problem; If So, How Can It Best Be Solved?," in terms of precisely this matter of difference. In both essays, Cooper advances pluralism and community as means to counter two cornerstones of liberal thought: individualism and binary opposition. As I have argued throughout this book, strictly racialized and gendered notions of the self-possessed, contained, rights-bearing individual engaged in an inevitable march toward progress denote hallmarks of Western rational modernity. And yet, blacks' access to the realms of sovereignty and entitlement following Emancipation remain severely compromised. Cooper confronts the circumscribed nature of the post-Reconstruction era in "Has America a Race Problem" by supplanting the reigning liberal telos of what she eventually terms singular, "despotic" development with a palpably textured theorization of harmony.

The section in question, "Has America a Race Problem," commences audaciously: "There are two kinds of peace in this world. The one produced by suppression, which is the passivity of death; the other brought about by a proper adjustment of living, acting forces" (Cooper 149). The "secret of true harmony," she suggests then, necessitates not merely the presence of diversity, but constituents' mutual sustenance and simultaneous capacities to thrive (ibid.). Adopting an array of symbols to represent often-competing, yet finally indispensable, parts of a whole—from a macro-level metaphor of planets and suns to a micro-level comparison of negative and positive electrodes in elements such as water and air—Cooper sculpts a conceptual space for peace and harmony secured not by violence or individual tyranny, but by an effectual combination of multiple identities and perspectives. Overall, difference and conflict prevail in Cooper's model at the expense of "unity without variety," "sameness," "stagnation," or "death" (Cooper 152).

Though for Kevin K. Gaines, Cooper's intervention via harmony bears pastoral and paternalistic connotations, corresponding to a pandering to white elites not uncommon among prominent black writers and public intellectuals of the period, I argue that it in fact departs from wide-spread notions of harmony as pleasant unity by striking at the heart of dominant discourses of possessive individualism that pivot upon an abjection of blackness.[12] As Penny Weiss corroborates, "[Cooper's] work contains a deep critique of individualism and constantly appeals to more communitarian concerns, emphasizing women's social influence and responsibilities and stressing the importance of civility, humility, and commitment to helping others" (84). With a discerning eye to Cooper's strategic mobilization of discourses around conventional gender roles and complementarity, as well as to the layeredness of Cooper's appraisal of American liberal ideology, I suggest the importance of examining the rhetorical effects of Cooper's insight, rather than focusing solely on its possible use-value as a mechanism of appeasement.

"[I]t is both the simultaneity and the sounding against one another that Cooper emphasizes in her argument," affirms Janice Fernheimer (Waters and Conway 293). Ultimately, Cooper contradicts liberal pre-scription toward individual achievement and advancement above the needs of a heterogeneous collective. For Cooper, "healthy, stimulating, and progressive" conflict yields a harmonious juxtaposition of "radically opposing or racially different elements," thereby locating resistance and productive dissonance as central to the democratic project (Cooper 151).[13]

In this vein, Cooper's theories of conflict and community likewise destabilize binary modes of thought. The non-dichotomous approach of her writing, Cooper's issuing of multiple points of view to multiple audiences, posits a "both/and" approach to knowledge production an-tithetical to the Western rational tradition. As Gloria Anzaldúa asserts, acceptance of divergent, plural, even overtly ambiguous thought—of occupying and embodying a crossroads—facilitates awareness and gen-erates political consciousness, while "either/or" logic perpetuates and naturalizes violence, tethering oppressed populations to their oppres-sors (100). Exploring Cooper's critiques of American liberal ideologies of individualism and binary opposition—of how one can be at once op-pressed and privileged, simultaneously disempowered as black and as a woman—situates her as a participant within a confluent black and Chi-cana feminist dialogue crossing time and space, underscoring the ongo-ing relevance of Cooper's interventions in the present.

Cooper also takes up the issue of difference in a manner resonant with contemporary feminist scholarship in "Woman Versus the Indian."

In general, a crucial dimension of her argument in this chapter is the perversity and pervasiveness of "Southern influence, Southern ideas and Southern ideals" upon post-Reconstruction governance at the federal level (Cooper 101). In perhaps Cooper's most scathing indictment of the South—emerging from a memorable stew of metaphors of race, ethnicity, family, and blood—she offers a striking analysis of societal co-opting and suppression of diversity:

> For two hundred and fifty years [the Southerner] trained to his hand a people whom he made absolutely his own, in body, mind, and sensibility. He so insinuated differences and distinctions among them, that their personal attachment for him was stronger than for their own brethren and fellow sufferers. He made it a crime for two or three of them to be gathered in Christ's name without a white man's supervision, and a felony for one to teach them to read even the Word of Life; and yet they would defend his interest with their life blood; his smile was their happiness, a pat on the shoulder from him their reward. The slightest difference among themselves in condition, circumstances, opportunities, became barriers of jealousy and disunion. He sowed his blood broadcast among them, then pitted mulatto against black, bond against free, house slave against plantation slave, even the slave of one clan against like slave of another clan; till, wholly oblivious of their ability for mutual succor and defense, all became centers of myriad systems of repellent forces, having but one sentiment in common, and that their entire subjection to that master hand. (Cooper 102)

Importantly, this passage is hinged to Cooper's subsequent characterization of white paternalism as fundamentally manipulative, and, in her words, a mode of "manage[ment]" and "hoodwink[ing]," the result of which blacks supposedly "wouldn't be free if they could" (103). Cooper's depiction of the surveillance and deprivation endured by black bondsmen and women at the hands of Southern whites clarifies the violent structure of feeling undergirding fin-de-siècle racial politics, an ethos predicated upon an eradication of black distinction.

However, this passage also historicizes the ways in which particularity is often reduced to a site of pathology, or erased altogether, rather than being viewed as a force of sustenance or social change. Intra-racial suspicion, a mode of control Audre Lorde refers to as "horizontal hostility," signals precisely such appropriation of ethnic, sexual, and class variance, and a dissimulation of patriarchal ideology and racial subjection.

Such fixations, Lorde establishes in *Sister Outsider* in an echo of Cooper's initial critique, foreclose possibilities for collective justice and reproduce white supremacist values.

A becoming together of Cooper, Anzaldúa, and Lorde reveals possibilities of Cooper's attenuated focus on her own complicity with hegemonic structures, but also of the scholars' mutual carving out of a necessarily heretical space for coalition. An understanding of the ways in which Cooper's insights into a liberal politics of objectivity and universality, possessive individualism and binary logic overlap with the vision of contemporary women-of-color feminists necessarily expands the framework through which black resistance attains legibility.

Coming to Voice

Along with a theorization of harmonious difference, the very organizational structure of *A Voice* is suffused with a songful politics that undermines the liberal problematic. The first section of the text bears the title "Soprano Obligato" and contains the following chapters: "Womanhood a Vital Element in the Regeneration and Progress of a Race," "The Higher Education of Woman," "Woman Versus the Indian," and "The Status of Woman in America." "Tutti Ad Libitum" is the heading of the second part of the volume, in which the chapters "Has America a Race Problem; If So, How Can It Best Be Solved?," "The Negro as Presented in American Literature," "What Are We Worth?," and "The Gain from a Belief" appear. Thus, in a nod to the title of the collection as a whole, Cooper uses a fluency in musical theory to situate "Soprano Obligato" and "Tutti Ad Libitum" as components of an intervention that is at once textual and also acutely preoccupied with sound and voice.

Aptly, Cooper qualifies soprano—the highest and most overwhelmingly feminized of the vocal registers—with the term *obligato*, which refers to the essential nature and crucial contribution of a particular melody to the fullness of a musical performance. Hence, as a vestibular site denoting distinctiveness and independence—in particular, a cue that a part be played only by a specified instrument—soprano obligato ushers in the exact segment of *A Voice* grounded by Cooper's caveat that "Only the BLACK WOMAN can say 'when and where I enter.'" In defiance of the silencing constraints of racist and sexist subjection, and of the evasion of contrast buttressing dominant liberal norms, Cooper emphasizes the singularity of black women's voices. Her articulation of soprano obligato

Figure 7. Sheet music for "Ethiopia's Paean of Exaltation," score by H. T. Burleigh and lyrics by Anna Julia Cooper (Call Number "Sc Scores Burleigh," Section "E-J," Box 115, Schomburg Center for Research in Black Culture, New York Public Library).

speaks to black women's leadership capacities, and to possibilities of overcoming both outwardly hostile and more subtly oppressive regimes.

"Tutti Ad Libitum," conveying a more ensemble-like and improvisational tenor, both supplements and reinforces Cooper's initial claims in "Soprano Obligato." With a focus on a group quest for human rights and an intersectional attentiveness to issues of gender, race, and class, the latter half of the text denaturalizes a privileging of the individual extant in the American liberal tradition. Across both portions, Cooper makes repeated mention of such terms as (key)note, tone, harmony, rhythm, musical, cadence, voice, strain, chorus, lyric, carol, echo, song, and (dis)cord. Read with and against one another, the two sections foreground a fundamentally dialogic system imagining black women as agents.[14]

Cooper's acts of choral self-definition are also related to the genre of black spirituals. Theological scholar Karen Baker-Fletcher supports such a position, making mention of W.E.B. Du Bois's characterization of spirituals as "sorrow songs" as she recommends that "Womanist theologians must turn to African American song as one of the cultural forms in which Black Americans have expressed and recorded their feelings and thought about Black experiences in America" (194). I conjure Du Bois's *The Souls of Black Folk*, on the other hand, for its specific reverberation with Cooper's distinct musical poetics.

Indeed, *A Voice from the South* and *The Souls of Black Folk*, as confluent analytics, reflect interrelatedness on multiple levels. Du Bois's "problem of the Twentieth century" is Cooper's "perplexing cul de sac of the nation." However, I draw attention in this instance to a key contention extended by Hazel Carby in *Race Men* regarding *Souls*—that is, that the aural framing in which Du Bois engages at the start of each chapter carries out a particular form of epistemological and rhetorical work that the text then reinforces. In contrast to ethnographic readings of the sorrow songs, Carby argues, "I believe that the text of each chapter has a specific performative role: each is a composition of improvised lyrics upon the musical fragments that precede them. Du Bois does not reflect directly upon the lyrics of the sorrow songs prior to his conclusion precisely because he intends that his chapters be regarded as new lyrics, new improvisations" (88).[15] As a consequence, the project of *Souls* is inherently political, while also signaling "the actual imaginative creation of a national, African American . . . cultural presence, a presence which becomes a forceful participant in a cultural struggle over defining exactly what should constitute not just 'black culture,' but American culture" (Carby, *Race Men* 89). What has been overlooked in critical scholarship more broadly are not only the ways in which Carby's insights might extend to the poetry that concludes each of the chapters in Du Bois's 1935 volume *Black Reconstruction in America: 1860–1880*, composed at Cooper's behest, but how *A Voice* is likewise shot through with concerns with black music as theoretical, rather than purely sociological.

Sonic dimensions and effects, specifically, function as frameworks through which Cooper revises standards of national community, as she consistently extricates democracy and liberty from originary realms of Western European modernity. In fact, Cooper's Singing Something, the notion of an inherent (if as-yet unfulfilled) human impulse toward parity, marks an unreserved gift from God, a blessing discernible on the horizon of sound. Underscoring the texture and tangibility of God's tone, Cooper explores the nature of what it might mean to function as a channel for His democratic intonation, a vessel for His revelatory telling. Accordingly, "For Cooper humankind's creation in the image of God is more than merely imagistic," Baker-Fletcher argues; "It is vocal. It is musical. It is auditory. . . . She was interested in the sound, the words, the composition of God's voice" (191). Moreover, Cooper expressly links the meaning of speech with the power of physicality and embodiment.

That is, Cooper locates the "divine Spark" of the Singing Something as a dynamic that exceeds normative patterns of feminine passivity and masculine authority, finally rejecting patterns of mental transcendence over bodily groundedness that are redolent of the liberal problematic. Elizabeth Alexander apprehends as much in her own work on Cooper, maintaining, "Using the voice is a physical act, one that first announces the existence of the body of residence and then trumpets its arrival in a public space. The physicality of that metaphor ["of the unheard voice of the African American woman"] asserts corporeal presence in the space of imagined absence" ("We Must Be" 345). In evacuating aurality as an esteemed source of knowledge formation, liberal theory disproportionately primitivizes blackness, perpetually equating orality with simplicity. Nevertheless, by way of its "sly alterity," the black singing voice reclaims rational authority in the name of the body, exposing practices of ocularcentrism and detachment as flawed Enlightenment imprimatur.[16] A more explicit engagement with Cooper's auditory analyses in this regard, I argue, challenges the apparent discreteness of Western theology and rationality, simultaneously flouting a mind-body split endemic to Western ways of knowing.

In the end, critical consideration of the musicality of not only Du Bois's but also Cooper's spiritual strivings yields understanding of how the narrative of *A Voice* sounds, and insight into the ways in which its sounding undermines reliance on predominantly visual terms of order and coherence. In other words, Cooper's composition—its musical framing, metaphor, and theory—cannot be relegated to the cosmetic domain of style alone. Rather, Cooper's textual and phonic substances coalesce to produce new modes of valuing black womanhood and oppressed peoples more broadly. Her recovery of the body through music, her fin-de-siècle song, re-frames civic equality and American civil subjectivity. Therefore, Cooper's dissonance within larger rubrics of black resistive performance speaks less to her racialist accommodation and more to ossified practices of mishearing in need of transformation.

Of Liberal Utterance: Subverting Tropes of Intention, Inclusion, and Sorority

In Cooper's estimation, difference defies superficial consensus and liberal unanimity in favor of purposeful discord. Consequently, and as black feminist intellectuals have long argued, viable anti-racist coalition represents a joint context of oppression founded as much on precepts of commonality as on struggle and risk. Thus, in *Reconstructing Womanhood*, Hazel Carby problematizes and contextualizes late twentieth-century mainstream feminists' urge to "discover a lost sisterhood and to reestablish feminist solidarity" (Carby 6).[17] In particular, she leverages Cooper's keen sense of the provinciality and circulation of liberal affect within ostensibly progressive political movements to structure her reading of impediments to modern interracial coalition-building. Further, she taps into the power of Cooper's critique in the aforementioned "Woman Versus the Indian" to unearth the previous life of late twentieth-century (white) feminism's origin narrative of itself. Indeed, as I have suggested elsewhere, and as Cooper's analyses make abundantly clear, much contemporary feminist conflict marks "a reprisal of earlier hegemonic scripts, a reformulation of prior regimes of ownership" (Mann 576).

Accordingly, I argue that Cooper's third chapter opens in an only apparently celebratory tenor as she applauds Susan B. Anthony and Anna Shaw of *Wimodaughsis*—an elite organization of wives, mothers, daughters, and sisters supporting the cultural and professional advance-ment of women—for their censure of the group's secretary for refusing to admit a woman of color. Cooper's account of the Southern secretary's "grief" and "horror" at the prospect of permitting a black woman access to the club—of the "painful possibility of the sight of a black man coming in the future to escort from an evening class this solitary cream-colored applicant"—encapsulates quite compellingly what Vorris Nunley terms the "biopower of White comfort" (Cooper 81–82; Nunley 16). Concerned with the ways in which white middle-class ease and contentment func-tion as modes of policing blacks' "reputations, their jobs, their safety, and too often, their very lives," Nunley grapples with a vestige of cult (of true womanhood) ideology that Cooper's work ardently sought to disrupt, yet that still holds sway in present-day feminist debates (Nunley 16).[18]

Nevertheless, Cooper's fundamentally kairotic account, alerting us to the importance of what rhetorical scholar Shirley Wilson Logan terms "arrangement," in fact merely seduces her audience through outward relish for Shaw's compassion and a meditation on the moral failings of the South. According to Logan, "Arrangement is important in persua-sive discourse . . . because changes in the audience are contingent upon the order in which the elements in an argument are presented" (117). Indeed, kairos and arrangement alike reflect a complex manipulation of the elements of time, place, culture, audience, decorum, and style. At-tentiveness to rhetorical pace in these ways facilitates engagement by defusing potential audience skepticism or suspicion. In the long run, Cooper's project undercuts dominant notions of narrative progress and white Northern empathy, culminating in a stunning rhetorical skewer-ing of Shaw's privileged ethos of tolerance.

Hence, Cooper's initial assertion that "Miss Shaw is broad and just and liberal *in principal* is proved beyond contradiction," and the impre-cisely Native American undertone of *Wimodaughsis*, are key (Cooper 80; emphasis added). Granting Cooper a "fine opportunity to pun upon the arrogance and fallacy of [*Wimodaughsis'*] use" (Foster 188) in the first place, Cooper's strategic rhetorical manipulation in "Woman Versus the Indian" exposes Shaw's implicit endorsement of racial hierarchies. Indeed, Cooper collapses the distance between the venerable, liberal-minded "lady" of the North and the secretary "who really would like to help 'elevate' the colored people (in her own way of course and so long as they understand their places)" (Cooper 81). Cooper demonstrates Shaw's acute proximity to, rather than moral high ground over and above, her organization's Southern secretary.[19]

Furthermore, of Shaw's 1891 speech at the National Woman's Council in Washington, D.C., the namesake of Cooper's chapter, the latter argues forcefully, "Is not woman's cause broader, and deeper, and grander, than a blue stocking debate or an aristocratic pink tea? Why should woman become plaintiff in a suit versus the Indian, or the Negro or any other race or class who have been crushed under the iron heel of Anglo-Saxon power and selfishness?" (Cooper 123). That is, in a section of A Voice keenly attuned to the violence of American expansionism and imperialism, Cooper explicitly links the contexts of black, Native, and others' subjection under the force of the U.S. settler-colonial project, and signals mainstream white feminists' historic contribution to and ongoing complicity with such a system. "If the Indian has been wronged and cheated by the puissance of this American government," she adds, "it is woman's mission to plead with her country to cease to do evil and to pay its honest debts" (Cooper 124). Perceptively, Cooper sounds a critique against the ranking of oppression.

This intersects with Cooper's comments earlier in the volume: "We too often mistake individuals' honor for race development and so are ready to substitute pretty accomplishments for sound sense and earnest purpose" (29). As had Elizabeth Keckly before her, through the former's literary expression of anti-pastoral reach, Cooper attends to the limits of a palatable, exceptional blackness. Cognizant of the cruel underside of such "pretty accomplishments," Cooper indicts a liberal politics of singular ascent and inclusion predicated upon white supremacy.

Cooper also directs special attention to the violence enacted through language in ostensibly enlightened circles. In this vein, she asserts in "Woman Versus the Indian," "Woman should not, *even by inference, or for the sake of argument,* seem to disparage what is weak" (117; emphasis added). In a passage evocative of what I deem a broader epistemological move on the part of black female scholars of the period, including intellectual-activist Ida B. Wells, Cooper problematizes practices of "rhetorical imperialism."[20] Though Cooper is frequently compared to, and as often depoliticized as, Wells's antithesis on a continuum of radicalism, I argue that they extend analogous critiques of the limits of liberal ideological formations disseminated in and through language.

Significantly, Wells palpably echoes Cooper's claims regarding the denigrating impact of well-intentioned speech in the by-now classic

A Red Record, published just three years after *A Voice*, in 1895. In the eighth chapter of this crucial text of the anti-lynching movement, Wells directly addresses commentary dispensed by Frances Willard, president of the Women's Christian Temperance Union, at their annual convention in Cleveland in November 1894. In terms akin to Cooper's concerning Shaw, Wells states:

> I desire no quarrel with the W.C.T.U., but my love for the truth is greater than my regard for an alleged friend [Willard] who, through ignorance or design misrepresents in the most harmful way the cause of a long suffering race, and then unable to maintain the truth of her attack excuses herself as it were by the wave of the hand, declaring that "she did not intend a literal interpretation to be given to the language used." When the lives of men, women, and children are at stake, when the inhuman butchers of innocents attempt to justify their barbarism by fastening upon a whole race the obloque [*sic*] of the most infamous of crimes[, i]t is little less than criminal to apologize for the butchers today and tomorrow to repudiate the apology by declaring it a figure of speech. (Royster 147–48)

Wells strikes at the heart of mythologies of black bestiality, hypersexuality, white male chivalry, and the lynching-as-rape-prevention thesis, but also of tolerant white leaders' implicit reinforcement of such positions. Her crucial qualification—"through ignorance or design"—shifts the critical register away from intention and public apology as alibi and toward the realm of effects.

As discussed in chapter one, "While individual intention matters, [political] rationalities mediate intentionality, operating on the level of power, categories, and framing": that is, "framing who gets to speak as a citizen and how, and what behaviors, rhetorics, knowledges, and identities are deemed legitimate, acceptable, normative, and natural within the American imaginary as citizenship" (Nunley 12). Wells challenges Willard's governing assumptions of blackness as excess within the American polity, pinpointing the ways in which white privilege frames and informs precisely which lives hold value. Citing an ongoing tradition within liberal discourse of violent troping and effacement of blackness to metaphor, perhaps most (though by no means exclusively) evident in contemporary dehumanizing representations of Sojourner Truth, Wells underscores the dire stakes of even the most subtle of lynching apologia.[21] In an expression of epistemic continuity rather than polarity, then,

Cooper and Wells situate notions of blackness as expendable, though embedded as "inference" or mere "figure of speech," as forces of containment, an extension of a vicious if well-meaning agenda.

Critical Regard

Another means by which Cooper counters the limits of a manifestly instrumental ethos of inclusion reinforcing the liberal problematic, I would argue, is by positing an alternative social theory, a pubic pedagogy of civility I call "critical regard." By way of the latter, she undoes widespread cultural edicts of modesty and appropriateness, envisioning conduct at odds with liberal commonplaces of order and respectability. Playing with contemporary astronomer/writer Percival Lowell's theory in his *Soul of the Far East* that America is "the least courteous nation on the globe" (Cooper 99), Cooper sets the stage for her final condemnation of Shaw's prejudice.

Thus, she declares in "Woman Versus the Indian," "I have determined to plead with our women, the mannerless sex on this mannerless continent, to institute a reform by placing immediately in our national curricula a department for teaching GOOD MANNERS" (ibid.; emphasis in original). With this move, Cooper simultaneously engages prevailing definitions of refinement and appropriates entrenched dynamics of educability to subversive ends. Indeed, as Candice M. Jenkins observes in *Private Lives, Proper Relations*, "the dominant notion of 'civilization' is . . . a loaded one, heavy with the burden of white supremacy, Western imperialism, and the so-called 'savagery' of nonwhite people across the globe" (2). Yet Cooper extricates decorum from the gendered and racialized realm of etiquette alone. Instead, Cooper politicizes courtesy as an ethical performance grounded in faith in "substantial democracy."[22] Taken together with her emphases on difference, ambiguity, and conflictive "harmony" throughout *A Voice*, critical regard—Cooper's plea for reciprocal decency and respect—expands the space of comportment to one of imagining social change.

Accordingly, Cooper speaks of "the secret of universal courtesy," which she situates as at once an "art," "science," and "religion" (117). Rather than a disciplining formation concerned with naturalizing purportedly objective standards of behavior, critical regard functions within Cooper's framework as an agile font of subjectivity and worldview. She references "the art of courteous contact, which is naught but the practical application of the principal of benevolence, the back bone and marrow of all religion" (125). But courtesy also stands, in this sense, for collective justice. Decorum entails parity on the terrain of the human and on that of the citizen-subject.

"Though she seems to be calling for greater courtesy, she is actually demanding a better sense of 'self,' of personhood—one might even say of womanhood," confirms Lemert in his introduction to the most complete edited collection of Cooper's essays, papers, and letters to date. "She means, I think, to trifle with [Lowell's] half-baked theory of good manners in order subtly to emphasize the deeper values of personal character" (Lemert and Bahn 37). Formerly privatized by white "ladies" in the North and South alike, good manners serve in Cooper's project as sites of political consciousness and expression. Though Cooper takes pages upon pages to execute her critique of Shaw—a presentation of "studied uncertainty," Lemert observes, by one fully "aware of what she has been doing" (38)—her conclusion is plain: progressive liberal advocates' reliance on circumscribed notions of belonging enable violent practices of exclusion. By redefining civility, and precisely who can and cannot occupy such a domain, Cooper contests raced and gendered asymmetries of power, creating alternate ways of achieving freedom.

And yet, focused precisely on combating the structural subjection enacted across the domains of law and public policy, post-secondary education, religion, and popular culture, Cooper's philosophy of critical regard does not pivot upon liberal notions of uplift and self-help. She does not propagate distinctly individual correctives, promote a culture of self-policing, or fetishize volition as a conduit to civic mobility.[23] More accurately, Cooper underscores solidarity and accountability amid groups of various racial, gender, and class backgrounds and abilities. Not fundamentally therapeutic or ameliorative in orientation, but rather proactive, Cooper's approach poses a direct challenge to routine regimes of privilege. Therefore, her recuperation of the meaning of civil subjectivity shifts the epistemic frame of citizens' political relationships and responsibilities to themselves and to one another.

Furthermore, critical regard is buoyed not by false optimism or by naiveté on Cooper's part. Rather, it is rooted in and by an abundant faith. "Religion for this reformer was an embodied, intuitive form of reason," reflects Baker-Fletcher, enabling Cooper to harness non-empirical and material knowledge claims, New Testament scripture, Christian symbolism, and other redemptive figurations in an attempt to alter conditions dramatically within and outside of the public sphere (20, 169). That is, Cooper's faith surpasses institutional bounds. As her critique of abstract policies privileged by the Protestant Episcopal Church indicates, Cooper models a supple and discerning spirituality. She illuminates the imbrication of secular struggle and sacred ardor in securing black equality.

As Patricia Hill Collins affirms in *Fighting Words*, "faith constitutes a *process* whereby individuals and groups use an ethical framework grounded in deeply felt beliefs to construct meaningful everyday lives" (199–200; emphasis in original). Hence Cooper advances a sacredness that understands that belief contained by doctrine remains static. Cooper's own faith, by contrast, is abiding and processual, compassionate and communal. Political exigency and culpability ground Cooper's activist drive for a mutually sustaining society.[24]

Just as Cooper's notion of critical regard makes the liberal problematic—the disparity between liberalism's professed aims and its uneven effects—visible, Wells crystallizes a similar break between theory and lived black realities. Yet again in *A Red Record*, Wells demonstrates the slippage between abstract chivalry and the institutionalized rape of black women, as well as the harassment of Northern white teachers laboring to educate blacks following Emancipation. "Whatever faults and failings other nations may have in their dealings with their own subjects or with other people, no other civilized nation stands condemned before the world with a series of crimes so peculiarly national" (Royster 81–2), Wells declares, exploiting the aforementioned gap to censure America and to expose reverberations of civility that exceed the sphere of whiteness.

"It becomes a painful duty of the Negro," Wells continues, "to reproduce a record which shows that a large portion of the American people avow anarchy, condone murder and defy the contempt of civilization" (ibid.). In truth, civility eludes the U.S. nation-state. Throughout her work, Cooper demonstrates that the revolutionary promise of American egalitarianism does not correspond to the tangible experience of the most disenfranchised. In this way, she renders constitutional mandate hollow. More importantly, she forges a pathway toward democratization for Wells and others by opening up liberal propriety to possibilities for dissident reconfiguration. With the paradigm of critical regard, I contend, Cooper influences critical registers of embodied knowledge and black resistance in truly generative ways.

Jestice for All

There is one other quality of Cooper's prose that is both hard to miss, and, arguably, one of the primary sources of her inaudibility as a legitimate practitioner of resistance. Simply put, she's funny. Less simply put, her sarcasm at once indexes and diverges from an established trajectory of African-American hilarity.

Indeed, despite Cooper's translation of the notably parodic eleventh-century epic *The Pilgrimage of Charlemagne* from medieval to modern French during her lifetime (May 81), and contemporary cultural critics' (including Albion Tourgée's) public allusion to the sarcastic elements contained in *A Voice* (Hutchinson 103), sustained attentiveness to the rhetorical effects of such humor remains scarce. But what of Cooper's clever observations in *A Voice* of the trite excuses leveled by whites to disarm calls for racial equity, her claims that "one would think they were words to conjure with, so potent and irresistible is their spell as an argument [against integration] at the North as well as in the South" (101)? What of her acerbic anticipation of Ruthie Gilmore's incisive definition of racism, in which she asserts, "society, where it has not exactly said to its dogs 's-s-sik him!' has at least engaged to be looking in another direction or studying the rivers on Mars" (92)?[25] How might one account for her angry critiques of the privileging of blood ties in the South, her statement that "if your great great great grandfather's grandfather stole and pillaged and slew, and you can prove it, your blood has become blue and you are at great pains to establish that relationship" (103)? Or her commentary to the Episcopal priests, mentioned at the outset of this chapter, that "the doctors while discussing their scientifically conclusive diagnosis of the disease, will perhaps not think it presumptuous in the patient if he dares to suggest where at least the pain is" (36)?

In these moments, as with her oft-cited rejoinder to the question of how increased education might hinder women's chances for marriage, I maintain that Cooper upends conventional expectations of black comedic performance in order to pillory dominant alibis undergirding state-sanctioned violence and exclusion.[26] While participating in a broader tradition of African-American humor, one invested in laying bare the decimation of black lives, Cooper also refracts this legacy by opting for a multi-vocal approach with appeal for heterogeneous contexts and audiences. Comedically, Cooper disputes conditions and circumstances governing reason, crystallizing the limits of mainstream liberal ideological formations.

In the antebellum period, black wit often hinged upon exposing the absurdity of racism in both its institutionalized and more individualized manifestations. "The humor of absurdity worked through a straight-faced assumption of the rationality of the system and the belief structure upon which it rested," writes Lawrence Levine (310). Of black jokes about segregation, specifically a comic anecdote by a former slave woman regarding the pervasive, if illogical, anti-integrationist sentiment in the pre–Civil War North, Levine explains that "[t]he note of absurdity struck by Mrs. Prosser remained the chief thrust of black humor concerning American racial codes" (310), adding later, "These jokes acknowledged black fear and subservience even as they stressed the inanity and fantasy nature of the system which bound them" (311). Mel Watkins, too, speaks of African-American humor as an idiom, or the "shared ironic vision of a group," characterized by an exploitation of the very breach between procedural and substantive equality—or the liberal problematic—that *A Voice* brings cogently to the fore (568).

Moreover, orators including Frederick Douglass, William Cooper Nell, James McCune Smith, William G. Allen, and Martin Delany (especially in his novel *Blake*) often invoked sarcasm in order to defy Enlightenment, Christian, and sentimentalist dogma, and to problematize dominant historical and archival memory. In *The Amalgamation Waltz: Race, Performance, and the Ruses of Memory*, Tavia Nyong'o suggests that "Antebellum black activists used sarcasm to distance themselves from their present condition, not only in relation to an ostensibly glorious past in Africa but also in relation to an ambiguous future in which racial justice might indeed be secured" (155). Not before noting that "a recurrent outcome of a successful act of sarcasm is the metamessage 'I don't mean this,'" and that "what distinguishes sarcasm is the clarity and intentionality of the alienation of the speaker from his or her words" (158), Nyong'o demonstrates the assertive and overtly disruptive nature of particular forms of black irony.

Scholar Darryl Dickson-Carr nevertheless calls for an expansion of the very terms by which African-American humor is recognized. In particular, at least two theoretical dimensions of Dickson-Carr's analysis of *reductio ad absurdum* in black satirical practice hold significance for this project. I draw attention to his interrogation of the ways in which satire "transgresses boundaries of taste, propriety, decorum, and the current ideological status quo" (1), and in which certain veins of ironic perfor-mance are overwhelmingly gendered masculine (5). Accordingly, I argue that in a work penned by one rendered perpetually accommodating and restrained by critics in our contemporary moment, Cooper not only in-troduces her own subversive public pedagogy of critical regard in *A Voice*, but directly engages in an unruly mode of discourse that negates reign-ing cultural dictates and rationalities of politesse.

Cooper's wry remarks must be thought about and contextualized, then, within an explicitly raced and gendered sphere of black performa-tivity and emergent modernity, as her sly quips register contestation of normative readings of black ontology as lack and of women as inher-ently inferior to their male counterparts. Notably, nineteenth-century "scientific" racist prognoses often relegated black oratory to the realm of "feeling" or inadvertent comic relief. Black rhetors, especially, were cited for overuse of allegory and Biblical parable in public discourse. Given prevailing sentiments of their "grotesque inventions in grammar and rhetoric" and "'characteristic fondness for big words' that they did not understand," Todd Vogel contends that Cooper, via at-once humor-ous and deductive reasoning, "tackle[s] head-on ideas about blacks as unintentionally comic orators and accept[s] no compromise on her ar-gument" (92). For Vogel, Cooper's divergence from the seemingly more self-deprecating, deferential, and feminized rhetorical styles of other public intellectuals of the period, including Mary Church Terrell and Francis Willard, is predicated upon deeply deliberate and sardonic word play. Language and other rhetorical skills—specifically, signification and irony—functioned as Cooper's "cultural capital" (Vogel 86), the means by which she forged incisive social critique.

Given the etymology of *sarcasmus* as "a gnashing of teeth or tearing of flesh" (Nyong'o 157), I argue for an express linkage between early nine-teenth-century lampoons of American liberalism and Cooper's comic post-bellum politics. Although, in its male-centeredness, Nyong'o's al-ternative canon of nineteenth-century sarcasts reinforces patterns of gendered exclusion in black humor studies, by accounting for sarcasm as "a bodily practice as much as a spoken register" (ibid.), Nyong'o speaks to Cooper's and her contemporaries' critical investment in dismantling prime tenets subtending the liberal problematic: binaries between mind and body, emotion and intellect, Emancipation and freedom.

For instance, in one memorable scenario, Cooper casts women's sup-pression worldwide as a form of blindness—the equivalent of seeing out of just one eye—the elimination of which ensures that "the whole body is filled with light" (Cooper 122). Mimicking figures such as Elizabeth Cady Stanton, specifically their opportunistic self-appointment as the select bearers of any and all luminosity, Cooper ridicules the "travesty of its case for this eye to become plaintiff in a suit, *Eye vs. Foot*" (123).[27] "There is that dull clod, the foot, allowed to roam at will, free and untrammeled; while I, the source and medium of light, brilliant and beautiful," Cooper proceeds facetiously, "am fettered in darkness and doomed to desuetude" (123). Subsequently coupling anti-black and anti-native stances on suffrage adopted by prominent members of the mainstream Women's Movement, Cooper problematizes representations of racial and cultural difference as bestial or uncivilized.

"In a manner illustrative of prevailing discriminatory conceptions of rights," acknowledges Kevin K. Gaines in *Uplifting the Race*, "Cooper vehemently rejected the arguments of white women suffragists that they . . . were more entitled to the vote than what she sarcastically called 'the great burly black man, ignorant and gross and depraved'" (144). As Gaines rightly intimates, Cooper's sarcasm in "Woman Versus the Indian" signals deep-seated imbrications between black disfranchisement and cultural mythologies of black hypermasculinity, sexuality, criminality, and infantilization. Her ventriloquizing of demeaning tropes of blackness and maleness in this scenario insinuates complicity with the dominant ethos, but ultimately derides the emptiness of abstract rights discourse and of parochial feminist praxis.[28] Cooper later draws attention to a commonplace metaphorization of slavery deployed by well-meaning majority feminists well into the twentieth century in order to spectacularize conditions of gender discrimination. Through humor, Cooper testifies to the limits of liberal utterance, to notions of entitlement that negate the fitness of racialized bodies for citizenship.

Via a defiant mock deference, Cooper also marshals the patently gendered attribute of reserve to pinpoint the significant expense at which race and male privilege are customarily accrued. In "The Higher Education of Women," a speech initially delivered to the American Conference of Educators in 1890, Cooper offers almost overlapping sarcastic passages instigated in ostensibly deferential registers, both of which I quote at length:

It seems hardly a gracious thing to say, but it strikes me as true, that while our men seem thoroughly abreast of the times on almost every other subject, when they strike the woman question they drop back into sixteenth century logic. They leave nothing to be desired generally in regard to gallantry and chivalry, but they actually do not seem sometimes to have outgrown that old contemporary of chivalry— the idea that women may stand on pedestals or live in doll houses, (if they happen to have them) but they must not furrow their brows with thought or attempt to help men tug at the great questions of the world . . . The three R's, a little music and a good deal of dancing, a first rate dress-maker and a bottle of magnolia balm, are quite enough generally to render charming any woman possessed of tact and the capacity for worshipping masculinity. (Cooper 75)

Cooper follows this declaration with an autobiographical anecdote, what she refers to as "a little bit of personal experience" (76), which discerning readers understand as a euphemistic spin on her history of organizing at St. Augustine's Normal School and Collegiate Institute:

Finally a Greek class was to be formed. My inspiring preceptor informed me that Greek had never been taught in the school, but that he was going to form a class *for the candidates for the ministry*, and if I liked I might join it. I replied—humbly I hope, as became a female of the human species—that I would like very much to study Greek, and that I was thankful for the opportunity, and so it went on. A boy, however meager his equipment and shallow his pretensions, had only to declare a floating intention to study theology and he could get all the support, encouragement and stimulus he needed, be absolved from work and invested beforehand with all the dignity of his far away office. While a self-supporting girl had to struggle on by teaching in the summer and working after school hours to keep up with her board bills, and actually to fight her way against positive discouragements to the higher education. (77)

As Vivian May warns, "it is . . . important to realize the risk [Cooper] took in asserting such notions, even under the guise of a joke or under the irreproachable cover of theological reflection" (60). In these closely allied excerpts, Cooper's professed concerns with polish and poise defuse dominant audiences before giving way to biting analyses of pervasive sexism, the coerciveness of cult ideology, and purported male courtliness. Through strategic recourse to counterfeit docility, Cooper contests women's status as ornate instruments by which to shore up hegemonic masculine authority. Without minimizing gentlemanly protection as an uneven, privileged context (only "if they [women] happen to have them," she says of "doll houses"), and by gesturing toward the legitimacy of black women's desires for equitable and loyal relations with black men ("they leave nothing to be desired generally in regard to gallantry and chivalry"), Cooper effects a broad-based call for sociopolitical change. Indeed, she agitates for educational access in order to expand the realm of possibilities for women within patriarchy, but also for those beyond the bounds of traditional domestic configurations, including impoverished, single, and widowed women (Cooper 68). Foregrounding material and ideological impediments to racial and gender parity—and embedding this critical move away from peripherality toward collective social justice in witty overtures—constitutes a powerful and necessary intervention into liberal protocols of belonging.

Then and Now

Upon gazing out of the window of a railroad coach one final time in "Woman Versus the Indian," Anna Julia Cooper experiences a dilemma. "[L]ooking a little more closely, I see two dingy little rooms with 'FOR LADIES' swinging over one and 'FOR COLORED PEOPLE' over the other," she reveals, "wondering under which head I come" (96). Cooper concludes her meditation by puncturing the hypocrisy of a nation that condemns "Russia's barbarity and cruelty to the Jews," while denying even the most meager provisions to a black traveler "driven by hunger [to seek] the bare necessaries of life at the only public accommodation in the town" (Cooper 97). Signaling the existential, if by-now-mundane crisis occasioned by forever having to "wonde[r] under which head I come," Cooper pinpoints the crux of the liberal problematic, as well as the indispensability of understanding racial discrimination and gender bias as systemic rather than aberrant forces in the U.S. nation-state.

Rather than the paradigmatic liberal subject, then, Cooper joins the voices of Wilson and Keckly to account for how normative political reason is lived and felt, how it infuses the rhythms of everyday life in significant, often violent ways. Cooper's fin-de-siècle song, in its reclamation of embodiment and of civility as virtue, diverges from traditional discourses of rights and inclusion, even as scholars continually reduce the epistemological scope of her project to such parameters. Through sarcasm and aurality, among other means, Cooper sounds a productive critique of privilege and of power that links her to contemporary feminist intellectuals and activists, then and now. The following chapter examines the writings of one of the latter group, twentieth-century African-Americanist scholar Sherley Anne Williams, and her becoming together with nineteenth-century black women's critical thought, as resistance.

4

"Mammy Ain't Nobody Name"

Power, Privilege, and the Bodying Forth of Resistance

A substantial body of scholarship has emerged in the last thirty years pertaining to the literary genre commonly referred to as "neo-slave narrative." Coined to encompass texts as varied as Margaret Walker's *Jubilee* (1966), Ishmael Reed's *Flight to Canada* (1976), Edward P. Jones's *The Known World* (2003), and Attica Locke's *The Cutting Season* (2012), among others, neo-slave narrative as catchall pivots upon temporal logic, signaling a recurring, if heterogeneous, engagement with slave culture and nineteenth-century racial politics evident in modern-day fictional pursuits. In the essay "'Somebody Forgot to Tell Somebody Something': African-American Women's Historical Novels," for instance, black feminist intellectual and literary critic Barbara Christian returns to the work of writers and activists Harriet Jacobs, William Wells Brown, Frances E. W. Harper, and Harriet Wilson in order to contextualize, deeply and richly, the rise of neo-slave narrative in the late twentieth century. Christian situates such works as Toni Morrison's Nobel Prize–winning novel *Beloved* (1987) as modes of redress, as answers to the thick silences and strategic omissions that inform much antebellum slave narrative and even postbellum black poetry, fiction, and prose (89).

In a different vein, critics Marisa Anne Pagnattaro and Angelyn Mitchell understand neo-slave narrative, particularly those volumes penned by women writers, as extensions of contemporary unrest and social movement, and even more narrowly, of Second Wave feminist agitation.

Accordingly, both theorists underscore the urgency and opportunity embedded in "our" present moment. Indeed, artists "present . . . feminist
engagement with race, so that we can imaginatively consider what might
have been in terms of interracial feminist coalition during slavery as well
as what should be in terms of interracial feminist coalitions now," Mitchell maintains in relation to the writing of Sherley Anne Williams (65).
"For [Williams's] *Dessa Rose*, as a twentieth-century text, [the] future
is to recognize the value of interracial collaboration right now," affirms
Pagnattaro (135).

However, as Arlene Keizer's *Black Subjects: Identity Formation in the
Contemporary Narrative of Slavery* productively suggests, extant paradigms and reading practices around neo-slave narrative—those extended by Mitchell, Ashraf Rushdy, Bernard Bell, and Elizabeth Ann
Beaulieu, among others—remain limited. Issuing a call "to cast a wider
interpretive net," Keizer (a student of Christian's) instead posits a theory of "contemporary narratives of slavery" in both African-American
and Afro-Caribbean literary contexts (3). Notably, Keizer's concept of
contemporary narratives of slavery diverges from the work of Rushdy
and Bell by shifting aesthetic standards away from a mimetic relation
to teleological, first-person, literate, antebellum slave experience. For
Keizer, slavery constitutes an increasingly capacious vehicle through
which writers claim agency and reconceptualize the self.[1]

Following Keizer, I, too, tackle underexamined dimensions of neo-
slave narrative discourse. Specifically, I intervene in ongoing critical dia-
logue surrounding Sherley Anne Williams's aforementioned novel, *Dessa
Rose* (1986). That is, scholars have delved into the allusiveness of *Dessa
Rose*, mining its connections to Angela Davis's "Reflections on the Black
Woman's Role in the Community of Slaves" (1971), Herbert Aptheker's
American Negro Slave Revolts (1947), and William Styron's *The Confessions
of Nat Turner* (1967). In addition to these texts, each directly cited in
Williams's "Author's Note," Mae G. Henderson examines the novel's re-
lation to Williams's earlier short story "Meditations on History" (1976)
and Pauline Réage's *Story of O* (1965). Jacquelyn A. Fox-Good and Amy
K. Levin, on the other hand, locate *Slave Songs of the United States* (1876)
and *Jane Eyre* (1847), respectively, as critical reference points. Conversely, I deliberately position Harriet Wilson's *Our Nig* (1859), Elizabeth
Keckly's *Behind the Scenes* (1868), and Anna Julia Cooper's *A Voice from
the South* (1892) as key intertexts in this chapter in order to uncover
the ways in which Williams provokes interchange with her precursors'

legacies of resistance. I concede Christian's claim that texts including Gayl Jones's *Corregidora* (1975) and Octavia Butler's *Kindred* (1979) address gaps within nineteenth-century literature, but not at the expense of exploring contemporary texts' affinities with what previous narratives have explicitly said that has subsequently been misread or overlooked.

Given Williams's status as a lifelong student of the craft of writing, she likely came into contact with works by Wilson, Keckly, and Cooper addressed in the previous chapters of this volume. In her 1972 book of literary criticism, *Give Birth to Brightness*, Williams eschews what she terms "chronological surveys" (102), tendencies on the part of critics to impose narrow patterns of literary succession or descent instead of more nuanced networks of connection. Accordingly, a becoming together of Williams with earlier black women authors does not presuppose a literal encounter. Fundamentally, it denotes a framework of possibility. It yields a dialogic exchange that reveals more about the potential of unforeseen black association than the limits of circumscribed realities. Becoming together, as a temporary mode of assembly, unmasks liberal ways of being, including individualism and universality, as channels of disenfranchisement. Further, it undercuts a persistent ideological alibi by which hegemony is maintained across time and space. In spotlighting conceptual continuity in this way, becoming together deforms purportedly enlightened definitions of freedom and self-possession.

By foregrounding Williams's more recent problematization of coherence and interracial friendship, and by considering her theoretical representations of embodiment, commodification, and rage in relation to blackness, I demonstrate the enduring productivity of nineteenth-century black women's initial contestation of the liberal problematic. Indeed, apprehending neo-slave narratives as repositories of liberal ideology critique—as indebted to complex historical epistemologies regarding privilege and consent—confounds long-standing perspectives on black defiance. It likewise prompts an interrogation of the limits of American liberalism within a neoliberal present.

Reading "As-Told-To" Anew

Born in Bakersfield, California in 1944, Sherley Anne Williams spent much of her life as author and professor articulating to the world what she knew best. In genres as varied as poetry, fiction, children's literature, television, and drama, Williams focused a great deal of her writing

Figure 8. Sherley Anne Williams, photograph by Jim Coit. Courtesy of the photographer.

on themes of poverty and power, but also on the complexities of black history and the vernacular tradition. A daughter of migrant workers, she went on to earn a bachelor's degree in English from the University of California, Fresno in 1962, and later a master's degree from Brown University in 1972. National Book Award and Pulitzer Prize nominations for her 1975 collection *The Peacock Poems,* as well as an American Library Association Caldecott Award for 1992's *Working Cotton,* soon followed. *Dessa Rose*, Williams's only novel, was published in 1986.[2]

Dessa Rose chronicles the exploits of the novel's namesake, a young bondswoman of the U.S. South of the mid-1840s, in the wake of the brutal murder of her husband, Kaine. As violence begets violence in the context of enslavement, Kaine's attack on his master, Terrell Vaugham—for breaking a hand-crafted banjo symbolizing the former's sense of home and identity—results in his death, while Kaine's demise incites Dessa to assault her mistress, Mary. The latter confrontation consigns Dessa to the "sweatbox," wallowing in her own excrement and grief, bearing deep lacerations and later such extensive keloid scarring across her genitals that "no hair would ever grow there again" (Williams 154). Eventually dispatched deeper South, a pregnant Dessa mourns the loss of her partner, mother, and siblings, only to join a vicious uprising in east

Alabama after a white man who ventures off into the woods to rape a mulatta slave girl, Linda, whom he has temporarily freed from the coffle, neglects to properly re-secure the slaves' chains. Severely wounding the slave trader, Wilson, and assisting in the killing of five other white men, Dessa ultimately surrenders in the hopes that some of her accomplices, unencumbered by impending childbirth, might escape.

However, aside from an "Author's Note" and brief prologue, all that readers first glean about Dessa and her story is filtered through the diaristic perspective of Adam Nehemiah, a character based on Boston clergyman Nehemiah Adams (1806–1878). The fictional Nehemiah, a white aspirant to the wealthy planter class and author of *The Masters' Complete Guide to Dealing with Slaves and Other Dependents*, meets regularly with an imprisoned Dessa in order to interrogate her about her experiences on the coffle.[3] In fact, Nehemiah's ruminations about Dessa for his newest masterpiece, *The Roots of Rebellion in the Slave Population and Some Means of Eradicating Them* (or suggestively, *Roots*, for short) structures the entire first section of the novel, titled "The Darky." The remaining two-thirds of the work, designated "The Wench" and "The Negress" respectively, detail a transformation of Dessa-as-epithet—as an object refused a legitimate name—to Dessa as a self-defined subject. Indeed, as her comrades surreptitiously return to liberate Dessa from confinement, as she enters into motherhood, and, ostensibly, to a life post-servitude at Sutton's Glen, readers witness the painful process by which the protagonist attains a measure of interiority.

A homestead controlled by a white woman named Miss Rufel—also known as Ruth, Miz Lady, and Miz Ruint, among other names—Sutton's Glen operates as a liminal space in which Dessa's notions of labor, love, community, and power are all called into question. The narrative concludes with an Epilogue in which an aged Dessa reflects on earlier turmoil and trauma, including the trickster scheme whereby the blacks at Sutton's Glen sell themselves back into slavery in order to extort enough money from local whites to run away for good. A novel preoccupied, with varying degrees of success, with laying bare dense networks of racial and gender domination in the antebellum period, *Dessa Rose* marks a pivotal text in the arc of contemporary narratives of slavery.

Early exchanges between Dessa and Nehemiah in the segment of the novel titled "The Darky" personify Williams's sharpest indictment of rationality and objectivity, two key facets of the liberal problematic. Referencing democracy as an idealization, the liberal problematic names a range of constitutive sociopolitical contradictions, including guarantees of equivalence and autonomy, that in the end give rise to damaging forms of Otherness and differential entitlement. Just as she decries the "ill-fitting guise of objectivity and critical authority" (233) in *Give Birth to Brightness*, Williams denaturalizes the mind-body split endemic to the project of traditional liberal humanism in *Dessa Rose* as she starkly dramatizes the trope of antebellum white mediation.

"Always above [Dessa], behind her if she turned her head," observes the narrator, "she heard tapping, in the silence between [Nehemiah's] questions, his finger flicking proudly against the gold chain he wore at his waistcoat" (Williams 56). Juxtaposing Dessa's dark, chained, brutalized body—a figure positioned on the ground during the interviews, and thus, as always already below—with Nehemiah's duly arrayed, authoritative, civil form, Williams accounts for the bias and privilege embedded within the amanuensis relation. Indeed, Nehemiah's quest for "facts" and "research" about black treachery and insurrection remains fundamentally tethered to gestures of dehumanization. "He had been told they fell asleep much as a cow would in the midst of a satisfying chew" (36), relates the narrator of Nehemiah's private musings. Further, "He wouldn't have thought the darky's face so expressive" (38), Williams adds via narration, echoing broader cultural presumptions of an inherent dearth of black sentience and intellect.[4]

Nevertheless, I argue that Dessa's eventual admission that "She couldn't always follow the white man's questions; often he seemed to put a lot of unnecessary words between his 'why' and what he wanted to know" (Williams 56) signals not Dessa's ignorance, but rather possibilities of Nehemiah's identity as a performance, his knowledge as conjectural rather than purely "theoretical." In the words of Roderick Ferguson on canonical sociology, a related racialized enterprise and outgrowth of the Enlightenment, Nehemiah "invests in rational reflection ostensibly to record, but actually to construct" (98) ideas of blackness as excessive and deviant. Nehemiah's feigned impartiality and concern install an unequal set of power relations along racial lines by displacing Dessa's personality with his own production of her sense of self. Accordingly, as critic Emma Waters-Dawson contends, "Nehemiah records Dessa's description in words that *he* would use" (20; emphasis in original), and, as the narrator later reveals, "it was soon apparent to [Dessa] that the white man did not expect her to answer" (Williams 56). Ultimately, Nehemiah veils prejudice under the cover of detached, conceptual jargon.

Paul Gilroy corroborates precisely such a reading in *The Black Atlantic: Modernity and Double Consciousness*. "The desire to return to slavery and to explore it in imaginative writing," argues Gilroy, "has offered ... contemporary black writers a means to restage confrontations between rational, scientific, and enlightened Euro-American thought and the supposedly primitive outlook of prehistorical, cultureless, and bestial African slaves" (220). Williams's novel directly engages in such an undertaking, locating Dessa's body—her wounds, her pregnancy, her voice—as a site that contradicts dominant standards of knowledge formation and comprehension. While Nehemiah repeatedly emphasizes the distinctiveness of the realm of reason, reinforcing the significance of eliminating ambiguity and maintaining coherence at all costs, his eventual plunge into madness when his calculated assessments of Dessa do not bear out establishes the instability of mainstream, "scientific" bases for interpreting black experience. "I never will forget Nemi trying to read me" (236), Dessa discloses at the conclusion of the novel, and yet, when called on to prove the validity of his research, Nehemiah turns up little more than a blank page.[5]

While Dessa's flesh testifies to encounters with love and loss, to a sense of righteous anger and of boldness, rationality operates as a state-sanctioned apparatus whereby black pain and subjection are disavowed and instead codified as evidence of unassimilable difference and pathology. As Hortense Spillers understands in "Mama's Baby, Papa's Maybe: An American Grammar Book," the Middle Passage fortified institutionalized hierarchies of value and racial meaning by reducing captives from feeling, knowing beings to property and cargo. Without authorized kinship systems or a legitimate capacity to mother or father one's offspring, Spillers maintains, captive bodies are relegated to a space of vestibularity before culture, to the domain of the flesh. "If we think of the 'flesh' as a primary narrative, then we mean its seared, divided, ripped-apartness, riveted to the ship's hole, fallen, or 'escaped' overboard," Spillers writes (67). Ungendered flesh, then, becomes an archive of memory, a manuscript in itself that is passed down across generational lines.

"Williams is primarily concerned with the differences between the marks inscribed on paper by Nehemiah's pen and the marks inscribed on or rather incorporated into Dessa's body," confirms Gilroy. "Each supports a distinct system of meaning with its own characteristic forms of memory, rules, and racialised codes. They cross each other in Dessa herself" (220). By framing Dessa and Nehemiah's discourse in this way,

Williams undermines critical abstraction and neutrality as singular fonts of wisdom and understanding, crystallizing how each contributes to the dissimulation of power.

Importantly, Williams's incisive departure from a romanticization of the interracial "as-told-to" dynamic, her parody of such a framework even as she exposes its sexual undercurrents, denotes a refusal of the cultural capital and rewards typically associated with pastoral illogic.[6] The success of the 2011 blockbuster film *The Help*, an adaptation of Kathryn Stockett's 2009 novel by the same name, to take just one example, demonstrates the tenacity and allure of such problematic popular cultural renderings. Grossing more than twenty million dollars in its opening weekend alone, as well as ample Academy Award recognition, *The Help* recounts the journey of a young white woman, Skeeter Phelan (Emma Stone), to publish a narrative exposing the conditions faced by black domestic workers Aibileen Clark (Viola Davis), Minny Jackson (Octavia Spencer), and others, in Jackson, Mississippi in the 1960s. Yet this "lovely little coming-of-age-story" fixes whiteness as the sole origin of viable sociopolitical action—despite the film's setting in a veritable hotbed of formal and informal black civil rights organizing and resistance—and elides lived realities of lynching and sexual abuse, finally scapegoating black masculinity, rather than white privilege, as villainous.[7]

Unlike Williams's rendition, *The Help* installs a sanitized plot of (white) upward mobility, one that pivots upon a larger liberal mythos of writing as essentially liberatory, as well as upon illusions of consensuality and collaboration that inexplicably transcend rigorously policed racial and class distinctions. Read with and against a film in which the image of a white hand on a white page tellingly occupies the entirety of the opening frame, "The Darky" section of *Dessa Rose* instead sets up the novel as an intervention into gendered and raced discourses of reason, challenging the notion of white intermediacy as a precondition for legitimate knowledge production. Indeed, Williams foregrounds disembodied and disinterested, if liberal, modes of construal as simultaneously violent and reductionist in scope.

Re-Cooper-ating Black Sound

As much as Williams's deconstruction of hegemonic modes of thought contests valorization of the mind-body split, and deposes amanuenses as indelible agents of democratic promise and possibility, becoming together also accounts for the ways in which *Dessa Rose* speaks to similar efforts by nineteenth-century black activists, including Anna Julia Cooper, to disrupt the liberal problematic. As I argued in chapter three, Cooper's *A Voice from the South* deploys aural framing and musical metaphor to undercut Western reliance on predominantly visual terms of order and to recognize neglected intersections between embodiment and rationality. In fact, Cooper's fin-de-siècle song attests to the failure of reason to transcend material presence, contributing to a subversive reconceptualization of U.S. civil subjectivity and of reigning valuations of black womanhood.

Notably, Cooper's representation of harmony and of voice also resonates with modern-day black feminist engagement with and through sound, demonstrating an ongoing need to understand black music in excess of purely sociological imperatives.[8] A dialogical encounter between Williams's novel and Cooper's archive, I suggest here, achieves this aim. Indeed, as the lyrics of a love song from Kaine to Dessa open the Prologue of *Dessa Rose*, melodies of black spirituals and other rhythms steadily infuse its pages. Further, as a means of concealing slaves Nathan, Cully, and Harker as they return to spirit Dessa beyond Nehemiah's grasp, a call-and-response blend of contralto, tenor, and baritone notes is heard: "one voice calling, another answering it, some other voice restating the original idea, others taking up one or another line as refrain" (Williams 63). The pivotal scene then culminates in the hymn, "Good News, Lawd, Lawd, Good News" (67).

Not insignificantly, though Nehemiah attempts to write off ballads performed by Dessa as "only a quaint piece of doggerel which the darkies cunningly adapt from the scraps of Scripture they are taught" (Williams 52); to reduce her compositions to mere "annoying melody" (52); or to conclude alongside the slave owners in his midst that, simply put, "a loud darky is a happy one" (29), Nehemiah obviously struggles to register and to repress the intricacy of Dessa's voice. On one occasion, Nehemiah recalls that "He and Hughes had heard upon approaching the cellar [where Dessa resides awaiting execution] a humming or moaning. *It was impossible to define it as one or the other*" (29; emphasis added). When Nehemiah tries to clarify that "The *noise* had sounded like some kind of dirge," Hughes rebuffs the notion and attributes the racket to Dessa's indiscriminate happiness, perceiving no need to distinguish between moaning and singing when "The niggers don't" (29; emphasis added). Yet Nehemiah remains continually perturbed by Dessa's "absurd monotonous little tune[s] in a minor key, the melody of which she repeated over and over as she stared vacantly into space" (Williams 35). What's more, "each morning Nehemiah was awakened by the singing of the darkies and they often startled him by breaking into song at odd times of the day," the narrator observes (35).[9]

Dessa's inflection and cadence flout Nehemiah's impetus toward normative lucidity and coherence. According to the narrator, due to the "quiet rasp of her voice," he "hadn't caught every word; often he had puzzled overlong at some unfamiliar idiom or phrase" (Williams 18). Plus, "she answers questions in a *random* manner, a loquacious, *round-about* fashion—if, indeed, she can be brought to answer them at all," writes Nehemiah in his journal (23; emphasis added). As Jacquelyn A. Fox-Good apprehends in an important essay, "Singing the Unsayable: Theorizing Music in *Dessa Rose*," Dessa's modulation, her manipulation of timbre and tone, inhibits prevailing codes of listening: her voice/song "clearly prevents, disrupts, and resists [Nehemiah's] 'comprehension' of her" (15). Though Nehemiah eventually begins to collapse Dessa's cries and chants into the natural soundscape—as akin to "the clucking of the hens or the lowing of the cattle" (Williams 51)—the knowledge encoded in her song, I argue, comprises a distinct terrain of articulacy, one that runs counter to liberal preoccupation with outwardly logical or otherwise methodical lines of thought.

In other words, music produces more than audible effects; it bears ideological resonance. Fox-Good contends, as have others, including Gilroy and Lindon Barrett, that "One must work against . . . conventional assumptions about music: that it is nonrepresentational and cannot carry ideological, political, or other kinds of content; that it is formally and aesthetically replete, well-made sound and fury, signifying nothing" (9). Thus, Williams exploits music's own materiality—that is, the "density, simultaneity, and sense of movement into and away from the tonal center" of song (Fox-Good 25)—to influence governing structures of language and signification. Not unlike Cooper, then, Williams (via Dessa) mobilizes a framework that resists narrow bounds of intelligibility. While Cooper's and Williams's musical poetics may not, in fact, facilitate a complete transcendence of alterity—leaving them effectively unsung—each indexes a commitment to survival, marking meaningful attempts to maneuver within and beyond the constraints of the existing liberal order.

Such a reading, I would add, might also be extended to Williams's representation of the act of braiding. No doubt an Africanism, the process of black hair styling/dressing also disrupts individual, ocularcentric pathways of knowing that sustain the liberal problematic, in a manner similar to song.[10] As Dessa struggles to return to full consciousness and come to grips with her new surroundings at Sutton's Glen, it is a trance-like remembrance of her older sister, Carrie Mae, corn-rowing her hair that she immediately conjures: sensations of the bite of the comb and the massage of her sister's fingers on her scalp alternate as she attempts to process the proximate, overwhelming whiteness around her (Williams 83–86). Dessa and her sister-truant, Ada, labor to cultivate their own definition of trust and commitment to one another, subsequently forming a bond through the act of corn-rowing. Dessa's "head rested on Ada's knee as Ada's fingers wove rhythmically through the stubby strands of the girl's hair," the narrator remarks (147). "They looked so companionable and content that Rufel almost felt an intruder," much to Rufel's chagrin (147–48).

And in a fractured, halting recital in the Epilogue, Dessa recalls,

> *I missed this when I was sold away from home.*—"Turn your head, honey; I only got two more left to do."—*The way the womens in the Quarters used to would braid hair. Mothers would braid children heads—girl and boy— until they went into the field or for as long as they had them. This was one way we told who they people was, by how they hair was combed. . . . Child learn a lot of things setting between some grown person's legs, listening at grown peoples speak over they heads. This is where I learned to listen, right there between mammy's thighs, where I first learned to speak, from listening at grown peoples talk. . . .* (234; emphasis in original)

From Dessa's perspective, plaiting becomes an expression of place, belonging, and as she will go on to elaborate, decorum, and even pleasure (Williams 235). Yet she simultaneously locates the quotidian, embodied practice as a means of transmitting memory and experience. Citing braiding as a textured mode of discourse, Carole Boyce Davies identifies this specifically "nonscribal way of storytelling and maintaining history" as a profound strategy by which Dessa transforms from "the-mother-as-she-is-written to being the-mother-as-she-writes" (56). Indeed, Dessa's son, Mony, acquires a deep sense and awareness of his mother's pain and pride on her path from bondage through this special performance of reclamation and connectedness. Additionally, throughout the Epilogue,

Dessa's articulation of wrapping and weaving hair is filtered through reminiscences of her family, as well as of fellow Sutton's Glen runaways Annabelle, Debra, Flora, and Janet, and their involvement in the braiding process, underscoring the communal character of this approach to meaning-making. Through both music and hair care, then, Williams offsets dominant systems of rationality and literacy, in tune with epistemological ground activated by black women writers and activists over a century ago.

Elizabeth Keckly: Restyled

Though less secondary critical focus attends Williams's aforementioned renarration of liberal abstraction and associated discourses of reason, much has been made (and aptly so) of her problematization of the "Mammy" figure. Drawn to the representation of Rufel caring for Dessa's newborn at Sutton's Glen in the wake of the title character's recovery from her latest harrowing flight from captivity, scholars have situated this particular scene within diverse interpretive milieux. "The image of the white nursemaid and the black infant dismantles a long tradition in American sentimentality naturalizing the ur-image of the black mammy and the white child," theorizes Mae G. Henderson (297). "Such a reversal has the subtle effect of transcoding a traditionally sacred iconographic representation of Madonna and child into an obscene image by reinscribing it into the context of a suggestively pornographic scenario" (ibid.). According to Elizabeth Ann Beaulieu, in a study of the neo-slave narrative's prioritizing of motherhood as a central drive for black resistance and survival, Dessa's hostility toward the white mistress to whom she must forfeit the capacity to nourish her child constitutes an "ironi[c]" show of "reverse prejudice" (39), while consent to interracial breastfeeding, on the other hand, "signals [Rufel's] growing courage to be true to her feelings" (38).[11]

Specifically, I question a broader analytical trajectory that understands Williams's subversion of the sedimented Mammy trope as attributable almost exclusively to an inversion of wet nursing roles. This, I suggest, circumscribes the epistemological import of Williams's intervention, finally obscuring its relation to early African-American women's literature, including that of Elizabeth Keckly. Hence I offer a becoming together of Williams's *Dessa Rose* and Elizabeth Keckly's *Behind the*

Scenes within a larger framework of resistance to liberalism at the scene of black women's writing. I argue that the two texts, though distinct in their own right, critique the liberal problematic in comparable ways.

The heart of Williams's premise regarding motherhood, in fact, surrounds a charged conversation between Rufel and Dessa in the master bedchambers of Sutton's Glen. In an altercation prompted by Rufel's rapt reverie about her recently deceased Mammy, a bondwoman named Dorcas who had labored for Rufel's family for years, Dessa rouses her nearly broken frame in bitter objection to the white woman's meandering recollections. "'Mammy' ain't nobody name, not they real one," spits Dessa, enraged. "You don't even know 'mammy's' name. Mammy have a name, have children," she declares (Williams 119). Though Dessa "knew even as she said it what the white woman meant" (Williams 118)—that she was not referring to Rose, Dessa's mother—she proceeds angrily to quash Rufel's cherished icon. Indeed, she speaks her own mother's name and testifies to the lives (and deaths) of nearly all ten of the woman's children, "lest her poor, lost children die to living memory as they had in [Rose's] world" (119). While critic Gunilla Theander Kester notes in her comparative work on the fiction of Williams and Charles Johnson that this incident produces "'Mammy' as a semiotic sign," as a "sign [that] is in a sense meaningless" with "no transcendent or immanent truth value" (132), I read this moment as a vehicle for the urgent imperative that Mammy be at once materialized and historicized.

Contrary to Kester's notion that Mammy "escapes both the white and the black woman's need for a symbolic or a metaphoric history, and . . . consequently frees the women from their constructed genealogies" (132), I discern Williams's strident negation of Mammy as a disembodied reserve of surrogacy as a repossession of the value and the truths of her life as someone's daughter, as someone's mother. Simply put, Kester's determination takes for granted an analogous relation between the constructed-ness of each woman's respective genealogy. Through her theoretico-narrative enterprise, Williams illuminates Rufel's liberal claim to reciprocal fidelity between her and her Mammy as little more than a consolidation of white privilege.

As outlined in chapter two, the memoir *Behind the Scenes* contains performances of countermemory, or anti-pastoral reach, by which the author upsets seemingly intractable fantasies of Keckly-as-mammy. Keckly's quiet resistance clarifies the violence perpetuated by mythologies of superhuman black female strength, particularly their simulation of

black volition and consent, without tangible variation in existing political and affective regimes. Ultimately, Keckly and Williams carefully
undo liberal fictions of dehumanized, consumable black motherhood,
exposing Mary Lincoln and Miss Rufel, respectively, as self-interested
rather than charitably inclined. Williams's becoming together with Keckly's text in this way, moreover, speaks to the institutional hold of racial
privilege, without reifying it as absolute, pinpointing an ongoing site of
black feminist inquiry in the twentieth and twenty-first centuries.

Similarly, Keckly's life and writings undermine prevailing models of
interracial friendship and intimacy. Arguably, the ambivalence of intimacy—an ideologically and materially violent institution—is often
minimized, if not covered over entirely, in liberal renderings of compan-
ionship and rapport. Productively, *Behind the Scenes*' restaging of the un-
inhabitability of normative reason and liberal being (for black women, in
particular) intervenes in a widespread misnaming of complex social and
emotional ties that traverse, though rarely transcend, racial and class
boundaries in the context of the nineteenth century. As modern historical scholarship and commercial publications alike consistently reiterate
myths of interracial amity and acquaintance when addressing Keckly's
legacy, related claims are often staked in the literary relationship between Dessa and Rufel.[12]

In a stance perhaps most symptomatic of the limitations of this
framework, Beaulieu insists that at Sutton's Glen, "a place where no race
hierarchy is recognized" (33), the "disenfranchised blacks and the white
woman deserted by her financially irresponsible husband form a group
that in some ways resembles an extended family" (35). For Beaulieu, by
the novel's end, "the enslaved persons and Ruth [Rufel] cooperate to
implement the moneymaking scheme [and] . . . realize that trust is an
essential element of the scam and that trust can develop only among
friends" (36), as "each [woman] has chosen friendship over race" (50).
Beaulieu and others' commentary in this vein places a premium on liberal notions of autonomy and self-determination.

Much of Dessa's own language throughout the novel, on the other
hand, bespeaks precisely who can and cannot opt out of racial difference.
"White woman was everything I feared and hated," declares Dessa just
prior to the plot getting underway (Williams 169). Indeed, "we didn't
talk too much that was personal," she recalls afterward. "I mean, I know
I mentioned mammy-nem, and she talked about Dorcas—or 'Mammy,'
as she called her. But this was a white woman and I don't think I forgot

it that whole, entire journey" (216–17). And in another incisive display of discernment and recognition, Dessa counters Miz Lady's suggestion that most whites were just like her and simply did not know any better when it came to the depths of despair subtending enslavement. "As far as white folks not knowing how bad slavery was—they was the ones made it, was the ones kept it" (212), Dessa clarifies, dismissing oblivion as a pretext for brutality and locating unexamined privilege as a considerable barrier to integration.

Dessa remains equally perceptive when Rufel flagrantly inverses the configuration of their trickster scheme, as the latter proclaims, "I don't want to live round slavery no more . . . What do you think about that, Odessa? About you-all coming [out West] with me?" (218) "It was like her to take for granted I'd want to be her friend, *that we-all would want her to come West with us*," Dessa corrects, "that she could have what she want for the asking" (219; emphasis added). As Keith Byerman corroborates, "Although Dessa saves Rufel from rape and later Rufel does everything she can to save Dessa from reenslavement through Adam Nehemiah, racial boundaries are ultimately left in place" (63). Thus, he concludes, "While Williams clearly refuses any simple white claims of knowledge or understanding of black experience, she also appears to be unwilling to grant the possibility of cross-racial community" (Byerman 63).[13] To be sure, an unqualified recuperation of Dessa and Rufel as allies elides the nuances and deep problematics of even the most seemingly progressive relationships.[14]

As Keckly had done with respect to her son, George, Williams also juxtaposes intimacy informed by dominant ideological impulses with that catalyzed by purportedly non-rational forces.[15] From the very beginning of her time on the coffle, Dessa remembers that "the negro driver the white men called Nate was paying attention to her," that "the young mulatto boy who often walked the chain in front of her was being kind" (Williams 59). Though their collective efforts to ensure that she never faltered on the journey, and to minimize her hunger by providing extra home-fries or molasses, initially lead her to expect that "one or both of them would come fumbling at her in the dark," Dessa soon "knew herself to be *enveloped in caring*" (ibid.; emphasis added). Williams, via Nathan's characterization, later names such intimacy as "sweetness": "You been through with someone what we been through together and you be 'sweet' on em, too," Nathan reveals to a mystified Rufel (Williams 149). Slavery, Nathan continues, turns blacks into "poor excuses even for they own selfs . . . I feels bad for all them that didn't make it, worse for all them that didn't die, that even now living in slavery after we been free. But us three—we did it and we made it. It's got to be some special feeling after that" (Williams 149). For Williams, this "sweetness" or "special feeling" represents less a sensation-driven, bounded, private mode of expression than an erotic, innately political one.

In this sense, Nathan, Cully, and Dessa's connection might well be mediated by what Imani Perry theorizes, in a slightly different context, as a praxis of care. Though her focus involves the "context of human creativity and productivity," Perry's call for an understanding of care as an ethic and a value, as a standard in our most basic terms of engagement with one another, parallels Williams's imaginative formulation in many respects. Significantly, Perry borrows from feminist philosophy to revive a species of care reflective of an "inherent communal interest," one which possesses a "requirement of integrity," and that functions as at once a "pedagogical, aesthetic, and creative endeavor" (20). Williams's insurgent care in developing the characterization of a story of a black female slave renegade, and in turn the manner of concern and affirmation with which those in bondage generally address one another in the narrative, challenges a broader impetus to order and define the intimacy of the narrative in normative ways.[16] In contrast to a default invocation of liberal tropes of interracial friendship and intimacy, Williams posits black sweetness as a resistant site of collective fulfillment and critical consciousness.

Enacting Black Subordination

In her memoir, Keckly also advances a conceptualization of American liberalism as a ritualized, embodied performance, rather than as a political or economic formation alone. That is, *Behind the Scenes* contests the public, if tacit, power dynamics and diverse modes of violence through which hierarchized relations are produced. As I argue in chapter two, Keckly's project reworks scripted custom and convention governing interracial affect and consent. Particularly striking is Keckly's manipulation of the masks of silence, docility, and deference as she articulates the tenuous intersection between liberal ideology and blackness. Williams, too, I maintain, makes visible the effects of such routinized scenarios in *Dessa Rose*. An analysis of Williams's becoming together with Keckly in her contemporary literary rendering of slave culture productively illuminates precisely how liberalism as a performative mode regulates black gesture and controls black being.

In chapter four of the section of *Dessa Rose* titled "The Wench," Rufel begins to come in increasingly close contact with the blacks in hiding at Sutton's Glen, particularly Nathan, to whom she will later become "romantically" attached. Notably, during the course of her initial interactions with him, the mistress of the liminal, would-be plantation remains vexed, for "[Nathan] did not say he would answer [a question she had posed to him], she noticed, just as he had made no excuse or move to go when she surprised him loafing yesterday" (Williams 132). For Rufel, Nathan appears out of sync with established patterns of etiquette and decorum. She, self-proclaimed as tolerant in comparison to other local whites, is confused by Nathan's reluctance to disabuse her immediately of her impression of idleness—a common charge leveled against blacks that she herself has fabricated in this instance. According to the narrator, "It was if they didn't know how they should act in front of a white person, she thought, amazed and uneasy. She had never met darkies who seemed so unversed in what was due her place as these" (Williams 132). Moreover, "Harker, Ada, Annabelle, none of them offered her anything that she had not specifically requested; they volunteered no act that she had not specifically directed; they never sought to oblige her," the narrator reveals (132–33). Desire for timely, mundane enactments of black subordination permeates Rufel's interior monologue here; their absence produces palpable uncertainty and disarray.

Significantly, Rufel distinguishes departures from prescribed behavioral codes, in the form of black diffidence, as especially troublesome and disruptive. "She felt, too, in [Harker] a certain reserve; he would give this much and no more," she reports, on one occasion, seething (Williams 133). Indeed, each time Ruth is lulled into a sense of comfort, of home, with the runaways at Sutton's Glen, the memory of her dispute with Dessa over Mammy arrests such feelings: "she knew the wench's reticence and timidity were feigned, and was angry and bewildered by the deception" (141).[17] "'Place,' [Miz Lady] say, 'place.' . . . 'That's how they answer everything,' she say, 'Ain't my place, Missy,' . . . 'Morning, Mammy,'; 'Ain't my place.' 'Afternoon, Dessa'; 'Ain't my place.' Well, I ain't talking no 'place,'" Dessa overhears Ruth yelling in exasperation (218). As the fugitives at Rufel's homestead navigate a dubious sovereignty, they rely on various techniques of subversion, methods often tethered to a performance of modesty and unassertiveness.

In this same vein, I maintain that Aunt Chloe's capitalization upon a keen awareness of racial scripts marks a crucial moment in the development of the novel, deepening Williams's interrogation of liberalism as affective performance. The figure of Aunt Chloe in *Dessa Rose*, as compared to Keckly's Aunt Charlotte, has elicited a considerable secondary critical response. Yet, contrary to emphases on Aunt Chloe's strength and courage—to those readings that suggest that "The fact that the sheriff trusts her is a measure of how powerful a woman she is" (Beaulieu 44)—I contend that her characterization permits Williams to literalize participatory and stylized, though frequently implicit, interracial traditions constitutive of the liberal problematic without presupposing black access or authority.

After Nehemiah recaptures Dessa, who had been walking the streets unaccompanied in a town where the group was implementing the latest version of their scheme, the sheriff sends for Aunt Chloe to verify Nemi's claims about Dessa's scarring. An "old woman [who] smoked a nasty pipe and mumbled a lot" and by the "way she hobbled round might've been a granny and then some," Chloe arrives and proceeds to examine Dessa behind the veil of a cloth she'd brought for the purpose (Williams 230). All the while, Chloe demonstrates expected gestures and signs of servility, bowing her head and never once speaking out of turn to the whites in her midst. After Dessa surreptitiously passes a quarter to the old woman behind the curtain—who bites it to ensure its authenticity before sliding it into the cover of her dress—Chloe surveys only the top portion of Dessa's body before concluding: "Masa Joel, Masa Joel . . . I ain't seed nothing on this gal's butt. She ain't got a scar on her back" (231). Via a complex manipulation of received notions of black obsequiousness and a veiling of the "truth" (that is, Dessa does not, in fact, have "a scar on her back"), Chloe profits while simultaneously enabling Dessa's evasion of Nehemiah for a second time. Nevertheless, Chloe then returns to her long-standing role as the sheriff's maid, evidenced by her prompt deletion from the narrative. In the end, Dessa advances toward a measure of independence Chloe may well never know.[18]

Further, Williams mobilizes Aunt Chloe's act to lay bare the sheriff's liberal pretensions. That is, the officer of the law seemingly strives to occupy a station antithetical to that of Nemi. As a crazed Nehemiah violently starts to restrain Dessa's weak frame following their arrival at the jail, the nameless sheriff pulls out a chair and allows her to sit (Williams 221). The sheriff likewise thwarts the efforts of Nehemiah and other white men congregated at the facility to strip Dessa naked to search for the scars that would confirm her identity as a runaway: "Damn it, Nemi, you had your last peep show in here . . . This is a jail, not no carnival" (222).[19] The sheriff also dispatches a messenger to the local hotel to retrieve Rufel (then traveling under the alias Miz Carlisle) to potentially verify Dessa's alibi (222), and reprimands Nemi after he proceeds to terrorize Dessa as she waits behind bars (224). In contrast to Nemi's exceedingly disheveled appearance since Dessa first absconded—"plumb wild, way he was throwing his head back like a horse and brushing at that brank of hair," observes the narrator—the sheriff emerges as "steely-eyed," reasonable, and fair (224). "The law handle this," the sheriff reiterates to a frenzied Nemi time and again throughout the exchange (228).

Nevertheless, the sheriff's discourses of justice and integrity ring hollow. He seems far more concerned with protecting his own reputation (and that of his precinct) from Nemi's lower-class antics and Miz Lady's accusations of chauvinist misconduct than with establishing Dessa's innocence. As it becomes clear that Nemi has abducted and detained scores of black women in his quest to recover Dessa, the sheriff's righteousness and legitimacy become even more suspect. Ultimately, the solicitation of his servant's aid indexes collusion in Nehemiah's plot and collaboration in Chloe's dehumanization, in spite of its aim to shore up the sheriff's status as progressive and understanding. Chloe's deferential, trust-inspiring performance crystallizes circuits of violent exchange in which this apparent spokesperson for uprightness and impartiality actively participates, fixing the two white men as conspirators, rather than foils. Indeed, inquiry into the becoming together of Williams's and Keckly's respective theorization of liberalism-as-ritual uncovers new, imaginative possibilities of subversion and critique.

Finally, Williams takes on one other critical theme from *Behind the Scenes*: selective self-commodification. As had Olaudah Equiano/Gustavas Vassa, Keckly acquires freedom through the creation of quality stock and the manipulation of a mercantile sensibility, making visible intersections between liberal notions of property and individual sovereignty. That is, Keckly's participation in the rational marketplace at once generates surplus demand for her product, problematizes her object status, and contravenes dominant modes of valuation. Moreover, her refusal of truancy, as previously theorized in this volume, extends a self-commodifying ethic reinforced by a sly, pecuniary fluency. By exploiting her acquaintance with prevailing standards of accumulation, Keckly exceeds accommodationist and conciliatory interests. Though frequently written off as submissive or elitist, Keckly posits an analytic of self-commodification that destabilizes gendered processes of chattel slavery. She foregrounds a liberal nexus of autonomy and possession, and exposes the conditionality of black freedom.

In *Dessa Rose*, Williams crafts a corresponding scenario, as Harker spearheads a plot in which the blacks at Sutton's Glen will trade themselves back into slavery over and again until they collect enough gold to flee west permanently. According to the scheme, originally developed by "Harker's old master [who] taught that the best lie is always the one closest to the truth" (Williams 206), Rufel will portray a distressed plantation mistress forced by unforeseen hardship to get rid of a few trusted hands. By wagon and by boat, the runaways plan to trek from Haley's Landing, on to towns across Tuscaloosa, Pickens, and Greene counties, and end up in Arcopolis, before returning to the Glen for final preparations.[20]

Immediately, Williams demonstrates the troupe's acute knowledge of the inner workings of the "peculiar institution." "Back in them days about all you had to do was put a rope and a collar on a negro and seem like every white person in seeing distance want to make an offer on him," remembers Dessa, pinpointing the ubiquity and pervasiveness of the antebellum market (Williams 206). "Most any of our peoples would bring eight or nine hundred dollars easy at public auction," they collectively appraise, though Harker, Castor, and Ned would likely garner even better prices (193). Yet, as "[t]he woman was valued more because her childrens belong to the master," the company begrudgingly consents to add Flora to the inventory of those sold (ibid.).

When the band arrives at Haley's Landing, they proceed to print up handbills, reflecting additional savvy regarding the commercial lexicon of the day: terms such as "private sale," "through no fault," "likely negroes," and "warranted sound" occupy prominent positions on each advertisement in order to entice just the right buyers. As Jennifer L. Griffiths corroborates, "The group's scheme to trick the white slave buyers involves a performance that denaturalizes the conditions and relationships buttressing the institution of slavery" (31), likewise signaling their broader attunement to the limitations of liberal discourses of equity and rights. Dessa even yells "Ware the goods!" in her effort to elude Nemi's clutches in the novel's concluding pages. "And this what stopped the white mens [from disrobing her to view her scars]: that [she] might belong to someone be upset about damaged goods," the narrator relates

(222). Ultimately, the party exhibits keen understanding of the relationship between ownership and citizenship, between authority and value, and a willingness to use such awareness to their advantage.

Notably, however, Williams extends Keckly's initial formulation, confronting tensions and costs associated with processes of selective self-commodification even more directly. Indeed, "[t]his was a scary thing to me," declares Dessa, "to flirt so close with bondage again" (Williams 194). In particular, Williams characterizes the public auction—perhaps the pinnacle of their performance of self-commodification—as a painful "mock[ing] of our manhood" (204). Detailing an auctioneer's proclamation to a full crowd of onlookers, Williams narrates: "'The gen-u-ine article,' pointing [then] at Castor's privates. All the white men laughed; this was a big joke" (204). Dessa, never before witness to a slave auction, is stunned by the gratuitous exhibition of racist pleasure, by the depths of Castor's humiliation and shame. In disregard of the cardinal rule of the scheme—that "We was slaves; wasn't posed to know nothing nor do nothing without first being told (194)—Dessa shoves Rufel's daughter into her arms and stalks away from the mob.

Nathan manages to catch up with Dessa before too long, however, dragging her into a nearby alleyway. Once out of sight, the two "rocked and crooned to each others, till [they] cried [them]selfs out, then leaned against the wall, laughing a little, kind of shamefaced" (Williams 204). This moment of tenderness, or of "sweetness" as Williams might have it, captures a shared sense of vulnerability and sorrow. As Keckly relays the complexities of at once circulating as flesh and as provider of specialized, embodied labor in the form of dressmaking, Williams theorizes the psychic toll on the group of becoming complicit, even if temporarily, in their own objectification. Accordingly, Dessa and Nathan grieve over all of the losses they have endured, expressing immense fear over gambling with the prospect of returning to slavery. Finally, they agree to help one another move forward together. As self-commodification enables proximity to freedom, Williams clarifies, it also entails great risk. By fashioning the scheme in this way, Williams inventively distorts normative boundaries of autonomy and choice, reshaping understandings of equality and personhood in the context of the nineteenth century and beyond.

Wilson and Williams: Understanding That Which
Dessa's Body Knows

As critical to the aforementioned scene as utterance—specifically, the unnamed hum or chant that passes between Dessa and Nathan—is touch. The act of rocking in one another's arms becomes transformative in the context of their experience; it represents an expression of knowledge production, strength, and possibility. This coincides, as I argue in this chapter's final pass, with much of Harriet Wilson's theorizing in her 1859 biomythography, *Our Nig*. While scholar Carole Boyce Davies explicitly cites an intertextual correlation between Wilson's *Our Nig* and Toni Morrison's *Beloved*, comparable interpretive frameworks have yet to be deployed to account for the relationship between *Our Nig* and *Dessa Rose*. This is especially concerning given their corresponding insights into questions of embodiment, in particular. Notably, a becoming together of writings by Wilson and Williams reflects meaning and discernment at odds with the liberal problematic.

As outlined in chapter one, embodiment functions as a fundamental source of sociopolitical awareness that contradicts Western patterns of rationality. Frado's ever-battered face and limbs attest to the provisional nature of the Protestant work ethic and the falsity of majority New England pastoralism in the antebellum period. Further, the testimony of her young body undercuts liberal discourses of progress and self-possession, as well as presumably neutral logics of nation and belonging predicated upon power and property. In critiquing the ways in which racial and class ascendancy are secured at the expense of laboring bodies, Wilson problematizes conditions of enforced materiality by reclaiming the body toward subversive ends.

In 1986, I contend, Williams demonstrates a familiar insistence upon understanding the black body in excess of stereotype and conventions of exclusion. Indeed, in the context of Aunt Chloe's feigned submissiveness at the prison, the touched body emerges as a site of articulacy and knowing, of recovery and resistance, especially in relation to Nemi's pseudo-scientific musings. Sensuality between black women—"She ran her hand over my back, heavy, calloused hands; never forget how gentle they felt," recalls Dessa (Williams 231)—rather than white ministration, yields opportunities to inhabit even the most seemingly intractable circumstances on altered terms. Though Nathan's and Dessa's fervent grasp crosses gendered lines, their laying of hands on one another remains imbued with non-sexualized eroticism. At times strained, at times complicated, Nathan's and Dessa's "sweetness" perhaps finds its richest manifestation in this amicable embrace. While the caress does not prove to one or the other that they will forever elude capture, the contact reestablishes their willingness to proceed with the plan, and more importantly, it restores their sense of their own humanity.

Farah Griffin's essay, "Textual Healing: Claiming Black Women's Bodies, the Erotic and Resistance in Contemporary Novels of Slavery," validates precisely such a claim when she writes of the importance of the "process of reimagining black women's bodies mov[ing] from focusing on a body that is constructed in history and that carries that history within and on it, to a body capable of being remade" (525). Particularly attentive to hazards associated with the erotic as a mode of resistance for women of color, Griffin distinguishes between sensual and sexual touch. The former, for Griffin, facilitates spiritual affirmation and a means of effecting change, or what she refers to as an "opening out to others" (524). A jailed Dessa's capacity to achieve orgasm as she remembers her slain husband is particularly significant as an agential act of self-pleasure upon which white hegemony cannot directly capitalize (528).

Griffin also makes plain my sense of the ways in which embodiment might serve as grounds for liberal ideology critique:

> Healing [as a product of sensual touch] does not pre-suppose notions
> of a coherent and whole subject . . . the healing is never permanent: it
> requires constant attention and effort. I am using the term healing to
> suggest the way in which the body, literally and discursively scarred,
> ripped, and mutilated, has to learn to love itself, to function in the
> world with other bodies and often in opposition to those persons and
> things that seek to destroy it. Of course, the body can never return to
> a pre-scarred state. It is not a matter of getting back to a "truer" self,
> but instead of claiming the body, scars and all—in a narrative of love
> and care. As such, healing does not deny the construction of bodies,
> but instead suggests that they can be constructed differently, for different ends. (524)

Embodiment in Williams's narrative at once intervenes in Enlightenment-refined discourses of ocularcentrism and contained selfhood. Critically, she revises mandates for coherence and objectivity reinforcing the liberal problematic in favor of a felt, corporeal consciousness. This lends support to one critic's conclusion that "With one gentle touch, [Aunt

Chloe] disrupts the primacy of the visual field. Her ability to feel and to know the meaning of Dessa's scars creates a new reading, one that bears witness to suffering without condemning the survivor to silence. Dessa's story finds its language in that encounter" (Griffiths 32).

Just as readers glean an appreciation of the body as a realm of knowledge formation in scenes with Nathan and Aunt Chloe, as well as through Williams's initial juxtaposition of Dessa's chained blackness with Nehemiah's civil rationality, the same might be argued in relation to the author's depiction of Dessa's initial escape from prison. Herein, via stream-of-consciousness narration, Williams articulates embodiment as a locus of black memory and perception. For instance, just after her arrival at Sutton's Glen, pieces of imagery from Dessa's present, such as "the white light the raftered ceiling," are shot through with fragmented reminiscences from her covert exodus with Nathan, Cully, and Harker (Williams 86). "It had taken a while for her feet to remember the gliding shuffle that, slow as it appeared, ate up ground. The coffle had taught her that," recalls Dessa of the escape, as she attempts to get her bearings at the Glen (87). For Dessa, as with many slaves, her feet retain patterns of movement, as well as a sense of the power and exploitative capacity of slave drivers, all while evoking uniquely racialized and gendered know-how.[21]

"Her feet were remembering," Dessa continues in retrospect. "The muscles of her calves and thighs protested some and it took all of her concentration to keep their protests from drowning out the remembrance of her feet" (87). Moreover, the narrator observes, Dessa "didn't speak [on the journey]. *She didn't think either.* She was free; maybe not as free as she would ever be but she knew, *without needing to think about it,* that she'd never be less free than she was now, striding, sometimes stumbling toward a place she'd never seen and didn't know one word about" (Williams 87; emphasis added). The runaways' clandestine passage represents at once the pain and the potential of liberation.

Significantly, this excerpt provokes an impression of both introspection and sheer absence of thought. Consistent with the Western philosophical tradition, the caveats "She didn't think either" and "without thinking about it," relinquish cognition to a transcendent intellectual or psychic sphere. Conversely, the body becomes associated with an instinctive, natural mindlessness. On the contrary, in this instance, it is precisely through Dessa's limbs that she begins to fathom her relationship to her violent past. It is precisely through her feet that she articulates

her expectation for a more capacious semblance of freedom. In this scenario, it seems more likely that normative rationality cannot keep pace
with that which Dessa's body knows. As a result, Dessa frequently references a gap between speech and literacy—two proper domains of liberal
rationality—and that which she feels, throughout the novel.[22]

In addition to representations of her appendages, several other mem-
ories are broached in avowedly bodily terms. Refusing to fix reason and
the visceral as antithetical, Dessa consistently cites the "tears sliding si-
lently down her cheek" during her trek away from the Alabama prison
as she "lean[ed] back against [Harker's] chest" (Williams 87). Further,
she cannot forget the "dull throbbing in her back, some pounding in her
head," or rather "starting up out of some unremembered dreams to feel
the sinewy arms around her, the beard-stubbled cheek against her face,"
expressions of awareness and consciousness without which she would
have otherwise "lost track of place, of time" (87). Meager, if nurturing
corporeal glimpses, too, are all Dessa has left of her father: "a prickly
cheek against her own small hand, a wide chest against her knees, hard
arms supporting her bottom" (83). In fact, "my own girlhood all I ever
had was the membrance of a daddy's smile," she notes (236). Within Williams's framework, then, materiality bears meaningful theoretical implications, granting the protagonist a space from which to interrogate a
sense of being and of belonging. Ultimately, it is through her body that
she attempts to conceptualize motherhood and to develop a measure of
community with the other fugitives in her midst.

A becoming together of *Our Nig* and *Dessa Rose* likewise demonstrates
engagement with larger representations of black rage. In terms of a politics of wrath, Wilson mobilizes the characterization of Frado-as-picaninny in her narrative in order to counter prevailing liberal discourses
of racialized anger as baseless or menacing. She renders fury as at once
an epistemological formation and a mode of survival by engaging black
anger on its own terms, and in conjunction with a "politics of joy," rather
than as a strictly illicit, pathological site. In positioning black rage in excess of liberal terms of order, Wilson interrogates insidious modes of discipline and social management by antebellum white Northerners while
positing both experience and feeling as legitimate terrains of meaning-
making and worldview. Through her theorization of the critical import
of black ire, as detailed in chapter one, Wilson anticipates black feminist
discourse articulated by the likes of Patricia Hill Collins and Audre Lorde.

Williams also addresses the irruptive force of an incensed blackness.

According to Waters-Dawson, "though the theme of the psychic rage of both the enslaved and the enslaver is present [in *Dessa Rose*] the novel itself [can be read] as a finished text or product of controlled rage by the novelist" (18). She is especially drawn to the scene of Dessa and Rufel's argument over Mammy, addressed earlier in this chapter. "In her angry response, Dessa represents multiple voices: for herself, for her mother, and for the nameless 'mammies' in the history of the slave woman . . . In other words, Dessa 'has the last word,' and Williams, as the creator of Dessa's story, is the medium of this enraged voice," Waters-Dawson observes (23). In a related scene in the novel, however, I argue that readers can apprehend even more precisely how liberal ideological imperatives attempt to sanitize expressions of black resentment.

Consumed on one occasion by thoughts of the increasing likelihood of her husband, Bertie's, death as opposed to his lingering absence, Rufel quietly enters the room in which Dessa is recovering following her escape. Catching Dessa unawares, who assumes it is simply another bondwoman, Ada, come to check on her, Rufel soon realizes Dessa is nude. However, "her bottom was so scarred that Rufel had thought she must be wearing some kind of garment," the narrator reveals (Williams 154). Indeed, "The wench had a right to hide her scars, her pain, Rufel thought, almost in tears herself" (ibid.). Characterized as alternately sympathetic, surprised, embarrassed, faint, and regretful, Rufel quickly closes the door as gently as she had entered it.

Nevertheless, rather than fully retreating, as a sign of respect for Dessa's "right" to privacy, Rufel proceeds to open the door a second time. Immediately, Rufel "sensed the *smoldering hostility* beneath the girl's obvious embarrassment," as a previously oblivious Dessa "had [now] snatched up a dress and stood stiffly with it clutched in front of her bare chest" (154; emphasis added). In the face of Dessa's indignation, Rufel responds anxiously: "That other day . . . that other day, we wasn't talking about the same person. Your mammy birthed you, and mines, mines just helped to raise me. But she loved me. . . . She loved me, just like yours loved you" (154). Subsequently, Williams depicts a problematic diffusion of black anger as Dessa "watched her narrowly for a moment" before "slowly her tensely held shoulders relaxed": "'I know that, Miss'es,' she sighed. 'I know that,' she said without anger or regret" (155).

Arguably, Dessa's lack of anger or regret in this moment signals an evacuation of black intensity and suspicion; the development of Rufel's liberal sense of self is secured at the expense of a slave woman's interiority and of her longstanding objection to uncritical white encroachment upon her life, her maternity, and upon the story her body tells. Notably, Rufel had outright dismissed other blacks' accounts of Dessa's barbaric treatment on the Vaugham plantation as propaganda, or else as completely warranted by the slave woman's own malevolence, prior to this exchange. Her refusal to acknowledge Dessa's experience without evidence relies upon sedimented tropes of black female hypersexuality and excessiveness.[23] In the end, Rufel's capacity to establish the veracity of black pain at will denotes a hallmark of racial and class privilege. Rufel's acceptance, Williams's construal, or both, of Dessa's tone as suddenly "without anger or regret," rather than as a vehicle of sustained critique, indexes a fundamental unintelligibility of black rage within liberal matrices of domination and control.

Williams likewise portrays a misapprehension of black anger within intra-racial community dynamics. For instance, as the fugitives at Sutton's Glen congregate one evening to discuss the merits of Harker's plan to sell themselves back into slavery, Dessa and another runaway, Janet, cast doubt on the scheme in light of Nathan's sexual liaison with Rufel. "How long you think we going last amongst white folks with Nathan in her bed?" Dessa queries. "Yo' all just jealous cause he not diddling you . . . Don't nobody want no old mule like you," counters a bondman named Ned, amid stifled laughter (Williams 183).

Though Williams confirms that Dessa was not merely "jealous-hearted," "making what [Ada] called a fool of [herself] over a negro didn't have no better sense than Nathan" (Williams 177), Dessa explodes. The charge, reminiscent of Nanny's declaration to Janie in the opening pages of Zora Neale Hurston's novel *Their Eyes Were Watching God* (1937), stirs deep-seated emotions.[24] Straightaway, Dessa "had to close [her] eyes"; she "was so choked [she] couldn't speak" (183). Her response is at once visceral and volatile.

Not easily repressed, Dessa's anger manifests itself as "a fire-burst where Ned's head should've been" (Williams 183), a "flash" that makes time stand still, after which she "was still shaking from remembrance, from feeling" (184). Dessa recalls this sense of outrage—similarly personified as "a bloodhound in my throat, a monster that didn't seem to know enemy or friend, wouldn't know the difference once it got loose" (ibid.)—as the force motivating her earlier attacks on her mistress, Mary Vaugham, in the wake of Kaine's murder, and on Wilson, the slave trader, during the uprising on the coffle. She eventually laments directing such umbrage at a fellow slave: "It scared me to see it almost loosed against one of us; and, pesky as he was, Ned was part of us," confesses Dessa (ibid.). Her reaction is consuming and fierce, formidable and destructive.

But while Ned mistakes Dessa's wariness for envy, I argue that her mad, possessive display registers something else entirely. In this instance, Dessa produces a mode of contestation incumbent not on garnering black male favor, but on problematizing blanket devaluations of black womanhood. After lodging an initial complaint based on her discernment that Rufel's willingness to participate in the ruse marks, in effect, "her trusting in her whiteness and not our blackness" (Williams 189), Dessa heatedly rejects the demeaning, if commonplace, appellation imposed by Ned. Just as with the terms "darky" and "wench" deployed by Nehemiah and Rufel, "mule" as intra-racial epithet misnames black women's lives and labor at the same time as it minimizes their exploitation. "Oh, we was mules all right. What else would peoples use like they used us?" (183) Dessa broods angrily, implicating liberal black masculinity in the context of her oppression and that of countless other bondwomen.

This exchange disputes rampant misappropriation of black women's bodies under enslavement. Dessa's invocation of the beauty of her own rough heels, of Janet's tough, hickory-inflected skin, and of Flora's big, hard hands, in the midst of her exasperation also refutes broader patterns of dehumanizing black women from which black men are not exempt. Moreover, Dessa's bitter reflection upon the dispersal of seventeen of Milly's children in eighteen years, and upon Ada's rape at the hands of a master who later began to pursue Anabelle, the product of that initial union, in fact demonstrates a singular passion. It is precisely through this intensity that Dessa wrenches possibilities of black worth from the depths of sorrow and anguish. Akin to Wilson before her, Williams restores meaning to black antagonism beyond the bounds of liberal ideology. Both writers channel enmity as an agent of knowledge production and redress.

"You-All in This Together"

The conclusion of *Dessa Rose* is, in certain respects, an ambiguous one. Infuriated that Dessa has eluded his grasp yet again, Nemi curses his perceived tormentors: "'You-all in this together'—grabbing at [Dessa and Rufel]—'womanhood.' . . . 'All alike. Sluts.'" (Williams 232). Retreating from an earlier, vigorous defense of sanctified white femininity, Nehemiah vengefully casts all "womanhood" in derogatory, sexualized terms. Significantly, the term "slut" is deployed by various progressive whites throughout the novel to signal a collapsing of the hypersexual and the black feminine, locating black women's bodies as constitutive of the wantonness and depravity against which the normativity of whiteness is secured. Instead, in this scenario, an incensed Nemi yokes black slave and free white women together in ignominy. The prospect of their collaboration inspires his utmost dread. Their purported alliance threatens and violates all he has come to know about race and power.

However, Williams's novel concludes without fully exploring what this union—one striking palpable fear into the heart of white patriarchy—might become. The two women depart from the Southern jail expectant, yet ever reticent. "This was the way she was, you see, subject to make you mad just when you was feeling some good towards her. And she was good" (Williams 232), Dessa thinks to herself, following another of Rufel's sharp reprimands for Dessa's continued use of the title "mistress" after all they had just experienced together. "Maybe we couldn't speak but so honest without disagreement," she adds, citing evolving, material obstruction to their bond, "but that didn't change how I feel" (233). Williams seemingly extends a redemptive alternative, fraught and incomplete, to the coerciveness of the liberal problematic. Not unlike Wilson, Keckly, and Cooper, Williams gestures toward what it might look and feel like to undo fundamental contradictions constraining black life in the United States, but not without doggedly interrogating the structural conditions facilitating such exclusions in the first place. Refusing flat, idealized renderings of tolerance and inclusion, *Dessa Rose* emanates, fleetingly, a mode of relation yet to be realized in Williams's era or our own.

Overall, Williams's fiction disturbs reigning politics of order and fraternity. In this sense, returning to her late twentieth-century literary imaginings of sound, materiality, self-commodification, and black indignation reveals a greater incumbency to read nineteenth-century black women's narratives differently. Indeed, a more capacious understanding of the latter's contestation of the liberal problematic, as I have intimated throughout this book, revitalizes venerable standards of black resistance. Any accounting of the limitations of American liberalism in our current neoliberal moment must learn from this past.

Conclusion
Roll Call

Rekia Boyd. Tanisha Anderson. Sandra Bland. We are living in an era—
not emergent, but eerily familiar—in which state-sanctioned terror
against black women and girls proliferates daily. In its wake, and with
the aim of recuperating the full meaning and value of black women's lives
from the precipice of oblivion, charges to #SayHerName abound. Leveraging computational thinking to signal an unrighteous accumulation of
names and of bodies, the hashtag SayHerName honors the dead while
compelling transformative sociopolitical action and awareness from the
living, the spared. According to the African American Policy Forum, "Say
Her Name [as a formal report and a movement] responds to increasing
calls for attention to police violence against Black women by offering a
resource to help ensure that Black women's stories are integrated into
demands for justice, policy responses to police violence, and media representations of victims and survivors of police brutality." As one prong
in a multi-layered praxis targeting the political Left, Right, and beyond,
#SayHerName reminds us that interrogating black women's experiences
does not fulfill an additive function in relation to mainstream narratives. Rather, it is vitally important to centralize and give voice to black
women's trauma, violation, coercion by and contestation of state power,
in order to revolutionize how we apprehend meaningful change for all.

A more expansive roll call of who we are and who we have been, as
#SayHerName clarifies, necessitates more than symbolic name recogni-

tion. #SayHerName binds mass mobilization and policy reform to apparently less-spectacular genres of agitation, including the incitement of collective understanding. The collaborative entity demands accountability for patterns of black vulnerability via direct action and develops social media campaigns pivoting upon forthright dialogue, contextual frames, and information-sharing. Theorization and analysis, too, mark politicized means of cultivating dissent, while storytelling anchors comprehensive approaches to protest and community involvement. Intrinsic to these efforts are questions pertaining to what forms of black life and experience are disposable and why, alerting us to the enormous cost of erasure and to the insurgency of broader models of recovery.

#SayHerName and *Resistance Reimagined* are akin in their respective commitments to articulating ways of knowing by and about black women, past and present. As I have attempted to argue in these pages, a more capacious roll call of instigators of black opposition encompasses sustained engagement with the philosophies and social achievements of intellectuals too frequently deemed incomprehensible as such. Accordingly, refusing to leave the works of Lucy Terry, Maria W. Stewart, Frances E. W. Harper, and Victoria Earle Matthews unsung entails grappling with fierce intricacies of black interiority and unwavering imagination, thereby upsetting time-honored biases regarding resistance and power. Reading Harriet Wilson's, Elizabeth Keckly's, and Anna Julia Cooper's literary endeavors differently likewise involves theorizing a counter-hegemony as concerned with vicious racial antagonism as with subtle micro-aggression, with a theft of the black body as with a theft of black joy. By neglecting black knowledge production in its myriad forms, we perpetuate a history bereft of ambiguity and contradiction, and consequently, of humanity.

Hence, my aim in this book has been to name one of the pivotal, if complex, legacies of black women's ideology critique. This has meant abandoning a politics of representation and canonization circumscribed by race, gender, and class norms. Limited definitions of radicalism—those unable to account for historical black thought leaders other than David Walker, Frederick Douglass, Sojourner Truth, or Ida B. Wells, for instance—diminish black possibility. Rendering political cognizance in utterly diminutive terms, such perspectives situate black being as monolithic, rather than as increasingly various and wide-ranging.

The range undertaken in this project resists firm strictures of genre or periodicity, even constraints of region, era, or class status, analyzing difference less as a site of contradiction than as one of creativity. Indeed, the range of authors featured in *Resistance Reimagined* evokes the heterogeneity at the heart of black feminist consciousness as the latter confronts historic patterns of exclusion. For example, the book's focus comprises Wilson's awareness of sentimental and Christian pretexts for racialized abjection, and of links between abstract rationalism and hierarchized property and contract relations. It also includes her mobilization of experiences of enforced materiality to alternate, strategic ends. Further, through her representation of underclass exploitation across Northern antebellum environs, she complicates normative frameworks of self-help and autonomy and problematizes rituals of interracial charity. Via calculated invocations of blackness and fugitivity, Wilson also intervenes in Western liberal protocol that prioritize coherence and associated ocular metrics, finally disquieting standard tropes of childhood innocence.

Such a range also contains Keckly's dislocation of hegemonic paradigms of development and individual sovereignty by way of stirring depictions of harassment and indigence. In this way, she contributes to vital discourse-disrupting views of majority culture in the North as idyllic racial refuge. Keckly's portrayal of her own acts of witnessing and mediation similarly expose the tenuousness of black freedom in light of conspicuous continuities between slavery and post-Emancipation life, while opening up opportunities for critical resistance. Her selective self-commodification, and sly revelations of the effects of interracial intimacy besides, target insidious modes of control enacted under guises of inclusivity and voluntarism.

Cooper adds to this company by criticizing literary, religious, and governmental performances of abstraction. She extends nuanced insights into the limits of avowedly progressive politics evident in a later, turn-of-the-twentieth-century publication moment, including occasions of inter- and intra-racial prejudice and gender stereotyping. Her thematic foregrounding of pluralism and conflict, summoning of musical metaphor, and theorization of what I have been calling "critical regard" threaten the solidity of liberal institutions of civility and rights. Moreover, her censure of the elitism of mainstream Women's Movements bears as much relevance to early black women activists' challenges to liberalism as to our current milieu.

The becoming together of novels such as Williams's *Dessa Rose* with the diverse literary catalogue of Wilson, Keckly, and Cooper aptly

demonstrates engagement with the liberal problematic as a valid manifestation of black refusal. Particularly significant are Williams's interrogation of the mind-body split, in addition to allied exercises of mediation such as the "as-told-to" dynamic, in a matrix within and against
previous legacies of survival. Williams, of like mind with Wilson, also
explores a negation of black anger according to liberal criteria of appropriateness steeped in privilege. In dialogue with Keckly, Williams lays
"Mammy" bare as a fiction of surplus sustenance, while simultaneously
chipping away at dangerous, if romanticized, cases of interracial empathy and fellowship. At the same time, Williams's work coincides with
that of Cooper in writing black being into sound. In staging a temporary
encounter among Wilson, Keckly, Cooper, and Williams, I have sought
to highlight black women's incursions upon Enlightenment-era prerogatives of liberty and selfhood in order to position blackness beyond both
traditional mechanisms of containment and conventional expectations
of contention.

Still, thoroughly reckoning with a becoming together of black feminist thought exceeds the confines of a single scholarly monograph. There
is much more to say about nineteenth-century black women's divergences from liberal thought, and the contours of their relationship to
contemporary neo-slave narrative. My hope is that this text will serve
as a catalyst for subsequent critical inquiry, especially concerning intersections between textual manipulation of citizenship in the past, and
twenty-first century literatures attuned to antebellum life yet produced
in a patently neoliberal age. As we advance toward the end of the second
decade of the twenty-first century, authors struggle with the effects of
slavery in a manner distinct in many respects from that of Sherley Anne
Williams and amid an all-the-more entrenched ethos of corporatism and
exchange in the context of global capitalism. The pervasiveness of market ideology and the specificities of state violence of this moment permit
writers to engage former black feminist constructions of self-possession
and community in even more unique and productive ways.

Nevertheless, in undermining the liberal problematic, in particular,
the nineteenth-century black women activists and twentieth-century
writers reconceiving of antebellum America discussed here destabilize
discourses of individualism and universality that give the lie to blackness. They defy, more specifically, modalities of reason and equity that
contribute to striking patterns of disparity and racial Otherness. Contrarily, as Barbara Christian might have it, Wilson, Keckly, Cooper, and

Williams generate sarcasm and aurality. They deploy embodiment and difference in dense ways to unmake reigning cultural mythologies of progress. Moreover, they mobilize opacity and anti-pastoral reach to contend with troubling conceptions of decorum, objectivity, and choice. Nineteenth-century black women, in essence, are the bearers of epistemology. What we do with their knowledge, from this point forward, is up to us.

Notes

Introduction

1. Kevin Quashie's project *The Sovereignty of Quiet: Beyond Resistance in Black Culture* constitutes a companion piece of sorts. As I've argued elsewhere, it

> speaks to an enduring incumbency of theorizing race differently. Troubling conditions under which "[r]esistance is, in fact, the dominant expectation we have of black culture" (3), [Quashie] cites the agency embedded in awareness, quiet, and surrender. Deploying an archive from Du Bois to Zora Neale Hurston, Marita Bonner to Gwendolyn Brooks, James Baldwin to Elizabeth Alexander, he renarrates broader cultural tropes of signifying, dissemblance, double consciousness, and masking. He resituates politicized action in the terrain of imagination, waiting, and prayer. In recuperating spaces of inner pleasure, desire, and vulnerability, Quashie complicates easy equations of blackness with public expressiveness, calling attention to modes of black articulacy previously overlooked. (Mann, "Forever Perverse, Queer, Askew" E1)

2. Aside from the critics cited by name in this introduction, see writings listed in the bibliography by Alice Walker, Paula Giddings, William Andrews, Farah Griffin, Mae Henderson, Louise Hutchinson, Vivian May, and Keith Byerman, among others, including Angela Davis's *Women, Race, and Class*.

3. The distinction I make here between the aforementioned liberal aims as "attainments," as opposed to being ever "attainable," is critical here. Integral to the liberal dream, I argue, is the intimation of its already successful completion. Calls for attentiveness to the specificity of experience from an intersectional perspective can thereby be positioned by the state, or its beneficiaries, as threats to purportedly steady progress and achievement.

4. This is a prominent irony evident in the writings of many subjects in this study, I argue: they attend to the violence of liberal humanist practice even as they assert their rightful place in the realm of the human. As Lisa Lowe confirms, "many of the struggles we would wish to engage are not only carried out in

the languages of liberty, equality, reason, progress, and human rights—almost without exception, they must be translated into the political and juridical spaces of this tradition" (41).

5. Here I draw on Saidiya Hartman's formulation of "becoming together," though insisting on an even stricter distinction between "becoming" and "belonging," and extending an at-once historical and methodological application. As she maintains, "The significance of becoming or belonging together in terms other than those defined by one's status as property, will-less object, and the not-quite-human should not be underestimated. This belonging together endeavors to redress and nurture the broken body; it is a becoming together dedicated to establishing other terms of sociality, however transient, that offer a small measure of relief from the debasements constitutive of one's condition" (61).

Chapter 1. "They Won't Believe What I Say": Theorizing Freedom as an Economy of Violence

1. According to Barbara Christian, in the essay "What Celie Knows that You Should Know," in the 2007 collection of her essays edited by Bowles, Fabi, and Keizer, Harriet Wilson "writing and publishing her subversive story underlines her insistence on her own existence, her insistence that it be acknowledged, respected, recognized by others. . . . It is her truth, despite the prevailing traditional or alternative modes of representing reality, that Frado knows, that Celie knows. It is that contrariness that is at the core of so much of Afro-American women's literature" (27). Wilson's insistence on "relating a truth contrary to what readers have come to believe," to borrow from Christian again, at once calls normative ideologies of race and nation into question and initiates new epistemological possibilities.

2. "Try to go to sleep, and you will feel better in the morning," James promises, likening raced, classed, and gendered subjection to the likes of the common cold.

3. In the thirty-three years since Henry Louis Gates Jr. re-released this largely forgotten title, Barbara White, R. J. Ellis, Reginald Pitts, and P. Gabrielle Foreman, as well as Gates himself (all featured in *Harriet Wilson's New England: Race, Writing, and Region*), among others, continue to destabilize Wilson's apparently negligible archival trace. Importantly, such scholars remain committed to interrogating the dynamic interplay between personal elements and fictionalization techniques at work in a literary text abandoned for over a century. Notably, Foreman argues, "Indeed, now that we have situated *Our Nig* in the even deeper critical and historical context that has emerged since its rediscovery, readers must acknowledge that the text functions as an autobiography characterized by

its complex novelistic qualities just as surely as it can be considered a brilliant novel that makes substantive autobiographical claims" (Boggis, Raimon, White 125).

4. For biographical information, see P. Gabrielle Foreman's essay in *Harriet Wilson's New England*, or her own critical work, *Activist Sentiments*.

5. Johnnie Stover advances a related claim in *Rhetoric and Resistance in Black Women's Autobiography*, arguing that "The antebellum autobiographers, Wilson and [Harriet] Jacobs, highlight the importance of the body as a site of oppression in their respective narratives, specifically those parts of the body that are relevant to the acts of oral communication: ear, mouth, tongue, and throat" (109). Stover offers, as does DoVeanna S. Fulton in *Speaking Power*, a reading attuned to the abuse of the body as a struggle to delegitimize black orality as a mode of knowledge production. The vicious suppression of black women's speech acts, for Stover and Fulton, marks their bodies as cultural texts that subvert "dominant transcripts" of cult ideology, black idleness, and liberal notions of the private.

6. Though we might situate Wilson within a broader antebellum archive that critiques Northern progressivism—Martin Delany, Henry Highland Garnet, and Frederick Douglass come to mind—her literary text remains unique for its attentiveness to interrelated experiences of gender and labor.

7. I use the term "ungendering" here to address the slippage in Frado's gender identity under Mrs. Bellmont's command. Mrs. Bellmont often comments on Frado's capacity to complete the work of a man, boy, etc.

8. Importantly, the object of Wilson's embodied analytic also transcends narrow racial classifications, targeting at once the white abolitionist vanguard and black community and abolitionist leadership. As Xiomara Santamarina reminds us, the latter were all too frequently unmindful of "uplift ideology's racially undermining potential, particularly in relation to the mass of black workers who, despite all efforts, really could not get up and leave their structurally disadvantaged occupational position as disparaged, menial workers" (96). Therefore, by "Representing black workers as failing to participate in the ideology of economic individualism," Santamarina maintains, Frederick Douglass and others "obscur[e] the structural conditions governing black workers' domination" (98).

9. "By this unexpected demonstration, her mistress, in amazement, dropped her weapon, desisting from her purpose of chastisement," Wilson's narrator reveals (54). Though it does not bring an end to Frado's subjection at the hands of Mrs. Bellmont altogether, it resembles a turning point, for "This affair never met with an 'after clap,' like many others" (ibid.).

10. Elizabeth Alexander confirms this in "'Can You Be BLACK and Look at This?': Reading the Rodney King Video(s)," as she writes of Douglass's, Prince's,

and Jacobs's respective narratives, maintaining, "these corporeal images of terror suggest that 'experience' can be taken into the body via witnessing and recorded in muscle memory as knowledge" (97). For Alexander, blackness constitutes not the way, but at least one way in which, as a collective, "traumatized African American viewers have been taught a sorry lesson of their continual, physical vulnerability in the United States, a lesson that helps shape how it is we understand ourselves as a 'we,' even when that 'we' is differentiated" (95).

11. This no doubt influenced *Our Nig*'s reception in the antebellum literary marketplace. On Wilson's critical reception history, see Carby 43–44, Peterson 154, Frink 198.

12. By contrast, Katherine Fishburn's critical project attempts to salvage the notion of benevolence in relation to Wilson's novel, stating that "By including in her text many instances of human compassion, gestures that serve to reduce if not eliminate her pain, Wilson does seem to invite us to reach out to her in a similar fashion" (109). While Fishburn does argue for a more capacious use of the term than that exhibited by the Bellmont clan, the basic premise of empathy as always already a productive formation remains intact. "Clearly it is compassion [Wilson] is after," Fishburn affirms, "an efficacious compassion that will manifest itself . . . in the pragmatic act of 'buying a book' and in understanding her travails" (110).

13. Another passage demonstrating this coercive capacity reads: "[James] felt sure there were elements in her heart which, *transformed and purified by the gospel*, would make her worthy the esteem and friendship of the world. A kind, affectionate heart, native wit, and common sense, and the pertness she sometimes exhibited, *he felt if restrained properly*, might become useful in originating a self-reliance which would be of service to her in after years" (Wilson 37; emphasis added).

14. In fact, Frado wishes for death on at least three other occasions in the novel (Wilson 25, 44, 60), suggesting the possibility of an evolving perspective rather than triviality or childishness.

15. Black captive bodies, in this instance, can be enslaved or free. For more on "fungibility," see Hartman (19).

16. Such conversations take place only during Mrs. Bellmont's absence from the family compound.

17. See Peterson 167, Stover 115, and Ronna C. Johnson's 1997 essay, "Said But Not Spoken: Elision and the Representation of Rape, Race, and Gender in Harriet E. Wilson's *Our Nig*."

18. See Ellis 114; Cassandra Jackson's essay, "Beyond the Page: Rape and the Failure of Genre," in *Harriet Wilson's New England*; and Martha Cutter's *Unruly*

Tongue: Identity and Voice in American Women's Writing, 1850–1930 (Jackson: UP of Mississippi, 1999).

19. Despite its focus on Southern slavery, Camp's project is relevant to this one. Its application here is not about essentializing blackness, or collapsing Southern enslavement and Northern indenture, but about capturing the nuances of resistance through the body, as well as through variously gendered, classed, and domestic spaces. I also follow Wilson's lead in this instance, her clear sense that the abject conditions of U.S. enslavement might be used to animate a narrative about labor and race.

20. Juxtaposing what she terms "spectacular opacity" with the "colonial invention of exotic 'darkness,'" Daphne A. Brooks argues, "We can think of [mid-nineteenth-century to turn-of-the-twentieth-century black artists'] acts as opaque, as dark points of possibility that create figurative sites for the reconfiguration of black and female bodies on display. A kind of shrouding, this trope of darkness paradoxically allows for corporeal unveiling to yoke with the (re) covering and re-historicizing of the flesh" (8).

21. See Tate 45–46 and Green 143–44. Even forging a brief but useful connection between Frado and Topsy of Harriet Beecher Stowe's *Uncle Tom's Cabin*, Green further articulates the ways in which "the disorderly girl," angry and rebellious, generates a space in which to convey truths others cannot (or will) not say.

22. As Jayna Brown observes, "The derivation of the term picaninny signals the interchangeability between the black child bodies and the small bits of money required for their acquisition. Not always purchased but often 'made' on the plantation, they embodied the very public marketplace politics of sexualized subjection at the heart of the domestic sphere. Slave children were living currency. The picaninny was a key symbol of the conflation of sex and commerce, which defined the peculiar institution" (24). While an overdetermined blackness seemingly subsumes Frado's mixed-race identity throughout much of the novel, her mulatta standing simultaneously invokes a specter of interracial sex akin to that signified by the picaninny.

Green, too, recognizes Wilson's departure from more mainstream writers, but finally adopts a different research focus from my own.

23. As Brown reveals, constructs such as the picaninny were buttressed by discourses of scientific racism, evolution, and eugenics in the public domain. "Black children were considered to embody metonymically the condition of the lesser races, locked in a perpetual state of childlike simplicity, prone to excess, always emotional and immediate in their responses. Their 'natural' behavior was irrepressible physical and vocal expression," contends Brown (48). Notably, Wilson turns precisely such essentialist prognoses and gross stereotypes on their heads.

24. Lindon Barrett would often cite a "politics of joy" in conversation with colleagues during his brief tenure at UC Riverside. I use it, then, as a critical springboard for thinking about the theoretical implications of Wilson's text.

25. Of Mary's temper as legitimate, see pp. 18 and 35. Similarly, of Mag's temper, see pp. 11 and 19. And of Mrs. Bellmont's temper as legitimate, see pp. 19 and 44 in Wilson's text.

26. As Sianne Ngai argues of the function of traits associated with outrage, including "animatedness" and "irritation"—ambivalent indexes of racial Otherness that consistently fix people of color as spectacle—"it is the cultural representation of the African-American that most visibly harnesses the affective qualities of liveliness, effusiveness, spontaneity, and zeal to a disturbing racial epistemology, and makes these variants of 'animatedness' function as bodily (hence self-evident) signs of the raced subject's naturalness or authenticity" (95). Extrapolating further from Aristotle's *Rhetoric* and the *Nicomachean Ethics*, Ngai observes the ways in which a broader Western "emphasis on proportionality and correctness [of anger] clearly raises the specter of the person angry in the wrong ways and at the wrong times" (182). Interrogating precisely how animatedness and irritation straddle borders between emotion and embodiment, and are as often as not imposed through violence, Ngai's ultimate conclusion that such affect constitutes a "nexus of contradictions with the capacity to generate unanticipated social meanings and effects" (125) resonates with various scenes throughout *Our Nig*.

27. Indeed, of this passage, Bernstein writes, "With this ugly racial flip-flop, the shocking image of a white girl . . . going to hell, turning black, and being seen, spectacularly, by her own mother as a 'nigger,' is an attack on the midcentury's most cherished ideologies of white childhood. Wilson, through Frado, tells the entire abolitionist debate over angel-children to go to hell" (60).

28. Fishburn likewise acknowledges the presence, via Mary Prince's editor Thomas Pringle, of Mary's own "somewhat violent and hasty temper" (qtd. in Fishburn 102).

Chapter 2. The Production of "Emancipation": Race, Ritual, and the Reconstitution of the Antebellum Order

1. According to James Emerson in *The Madness of Mary Lincoln*, "Historians have been misspelling Elizabeth Keckly's surname as *Keckley* since 1868. Jennifer Fleischner recently found her actual signatures and revealed the true spelling in her book *Mrs. Lincoln and Mrs. Keckly*" (193n13). I have chosen to retain the correct usage, rather than the spelling used in the copyright, in my own references to Keckly throughout this chapter, though I do not edit her name when referencing works of secondary criticism. Moreover, though Keckly is, in fact,

mixed-race, I refer to her "blackness" here and elsewhere not to elide this fact, but to remain consistent with how her body circulated in a nineteenth-century context. Lydia Smith, too, was reportedly of mixed-raced heritage.

2. On one occasion in the film, Keckly abruptly departs from Mrs. Lincoln's side in House chambers, only to return moments later, decidedly hopeful, leaving viewers to speculate as to the cause—fear, pain, possible resistance—of her flight. Though this fleeting screen time intimates that Keckly's life amounts to more than her interactions with the Lincoln family, in this case, it arguably dehumanizes, rather than politicizes her presence.

3. My characterization here applies to certain portions of Baker's and Schreiner's texts, as it does to that of Richard Stiller's 1970 *The Spy, the Lady, the Captain, and the Colonel*, among others. Joanne Braxton, too, identifies *Behind the Scenes* as "ghost-written" (43).

4. Keckly's exploration of the exploitative nature of liberalism is often vacated in order to authenticate the antislavery leanings and general broadmindedness of those in direct control of her labor. Jerrold M. Packard's *The Lincolns in the White House: Four Years that Shattered a Family* is likewise symptomatic of reductionist readings in its foregrounding of Mary Lincoln's interiority at Keckly's expense. Specifically, he situates the infamous widow's "attitude toward African-Americans" as "another aspect of Mary's that has largely gone unmentioned" (179). Centering her outlook on race as grounds upon which the former First Lady might, in retrospect, be redeemed, Packard suggests that her turn away from her upbringing in slave-holding Kentucky toward abolitionism can be attributed to the fact that "she finally saw a black person—Lizzy Keckly—as a fellow human being and friend rather than as a servant or an unfree possession" (ibid.).

5. The "Old Clothes Scandal" refers to Mary Lincoln's infamous attempts to auction off her extravagant wardrobe in the wake of her husband's assassination in order to alleviate her debt.

6. According to Fleischner, "In the hierarchy of dressmaking, Lizzy soon rose to the top and could legitimately advertise herself as a mantua maker. Not all dressmakers could sew the complicated and popular mantua, a dress whose bodice was made to fit snugly through vertical pleats stitched in the back" (*Mrs. Lincoln and Mrs. Keckly* 134).

7. In this edition, published by Oxford University Press in 1988, see p. xxx of Olney's introduction.

8. See Robinson 130, 136, and chapter seven, "Nature of the Black Radical Tradition." She is also in conversation with Achille Mbembe's theory of "necropower." See Mbembe 12–14.

9. See David Theo Goldberg, *Racist Culture: Philosophy and the Politics of Meaning*, including 216.

10. Significantly, such representations parallel her labor as a pioneering relief organizer. As presiding officer of the Contraband Relief Association of Washington, D.C., Keckly served the community by procuring food, clothing, and shelter for those dubbed expendable, or mere "contraband of war." Under Keckly's leadership, the organization also secured funds for a flag for the first "colored" unit of the U.S. Civil War Infantry, thereby expanding strictly raced and classed notions of charity and goodwill. See Forbes on the activities of the Contraband Relief Organization (106).

11. See Saidiya Hartman, on the pastoral:

Generally, the representation of the performative has been inscribed in a repressive problematic of consensual and voluntarist agency that reinforces and romanticizes social hierarchy. The pastoral has been the dominant mode of this problematic of repression. In the social landscape of the pastoral, slavery is depicted as an 'organic relationship' so totalizing that neither master nor slave could express 'the simplest human feelings without reference to the other.' Thus the master and the slave are seen as, if not peacefully coexisting, at the very least enjoying a relationship of paternalistic dependency and reciprocity. In this instance, paternalism minimizes the extremity of domination with assertions about the mutually recognized humanity of master and slave. (52)

12. See Andrews's "Reunion in the Postbellum Slave Narrative" 14, Foster 127, Hartman 72.

13. See Fleischner, *Mrs. Lincoln and Mrs. Keckly* 298 and Andrews, "Reunion in the Postbellum Slave Narrative" 12. Frances Smith Foster's emphasis on the manifestation of progress in such scenes is symptomatic in this regard (125).

14. New York Times bestselling author Jennifer Chiaverini offers a productive re-visioning of this scene in her 2013 novel, *Mrs. Lincoln's Dressmaker*, writing: "They laughed together over the incident, although perhaps not for the same reasons" (279).

15. Elizabeth Young's important work on American Civil War narrative bears out such a reading. Usefully, she points to Keckly's immersion in a cultural imaginary convinced of the metonymic function of the presidential body, an atmosphere in which "meeting Lincoln signals . . . direct access to the prerogatives, white and male, of citizenship" (129). Moreover, Young identifies the distinct parallels Keckly draws between herself and Lincoln in her text, from the timing of their initial terms of service in the White House, to the deaths of their sons, to their second inaugurations as presidents of the United States and the Contraband Relief Association, respectively (121).

16. Zafar, in a similar vein, maintains that Keckly "needed no degree in

economics to gauge her own value as a black female *ex-slave* commodity in the book-buying market, and allotted space to her own life accordingly. That sense of the buyer's market, in terms of herself as a black female seller, forms or de-forms her book accordingly" (171; emphasis in original). And, in one of the earliest contributions to this critical conversation, Andrews argues, "Rejecting idealism and moral absolutism in favor of *a materialist and pragmatic measure of self-valuation* empowered Keckley to redefine the terms in which a black woman in a postbellum slave narrative might explain 'whether [she] was really worth [her] salt or not'" ("The Changing Moral" 236; emphasis added).

17. See Packard 123.

18. Camp and Jacqueline Jones echo this point, noting the imbrication of attire with feelings of black leisure, pleasure, and community. See Camp 80–83 and Jones 29.

19. According to Young, "Keckley's laughter underscores the other woman's ignorance, compounding it with ridicule. Despite Keckley's own committed efforts on behalf of the Contraband Relief Fund, this moment mocks the ex-slave who is unable to understand the fashion of the body politic" (128).

20. Of "apparently incoherent [slave] songs," Douglass observes in his *Narrative*, "They would sing, as a chorus, words which to many would seem unmeaning jargon, but which, nevertheless, were full of meaning to themselves. I have sometimes thought that the mere hearing of those songs would do more to impress some minds with the horrible character of slavery, than the reading of whole volumes of philosophy on the subject could do" (27).

21. See also Packard 120 and Stiller 51, for example.

22. Of Nannie Garland, Keckly writes, "She slept in my bed, and I watched over her as if she had been my own child" (239).

23. See Nunley 16.

24. See the author's note in Jennifer Chiaverini's *Mrs. Lincoln's Dressmaker* (352), among other sources, regarding the tombstone. Yet Chiaverini's text, a historical novel, likewise contributes to the aforementioned trend in certain respects. "[M]rs. Lincoln was no longer only a patron, or even just the First Lady. She had become a friend, and Elizabeth would rather die than betray her," the narrator observes (70). The novel's title and cover art, too, dispossess Keckly of authority, meaning, and presence apart from her relationship with Mary.

25. Of the eventual outcome of such tolerance, David Theo Goldberg observes, "liberals are moved to overcome the racial differences they tolerate and have been so instrumental in fabricating by diluting them, by bleaching them out through assimilation or integration. The liberal would assume away the difference in otherness, maintaining thereby the dominance of presumed sameness, the universally imposed similarity in identity" (7).

26. See Fleischner 293–94.

27. Here, Mary Lincoln acknowledges a gap between desire and enactment of equitable relations with Elizabeth, a fissure that corresponds with what I have been calling the liberal problematic. This seemingly occurs again in one of Mary's (edited) letters to Keckly, found in the appendix: "If we get something, *you* will find that *promises* and performance for *this* life will be forthcoming" (360; emphasis in original).

28. On the other hand, a few contemporary critics of the perceived closeness between Lincoln and Keckly purposely render it in sexualized or threateningly miscegenistic terms. See a political cartoon to this effect, "Political Caricature N?2," published by Bromley & Company in 1864, or D. Ottolengul's satire. In the latter, the author ventriloquizes Keckly, saying: "Mrs. Lincoln at once took a fancy to me, [and during our first meeting] embraced me, and kissed me affectionately (11), and later, "I'm with her all the time" (12).

29. Keckly is raped by a white man named Alexander Kirkland, rival of the "pious" slave-breaker, Mr. Bingham, depicted in the memoir. Her non-rational praxis is also evident in the naming of her son as George (after her enslaved father, rather than her master) Kirkland (after her rapist, rather than her master), as well as in her fight for pension payments (Keckly 236–37). For additional mention of George, see Keckly 239.

Chapter 3. "Wondering Under Which Head I Come": Sounding Anna Julia Cooper's Fin-de-Siècle Song

1. Importantly, an interdisciplinary cadre of scholars including Paula Giddings, Elizabeth Alexander, Vivian May, Hazel Carby, Karen Baker-Fletcher, Karen Johnson, and Kathy Glass, among others, have endeavored to recover and reclaim Cooper's life and writings more fully in highly productive ways. Hence, in Giddings's by-now classic 1984 text *When and Where I Enter*, she harnesses Cooper's initial iteration of those words—a direct challenge to the gender norms sutured into the black radical stance of one of Cooper's contemporaries, Martin R. Delany—to ground her inquiry. Ultimately, Giddings revises W.E.B. Du Bois's telling omission of Cooper's name, following an invocation of her remarks, in "The Damnation of Women" in 1920's *Darkwater*. Further, she mobilizes Cooper's antiracist praxis in order to give voice to black women's experiences with respect to migration, education, labor organizing, and tokenization. In "In the Quiet, Undisputed Dignity of My Womanhood," the fifth chapter of *Reconstructing Womanhood*, Carby mirrors Giddings's earlier channeling of Cooper's words in order to frame her own theoretical intervention into Cooper's incisive deconstruction of legacies of American racism and imperialism. Both Giddings and Carby, then, expand the archive of black feminist knowledge production by

establishing the ongoing relevance of Cooper's intellectual contributions in the present. This contrasts with, to take just a few examples, Houston Baker's emphasis in *Workings of the Spirit* on strains of essentialism in *A Voice*, Mary Helen Washington's uneasiness over Cooper's apparent elitism in her introduction to the Schomburg Library edition of the text, and Kevin K. Gaines's suspicion of Cooper's nativism and anti-labor views.

2. Given that Patricia Hill Collins commonly, though not exclusively, situates the "outsider-within" perspective within spaces of domestic labor, I argue here that it functions as a vestibular site as it relates to Cooper's political consciousness. Young Annie gains the opportunity for schooling, but also witnesses the many modes of violence to which her mother, among others, was frequently subject (*Fighting Words* 6).

3. One of the affiliated institutions within Frelinghuysen was the Hannah Stanley Opportunity School, named in honor of Cooper's mother, and as Mark S. Giles notes, the university was an important early model for the contemporary community college system.

4. Earlier, in 1859, Frances E. W. Harper also discussed the importance of "soul," in that instance, in relation to black folk more broadly: in her view, they wanted for "more soul, a higher cultivation of all our spiritual faculties" (Bay 115).

5. On objectivity as ruse, Patricia J. Williams again proves instructive, noting that "in a world of real others, the cost of such exclusive forms of discourse is empowerment at the expense of one's relation to those others; empowering without communion" (93).

6. Cooper does, however, more explicitly address histories of imperialism in other sections of the text, including "Woman Versus the Indian." See also Cooper's critique of the abstraction of philosophers such as Hume and Kant (*A Voice* 291–93).

7. I put pressure on Cooper in terms of exonerating even the most progressive nineteenth-century artists and public intellectuals of any racial bias. For instance, in Paula Giddings's most recent study of Ida B. Wells, the former qualifies portrayals of black experience by figures such as Tourgée as "encouraging," yet shortsightedly "hing[ed] on the breakdown of law and order and on questions about the ability of the South to reform itself" (*Ida* 216).

8. For a discussion of Keckly's analysis of racial representativeness, see chapter two of this volume.

9. See also Toni Morrison, *Playing in the Dark*, the central argument of which Cooper, in this instance, anticipates.

10. Cooper also addresses this point earlier in the volume in "Womanhood a Vital Element in the Regeneration and Progress of a Race," stating that "our

satisfaction in American institutions rests not on the fruition we now enjoy, but springs rather from the possibilities and promise that are inherent in the system, though as yet, perhaps, far in the future" (12). Moreover, "Such conditions in embryo are all that we claim for the land of the West. We have not yet reached our ideal in American civilization" (ibid.).

11. For an analogous critique of patriotism, see Ida B. Wells's *A Red Record* (Royster 131).

12. See: Kevin K. Gaines, *Uplifting the Race* (150).

13. Cooper also relies on evolutionist language to distinguish between the potential for the U.S. and that of vaguely defined "Asiatic types of civilization" to achieve harmony. In my reading, this does not denote pandering, but rather a cognizant, politicized appeal. In fact, it marks an only apparently ethnocentric lure by one perpetually mindful of her rhetorical context: that is, as to how and by whom she would predominantly be read and heard. See Bailey, "Anna Julia Cooper: Dedicated in the Name . . ." (59) and chapter three of Hartman's *Scenes* on narrative seduction. After drawing her audience in with America's inevitable fixity at the apex of a Western civilizationalist framework, Cooper extends a separate argument that "not all conflict is undesirable or destructive, just as not all absences of conflict represent egalitarian or communitarian victories" (Weiss 96).

14. Baker-Fletcher also deepens Cooper's archive for subheadings such as "Soprano Obligato" beyond the commonly observed allusion to the operas and oratorios of German-English Baroque composer George Friedrich Handel (1685–1759). Typically, such a reading traffics in discourses of authenticity as well as circumscribed understandings of Cooper as classist or elitist.

15. Regarding ethnographic readings of the sorrow songs, see Eric Sundquist's *To Wake the Nations: Race and the Making of American Literature*, or the anthropological bent implicit in some of Baker-Fletcher's interpretations.

16. See Lindon Barrett's *Blackness and Value* (57–58).

17. See also bell hooks, *Ain't I a Woman?: Black Women in Feminism*; Valerie Smith, "Black Feminist Theory and the Representation of the 'Other'"; Ann DuCille, *Skin Trade* and "On Canons: Anxious History and the Rise of Black Feminist Literary Studies"; and Deborah McDowell, "Recycling: Race, Gender, and the Practice of Theory."

18. In terms of present-day feminist debates, I'm thinking of one inaugurated by Susan Gubar's 1998 *Critical Inquiry* article, "What Ails Feminist Criticism?"

19. Another clue as to the tongue-in-cheek quality of Cooper's initial reference to Susan B. Anthony and Anna Shaw appears in the following passage: "It is only from the broad plateau of light and love that one can see petty prejudice and narrow priggishness in their true perspective; and it is on this high ground,

as I sincerely believe, these two grand women stand" (Cooper 83). Arguably, this is reminiscent of Keckly's deployment of light imagery to signal the saccharine nature and pretense of white liberal sentimentality, as outlined in chapter two of this volume.

20. Theorizing the means by which writing is tethered (historically and rhetorically, among other means) to colonial violence, Scott Richard Lyons defines "rhetorical imperialism" as "the ability of dominant powers to assert control of others by setting the terms of [the] debate" (452).

21. On Truth, see Mann, "Theorizing 'What Could Have Been' . . ." 579.

22. See Nunley, *Keepin' It Hushed*: "Substantial democracy goes beyond voting to create new or usable knowledge by members of the body politic that offers some possibility of altering the dominant political and social rationalities. Substantial democracy holds out the hope that, through various kinds of participation, citizens can have a measurable effect on their daily lives" (164).

23. In nuanced critical readings, scholars Cindy White and Catherine Dobris, Elsa Barkley Brown, and Elizabeth Higginbotham attend to both the effectiveness and the limits of such a politics among figures like Cooper, Fannie Barrier Williams, and Josephine St. Pierre Ruffin in the black women's Club Movement; among black female parishioners in post-Reconstruction era Richmond; and among the black women of the National Black Baptist Convention, respectively. Moreover, demonstrating specific attention to the association of individual behavior modification as a means to attain citizenship with histories of white supremacist civilizing discourses, Rod Ferguson's and Farah Jasmine Griffin's respective works speak to the ways in which ideologies of black respectability are strictly policed along the lines of gender, class, and heteronormativity. Serving a managerial function in relationship to often poor and rural black communities, those championing such positions in the nineteenth and early twentieth centuries frequently acted in complicity with the interests of state capital by holding out false promises of protection and papering over institutionalized modes of repression. Further, Candice Jenkins usefully characterizes instantiations of the politics of black respectability into the twentieth and twenty-first centuries as expressions of a "salvific wish," attaching salvation to a compulsory containment of desire, to the suppression of black women's bodies, and to the erasure of sexual nonconformity. See White and Dobris, "The Nobility of Womanhood"; Brown, "Negotiating and Transforming the Public Sphere"; Higginbotham, *Righteous Discontent*; Ferguson, *Aberrations in Black*; and Griffin, *If You Can't Be Free, Be a Mystery: In Search of Billie Holiday* (72–73). Nevertheless, the "politics of black respectability," as a rubric, is not broad enough to account for the capaciousness of Cooper's articulation of decorum as critical public pedagogy.

24. On the other hand, the severing of the spiritual from the erotic in *A*

Voice—the presence of which in black feminisms is by no means reducible to Cooper's oeuvre—forecloses on the unique potential embedded in deep sensuality. In fact, the erotic as an innately political, non-rational force yields a profound sense of fulfillment and understanding. It simultaneously inspires wisdom and change. Cooper's silence on this score, her rhetorical enactment and performance of middle-class black womanhood, at once signals a missed opportunity and reinscribes a false dichotomy between the production of knowledge and the production of joy. At the same time, Cooper's muteness around the erotic underscores the specific challenges black women face when presenting a public, sexual self, and the need to take seriously (rather than to pathologize) Cooper's personal affinities and intimacies apart from *A Voice*.

25. According to Gilmore, racism constitutes minorities' institutionalized exposure to premature death. See *Golden Gulag* 28.

26. To the point about marriage, Cooper quips that "strong-minded women could be, when they thought it worth their while, quite endurable" (72). Other prominent instances of sarcasm appear on pp. 38, 39, 49, 81 (discussed previously in this chapter), 104–5, 114, and 269 of *A Voice*.

27. On Stanton's opportunism, see Angela Davis, *Women, Race, and Class*.

28. According to Charles Lemert, "Though Cooper could be biting in her criticism of men, including men in general, she does frequently display a striking reluctance to denounce them altogether" (26). This arguably misses the point. That is, ironic critiques aimed in part at recuperating black masculinity are consistently hinged to calls for male accountability in *A Voice*. Overall, Cooper's enduring defense of her male counterparts amounts to more than the apparent fact that she "thought in the manner of the times" (Lemert 26). Cooper's determined justification of the value of black manhood must be read alongside, to borrow from bell hooks, an as-insistent demand that "men have a tremendous contribution to make to feminist struggle in the area of exposing, confronting, opposing, and transforming the sexism of their male peers" (83).

Chapter 4. "Mammy Ain't Nobody Name": Power, Privilege, and the Bodying Forth of Resistance

1. In line with my analysis throughout this volume, Keizer's project also consistently refuses restrictive definitions of black empowerment. Hence, of the writings of Morrison, Charles Johnson, and others, she offers, "As a response to the overvaluation of direct, armed slave resistance or successful escape, the contemporary narrative of slavery demonstrates how fraught with difficulty resistance is and has been" (9).

2. For additional biographical information, see the obituary, "Sherley Anne Williams, 54, Novelist, Poet and Professor."

3. Notably, Dessa's execution is postponed until her child with Kaine can be birthed into slavery.

4. Much of the danger, of course, lies in the ability of Nehemiah to translate these presumptions into institutionally sanctioned "truth." Relatedly, see Nehemiah's representation of blackness as lack (Williams 17); as sickly/pathologized (20); as criminal (30); and as bestial and objectified (36, 37, 45–46).

5. In his journal entry of July 4, 1847, a date deliberately selected by Williams, Nehemiah cites "reason" as the source of his current understanding of Dessa's escape, separating himself from Hughes and his "supernatural" premonitions (Williams 69). And in an echo of his earlier suspicion of discrepancies and loose ends when it comes to slave conduct (36), Nehemiah stresses a need for coherence in the wake of Dessa's exodus, even attributing the latter to the slave woman's manipulative opacity (70–71). Nehemiah begins to be referred to by the narrator as "Nemi" by the novel's end, a sign of how his obsession with finding Dessa has consumed him and precipitated his deterioration. For Rufel's discovery of the blank pages in Nemi's note pad, see *Dessa Rose* 232.

6. On Williams's use of parody and her exploration of the sexual implications of the "as-told-to" dynamic, see Byerman 55–56 and Henderson 299, respectively. Regarding parodic effect, Deborah McDowell concurs, offering: Nehemiah's "section is a veritable parody of the 'as-told-to' device of gathering empirical evidence and documenting events to construct historicist discourse" (148). Furthermore, McDowell adds, "In telling Dessa's story, Nehemiah creates an abstraction and assigns it a place distant from himself" (149).

On the other hand, Dessa serves not as passive victim, but manipulates her interlocutor, exposing Nehemiah's misapprehension of Kaine's name (among other things about her husband) by way of jest: "You don't 'smell' it; you say it" she corrects on one occasion (Williams 40).

7. Melissa Harris-Perry characterizes the film as a "lovely little coming-of-age story" in an interview on Lawrence O'Donnell's television program, *The Last Word*, airing on MSNBC on August 10, 2011. Collectives such as the Association of Black Women Historians have likewise extended essential critiques of the film.

8. The organizational structure of *Still Brave: The Evolution of Black Women's Studies* (2009)—a continuation of the classic anthology *All the Women are White, All the Blacks are Men, But Some of Us are Brave* (1982)—constitutes but one example. Editors of the former—Stanlie M. James, Frances Smith Foster, and Beverly Guy-Sheftall—"named each section, each neighborhood, each family of thought [in the volume], with a line from a song [they] believe represents, reaffirms, and reconstructs the pieces into a whole. In doing so, [they] acknowledge

and honor the presence and prescience of music in Black Women's Studies and other cultural contexts as well as in the history of African peoples" (xxi).

9. Likewise, "The darky's song burst in upon [his] reflections and before Nehemiah could react, she spoke," Williams observes (37).

10. On black hair styling as Africanism, see Amy K. Levin 145.

11. I find Beaulieu's apparent consignment of bigotry and magnanimity along stark racial lines troubling.

12. For example, "motherhood and sexual vulnerability," writes Angelyn Mitchell, "become the two sites of commonality for Dessa and Ruth in their bond of sisterhood" (78). Likewise, deeming Dessa and Rufel "true witnesses to each other as survivors," in her study *Traumatic Possessions: The Body and Memory in African American Women's Writing and Performance*, Jennifer L. Griffiths holds that several carefully crafted scenes by Williams "allow the women to know the other's struggle on multiple levels: emotionally, intellectually, and bodily as mothers, daughters, lovers, and finally, as friends" (23). "The categories of difference that construct black and white womanhood in opposition to each other and prevent witnessing are broken down through empathy," she adds later (ibid.).

13. Similarly, in citing potential resemblances between Dessa and Rufel, Fox-Good aptly characterizes their "approximation to identity" as fundamentally disconcerting and dangerous for Dessa (26). Even Mitchell grants that theirs is a relation "rooted in difference" (83). Other passages from the novel contradicting representations of friendship between the women include: "It chafed [Dessa] to be so beholden to [Ruth]" (Williams 164) and "That's what we was in white folks eyes, nothing but marks to be used, wiped out. . . . We wasn't nothing to them. I couldn't trust all we had to something could swallow us like so many drops" (172).

14. This is not to discount the obvious ambiguity in which Dessa and Rufel's relationship is at times embedded. This is evidenced by such passages as the following, each from Dessa's perspective: "Who wanted to be her friend anyway?. . . . I wanted to believe it. I don't think I wronged her at first, but the white woman I'd opened my eyes to at the start of the summer wasn't the one I partnered with on that journey; I admitted this to myself that afternoon" (Williams 219), and "My thoughts had changed some since that night at Mr. Oscar's. You can't do something like this with someone and not develop some closeness, some trust" (Williams 206).

15. See the conclusion of chapter two of this volume.

16. Of other instances of "sweetness," Dessa remembers: "Nathan and Cully, and Harker, too, sat with me the whole time I was out my head; Ada said that was the only thing kept me quiet—they hands, they eyes, they voice. These had stood between me and death or me and craziness. We'd opened to each others"

(Williams 168). And furthermore, "wasn't no pretense between us" (169), for "Nathan and Cully, and Harker, too, had risked something for me and I felt bound to them—and them to me—as tight as blood-kin" (174–75). This is not to say that there is no conflict or disagreement within the group. Yet I maintain that the ethic of care/sweetness supersedes such conflict.

17. This also signals Ruth's denial of a full spectrum of emotion to Dessa (that she, like Rufel, might feel angry on one occasion and less so on another). This confirms Rufel's belief in black insentience and participation in black dehumanization, as she refuses to allow Dessa to possess multiple habits of being.

18. Aunt Chloe differs from Williams's representation of Jemina, the black bondwoman on Hughes's farm in Alabama who attends Dessa in her jail cell after the rebellion on the coffle. Jemina is, in certain respects, her popular cultural counterpart, Aunt Jemima, with a twist. Jemina's performance in the wake of Dessa's initial escape, a plot in which she is complicit, invokes the theatrical and melodramatic. Marked by "the darky's throwing her apron over her head and howling, 'Oh, Masa, it terrible; they was terrible fierce'" (Williams 70), Jemina concocts an embellished account in which "except for one exclamation from Odessa, of surprise or dismay, [Jemina] could not tell which, they fled in silence," insisting that "she could not see well enough to describe any of the niggers, save to state that they were big and black and terrible" (71) and "pointing to her muddied gown to prove it" (70). Jemina's tale, which simultaneously exonerates an alternately "surprised" or "dismayed" Dessa and appeases whites' penchant for a mythic black bestiality, relies on a calculated spectacle of exaggerated emotion.

Though Williams's positioning of Aunt Chloe's quiet performance at the narrative's close might, for some, signal a hierarchy between competing modalities of black slave women's resistance, such an arrangement as readily invites an understanding of the multiplicity of black struggle, conflict, and surrender. Black appropriation of sedimented racial scripts of humility and meekness, then, denotes an at-once pivotal and fraught avenue of defiance not reducible to—if ultimately inextricable from—ostensibly more forceful means of confrontation.

19. Notably, this marks a reconstitution of the infamous challenge to Sojourner Truth in 1858 to bare her breasts to verify her gender identity. See Nell Painter, *Sojourner Truth: A Life, A Symbol* (141).

20. Importantly, Arcopolis evokes Greek notions of philosophy and logic, spheres that Dessa will—as she did in the novel's opening section—continue to undermine.

21. This is likewise evidenced in texts like *The History of Mary Prince, A West Indian Slave* (1831). On Mary Prince, see chapter one of this volume.

22. Dessa declares on another occasion: "I couldn't put into words all this that

was going through my head. I didn't have the words, the experience to say these things. All I could do was feel" (Williams 174).

23. This mirrors a previous instance in which Rufel refuses to believe Ada's story of sexual subjection to the latter's master, who then attempted to have his way with Ada's daughter, Annabelle, prompting the duo's escape. "Rufel didn't believe a word of that. She could see nothing attractive in the rawboned, brown-skinned woman or her lanky, half-witted daughter" (Williams 91). "White man, indeed! Both of them probably run off by the mistress for making up to the master," she continues self-centeredly: "the 'cruel master' was just to play on her sympathy" (93).

24. See p. 14 of *Their Eyes Were Watching God*: "De nigger woman is the mule uh de world so fur as Ah can see. Ah been prayin' fuh it tuh be different wid you. Lawd, Lawd, Lawd!"

Works Cited

Alexander, Elizabeth. "Can You Be BLACK and Look at This?: Reading the Rodney King Video(s)." *Black Male: Representations of Masculinity in Contemporary American Art*. Ed. Thelma Golden. New York: Whitney Museum of Art, 1994. 91–110. Print.

———. "'We Must Be About Our Father's Business': Anna Julia Cooper and the In-Corporation of the Nineteenth-Century African-American Woman Intellectual." *Signs* 20.2 (1995): 336–56. Web. 12 Apr. 2012.

Allen, William Francis, Charles Pickard Ware, and Lucy McKim Garrison, eds. *Slave Songs of the United States*. Bedford: Applewood Books, 1867. Print.

Andrews, William L. "The Changing Moral Discourse of Nineteenth-Century African American Women's Autobiography: Harriet Jacobs and Elizabeth Keckley." *De/Colonizing the Subject: The Politics of Gender in Women's Autobiography*. Eds. Sidonie Smith and Julia Watson. Minneapolis: University of Minnesota Press, 1992. 225–241. Print.

———. "Reunion in the Postbellum Slave Narrative: Frederick Douglass and Elizabeth Keckley." *Black American Literature Forum* 23 (1989): 5–16. Web. 15 June 2012.

Anzaldúa, Gloria. *Borderlands/La Frontera: The New Mestiza*. Third Edition. San Francisco: Aunt Lute Books, 2007. Print.

Aptheker, Herbert. *American Negro Slave Revolts*. New York: International Publishers, 1993. Print.

Bailey, Cathryn. "Anna Julia Cooper: 'Dedicated in the Name of My Slave Mother to the Education of Colored Working People.'" *Hypatia* 19.2 (2004): 56–73. Web. 1 April 2012.

Baker, Houston A., Jr. *Blues, Ideology, and Afro-American Literature: A Vernacular Theory*. Chicago: University of Chicago Press, 1984. Print.

———. *Workings of the Spirit: The Poetics of Afro-American Women's Writing*. Chicago: University of Chicago Press, 1991. Print.

Baker, Jean H. *Mary Todd Lincoln: A Biography*. New York: W. W. Norton & Company, 1987. Print.

Baker-Fletcher, Karen. *A Singing Something: Womanist Reflections on Anna Julia Cooper*. New York: Crossroad Publishing Company, 1994. Print.

Barrett, Lindon. *Blackness and Value: Seeing Double*. Cambridge: Cambridge University Press, 1999. Print.

Bay, Mia, Farah J. Griffin, Martha S. Jones, and Barbara D. Savage. *Toward an Intellectual History of Black Women*. Chapel Hill: University of North Carolina Press, 2015. Print.

Beaulieu, Elizabeth Ann. *Black Women Writers and the American Neo-Slave Narrative: Femininity Unfettered*. Westport, CT: Greenwood Press, 1999. Print.

Bell, Bernard. *The Afro-American Novel and Its Tradition*. Amherst: University of Massachusetts Press, 1987. Print.

Berlant, Lauren. "Intimacy: A Special Issue." *Critical Inquiry* 24 (1998): 281–88. Web. 30 June 2012.

Bernstein, Robin. *Racial Innocence: Performing American Childhood from Slavery to Civil Rights*. New York: New York University Press, 2011. Print.

Bowles, Gloria, M. Giulia Fabi, and Arlene Keizer, eds. *New Black Feminist Criticism, 1985–2000*. Urbana: University of Illinois Press, 2007. Print.

Braxton, Joanne M. *Black Women Writing Autobiography: A Tradition within a Tradition*. Philadelphia: Temple University Press, 1989. Print.

Brontë, Charlotte. *Jane Eyre*. New York: Bantam Classic, 1981. Print.

Brooks, Daphne A. *Bodies in Dissent: Spectacular Performances of Race and Freedom 1850–1910*. Durham: Duke University Press, 2006. Print.

Brown, Elsa Barkley. "Negotiating and Transforming the Public Sphere: African American Political Life in the Transition from Slavery to Freedom." *Public Culture* 7.1 (1994): 107–146. Web. 15 May 2012.

Brown, Jayna. *Black Women Performers and the Shaping of the Modern*. Durham: Duke University Press, 2008. Print.

Butler, Octavia. *Kindred*. Boston: Beacon Press, 1979. Print.

Byerman, Keith. *Remembering the Past in Contemporary African American Fiction*. Chapel Hill: University of North Carolina Press, 2005. Print.

Camp, Stephanie M. H. *Closer to Freedom: Enslaved Women and Everyday Resistance in the Plantation South*. Chapel Hill: University of North Carolina Press, 2004. Print.

Carby, Hazel, ed. *Iola Leroy, or Shadows Uplifted*. Black Women Writers Series, 1987. Print.

———. *Race Men*. Cambridge: Harvard University Press, 1998. Print.

———. *Reconstructing Womanhood: The Emergence of the Afro-American Woman Novelist*. New York: Oxford University Press, 1987. Print.

Chiaverini, Jennifer. *Mrs. Lincoln's Dressmaker: A Novel*. U.S.A: Plume/Penguin Group, 2013. Print.

Christian, Barbara. "'Somebody Forgot to Tell Somebody Something': African-American Women's Historical Novels." *New Black Feminist Criticism, 1985–2000*. Eds. Gloria Bowles, M. Giulia Fabi, and Arlene Keizer. Urbana: University of Illinois Press, 2007. 86–98. Print.

Collins, Patricia Hill. *Black Feminist Thought: Knowledge, Consciousness, and the Politics of Empowerment*. Revised Tenth Anniversary Edition. New York: Routledge, 2000. Print.

———. *Fighting Words: Black Women and the Search for Justice*. Minneapolis: University of Minnesota Press, 1998. Print.

Cooper, Anna Julia. *A Voice from the South*. New York: Oxford University Press, 1988. Print.

Cutter, Martha. *Unruly Tongue: Identity and Voice in American Women's Writing, 1850–1930*. Jackson: University Press of Mississippi, 1999. Print.

Davies, Carole Boyce. "Mother Right/Write Revisited: *Beloved* and *Dessa Rose* and the Construction of Motherhood in Black Women's Fiction." *Narrating Mothers: Theorizing Maternal Subjectivities*. Eds. Brenda O. Daly and Maureen T. Reddy. Knoxville: University of Tennessee Press, 1991. 44–57. Print.

Davis, Angela. "Reflections on the Black Woman's Role in the Community of Slaves." *The Massachusetts Review* 13.1 (1972): 81–100. Web. 15 Mar. 2013.

———. *Women, Race, and Class*. New York: Vintage, 1983. Print.

Dickson-Carr, Darryl. *African American Satire: The Sacredly Profane Novel*. Columbia: University of Missouri Press, 2001. Print.

Douglass, Frederick. *Narrative of the Life of Frederick Douglass, an American Slave and Incidents in the Life of a Slave Girl*. New York: The Modern Library, 2004. Print.

Du Bois, W.E.B. *Black Reconstruction*. New York: The Free Press, 1998. Print.

———. *Darkwater: Voices from Within the Veil*. New York: Harcourt, Brace, and Company, 1920. Print.

———. *The Souls of Black Folk*. New York: Barnes and Noble Classics, 2003. Print.

DuCille, Ann. "The Occult of True Black Womanhood." *Skin Trade*, 81–119. Cambridge: Harvard University Press, 1996. Print.

———. "On Canons: Anxious History and the Rise of Black Feminist Literary Studies." *The Cambridge Companion to Feminist Literary Theory*. Ed. Ellen Rooney. Cambridge: Cambridge University Press, 2006. 29–52. Print.

Ellis, R. J. *Harriet Wilson's* Our Nig: *A Cultural Biography of a "Two-Story" African American Novel*. Amsterdam: Rodopi, B.V., 2003. Print.

Emerson, James. *The Madness of Mary Lincoln*. Carbondale: Southern Illinois University Press, 2007. Print.

Ferguson, Roderick A. *Aberrations in Black: Toward a Queer of Color Critique*. Minneapolis: University of Minnesota Press, 2004. Print.

Fernheimer, Janice W. "Arguing from Difference: Cooper, Emerson, Guizot, and a More Harmonious America." *Black Women's Intellectual Traditions: Speaking Their Minds*. Eds. Kristin Waters and Carol B. Conaway. Burlington: University of Vermont Press, 2007. 287–305. Print.

Fishburn, Katherine. *The Problem of Embodiment in Early African American Narrative*. Westport, Connecticut: Greenwood Press, 1997. Print.

Fleischner, Jennifer. *Mrs. Lincoln and Mrs. Keckly: The Remarkable Story of the Friendship Between a First Lady and a Former Slave*. New York: Broadway Books, 2003. Print.

Forbes, Ella. *African American Women During the Civil War*. New York: Garland Publishing, Inc., 1998. Print.

Foreman, P. Gabrielle. *Activist Sentiments: Reading Black Women in the Nineteenth Century*. Urbana: University of Illinois Press, 2009. Print.

———. "Recovered Autobiographies and the Marketplace: *Our Nig's* Generic Genealogies and Harriet Wilson's Entrepreneurial Enterprise." *Harriet Wilson's New England: Race, Writing, and Region*. Eds. JerriAnne Boggis, Eve Allegra Raimon, and Barbara A. White. Durham, New Hampshire: University of New Hampshire Press, 2007. 120–135. Print.

Foster, Frances Smith. *Written by Herself: Literary Production by African American Women, 1746–1892*. Bloomington: Indiana University Press, 1993. Print.

Fox-Good, Jacqueline A. "Singing the Unsayable: Theorizing Music in *Dessa Rose*." *Black Orpheus: Music in African American Fiction from the Harlem Renaissance to Toni Morrison*. Ed. Saadi A. Simawe. New York: Garland Publishing, Inc., 2000. 1–37. Print.

Frink, Helen. "Fairy Tales and *Our Nig*: Feminist Approaches to Teaching Harriet Wilson's Novel." *Harriet Wilson's New England: Race, Writing, and Region*. Eds. JerriAnne Boggis, Eve Allegra Raimon, and Barbara A. White. Durham, New Hampshire: University of New Hampshire Press, 2007. 183–200. Print.

Fulton, DoVeanna S. *Speaking Power: Black Feminist Orality in Women's Narratives of Slavery*. Albany: State University of New York Press, 2006. Print.

Gaines, Kevin K. *Uplifting the Race: Black Leadership, Politics, and Culture in the Twentieth Century*. Chapel Hill: University of North Carolina Press, 1996. Print.

Giddings, Paula J. *Ida: A Sword Among Lions. Ida B. Wells and the Campaign Against Lynching*. New York: Amistad, 2008. Print.

———. *When and Where I Enter: The Impact of Black Women on Race and Sex in America*. New York: Bantam Books, 1984. Print.

Giles, Mark S. "Special Focus: Dr. Anna Julia Cooper, 1858–1964: Teacher, Scholar, and Timeless Womanist." *The Journal of Negro Education* 75.4 (2006): 621–34. Web. 31 May 2012.

Gilmore, Ruth Wilson. *Golden Gulag: Prisons, Surplus, Crisis and Opposition in Globalizing California.* Berkeley: University of California Press, 2007. Print.

Gilroy, Paul. *The Black Atlantic: Modernity and Double Consciousness.* Cambridge: Harvard University Press, 1993. Print.

Glass, Kathy L. *Courting Communities: Black Female Nationalism and "Syncre-Nationalism" in the Nineteenth-Century North.* New York: Routledge, 2006. Print.

Goldberg, David Theo. *Racist Culture: Philosophy and the Culture of Meaning.* Massachusetts: Blackwell Publishers, Inc., 1993. Print.

Green, Lisa E. "The Disorderly Girl in Harriet E. Wilson's *Our Nig.*" *Harriet Wilson's New England: Race, Writing, and Region.* Eds. JerriAnne Boggis, Eve Allegra Raimon, and Barbara A. White. Durham, New Hampshire: University of New Hampshire Press, 2007. 140–154. Print.

Griffin, Farah Jasmine. "Textual Healing: Claiming Black Women's Bodies, the Erotic and Resistance in Contemporary Novels of Slavery." *Callaloo* 19.2 (1996): 519–36. Print.

Griffiths, Jennifer L. *Traumatic Possessions: The Body and Memory in African American Women's Writing and Performance.* Charlottesville: University of Virginia Press, 2009. Print.

Gubar, Susan. "What Ails Feminist Criticism?" *Critical Inquiry* 20.4 (1998): 878–902. Web. 1 Oct. 2009.

Hartman, Saidiya. *Scenes of Subjection: Terror, Slavery, and Self-Making in Nineteenth-Century America.* New York: Oxford University Press, 1997. Print.

Helm, Katherine. *The True Story of Mary, Wife of Lincoln: Containing the Recollections of Mary Lincoln's Sister Emilie (Mrs. Ben Hardin Helm), Extracts from her War-Time Diary, Numerous Letters and Other Documents Now First Published.* New York: Harper & Brothers Publishers, 1928. Print.

The Help. Dir. Tate Taylor. Perf. Emma Stone, Viola Davis, and Octavia Spencer. DreamWorks Studios, 2011. Film.

Henderson, Mae G. "The Stories of O(Dessa): Stories of Complicity and Resistance." *Female Subjects in Black and White: Race, Psychoanalysis, Feminism.* Eds. Elizabeth Abel, Barbara Christian, and Helene Moglen. Berkeley: University of California Press, 1997. 285–304. Print.

Higginbotham, Elizabeth. *Righteous Discontent: The Women's Movement in the Black Baptist Church, 1880–1920.* Cambridge: Harvard University Press, 1993. Print.

hooks, bell. *Ain't I A Woman: Black Women and Feminism.* Boston: South End Press, 1981. Print.

————. *Feminist Theory: From Margin to Center*. Brooklyn: South End Press, 1984. Print.

Hull, Gloria T., Patricia Bell Scott, and Barbara Smith, eds. *All the Women are White, All the Blacks are Men, But Some of Us are Brave: Black Women's Studies*. New York: The Feminist Press, 1982. Print.

Hurston, Zora Neale. *Their Eyes Were Watching God*. New York: Harper Perennial Modern Classics, 2006. Print.

Hutchinson, Louise Daniel. *Anna J. Cooper: A Voice from the South*. Washington, D.C.: Smithsonian Institution Press, 1981. Print.

Jackson, Cassandra. "Beyond the Page: Rape and the Failure of Genre." *Harriet Wilson's New England: Race, Writing, and Region*. Eds. JerriAnne Boggis, Eve Allegra Raimon, and Barbara A. White. Durham, New Hampshire: University of New Hampshire Press, 2007. 154–165. Print.

Jacobs, Harriet Ann. *Narrative of the Life of Frederick Douglass, an American Slave and Incidents in the Life of a Slave Girl*. New York: The Modern Library, 2004. Print.

James, Stanlie M., Frances Smith Foster, and Beverly Guy-Sheftall, eds. *Still Brave: The Evolution of Black Women's Studies*. New York: The Feminist Press, 2009. Print.

Jenkins, Candice M. *Private Lives, Proper Relations: Regulating Black Intimacy*. Minneapolis: University of Minnesota Press, 2007. Print.

Johnson, Karen A. *Uplifting the Women and the Race: The Lives, Educational Philosophies and Social Activism of Anna Julia Cooper and Nannie Helen Burroughs*. New York: Routledge, 2000. Print.

Johnson, Ronna. "Said But Not Spoken: Elision and the Representation of Rape, Race and Gender in Harriet Wilson's *Our Nig*." *Speaking the Other Self: American Women Writers*. Ed. Jeanne Campbell Reesman. Athens: University of Georgia Press, 1997. 96–116. Print.

Jones, Edward P. *The Known World*. New York. Amistad, 2003. Print.

Jones, Gayl. *Corregidora*. Boston: Beacon Press, 1975. Print.

Jones, Jacqueline. *Labor of Love, Labor of Sorrow: Black Women, Work, and Family, From Slavery to the Present*. New York: Basic Books, 2010. Print.

Keckly, Elizabeth. *Behind the Scenes: Or Thirty Years a Slave, and Four Years in the White House*. New York: Oxford University Press, 1988. Print.

Keizer, Arlene R. *Black Subjects: Identity Formation in the Contemporary Narrative of Slavery*. Ithaca: Cornell University Press, 2004. Print.

Kester, Gunilla Theander. *Writing the Subject: Bildung and the African American Text*. New York: Peter Lang, 1995. Print.

Lemert, Charles, and Esme Bhan, eds. *The Voice of Anna Julia Cooper*. New York: Rowman & Littlefield Publishers, Inc., 1998. Print.

Levin, Amy K. *Africanism and Authenticity in African-American Women's Novels.* Gainesville: University Press of Florida, 2003. Print.

Levine, Lawrence. *Black Culture and Black Consciousness: Afro-American Thought from Slavery to Freedom.* 30th Anniversary Edition. New York: Oxford University Press, 2007. Print.

Lincoln. Dir. Steven Spielberg. Perf. Daniel Day-Lewis, Sally Field, and David Strathairn. DreamWorks Pictures and Participant Media, 2012. Film.

Locke, Attica. *The Cutting Season.* New York: Dennis Lahane Books, 2012. Print.

Logan, Shirley Wilson. *"We Are Coming": The Persuasive Discourse of Nineteenth-Century Black Women.* Carbondale: Southern Illinois University Press, 1999. Print.

Lorde, Audre. *Sister Outsider.* Berkeley: Crossing Press, 1984. Print.

Lowe, Lisa. *The Intimacies of Four Continents.* Durham: Duke University Press, 2015. Print.

Luciano, Dana. *Arranging Grief: Sacred Time and the Body in Nineteenth-Century America.* New York: New York University Press, 2007. Print.

Lyons, Scott Richard. "Rhetorical Sovereignty: What Do American Indians Want from Writing?" *CCC* 51 (2000): 447–68. Web. 19 Mar. 2010.

Mann, Regis M. "'Forever Perverse, Queer, Askew': Notes on Slavery and Resistance in African American Studies." *Journal of American Studies* 49.1 (2015): E1. Web. 15 January 2015.

———. "Theorizing 'What Could Have Been': Black Feminism, Historical Memory, and the Politics of Reclamation." *Women's Studies: An Interdisciplinary Journal.* 40.5 (2011): 575–99. Print.

May, Vivian M. *Anna Julia Cooper: Visionary Black Feminist: A Critical Introduction.* New York: Routledge, 2007. Print.

Mbembe, Achille. "Necropolitics." *Public Culture* 15 (2003): 11–40. Web. 15 Feb. 2008.

McDowell, Deborah E. "Negotiating Between Tenses: Witnessing Slavery After Freedom—Dessa Rose." *Slavery and the Literary Imagination.* Eds. Deborah E. McDowell and Arnold Rampersad. Baltimore: The Johns Hopkins University Press, 1989. 144–63. Print.

———. "Recycling: Race, Gender, and the Practice of Theory." *Feminisms: An Anthology of Literary Theory and Criticism.* Eds. Robyn R. Warhol and Diane Price Herndl. New Brunswick: Rutgers University Press, 2007. 234–47. Print.

McKoy, Sheila Smith, ed. *A Determined Life: The Elizabeth Keckley Reader, Volume One.* Hillsborough, NC: Eno Publishers, 2016. Print.

Merish, Lori. *Sentimental Materialism: Gender, Commodity Culture, and Nineteenth-Century American Literature.* Durham: Duke University Press, 2000. Print.

Mitchell, Angelyn. *The Freedom to Remember: Narrative, Slavery, and Gender in Contemporary Black Women's Fiction*. New Brunswick: Rutgers University Press, 2002. Print.

Morrison, Toni. *Beloved*. New York: Vintage Books, 1987. Print.

———. *Playing in the Dark: Whiteness and the Literary Imagination*. New York: Vintage Books, 1993. Print.

Ngai, Sianne. *Ugly Feelings*. Cambridge: Harvard University Press, 2005. Print.

Nunley, Vorris L. *Keepin' It Hushed: The Barbershop and African American Hush Harbor Rhetoric*. Detroit: Wayne State University Press, 2011. Print.

Nyong'o, Tavia. *The Amalgamation Waltz: Race, Performance, and the Ruses of Memory*. Minneapolis: University of Minnesota Press, 2009. Print.

Ottolengul, D. *Behind the Seams; by a Nigger Woman who took in work from Mrs. Lincoln and Mrs. Davis*. New York: National News Company, 1868. Web. 26 June 2015.

Packard, Jerrold M. *The Lincolns in the White House: Four Years that Shattered a Family*. New York: St. Martin's Press, 2005. Print.

Pagnattaro, Marisa Anne. *In Defiance of the Law: From Anne Hutchinson to Toni Morrison*. New York: Peter Lang, 2001. Print.

Painter, Nell Irvin. *Sojourner Truth, A Life, A Symbol*. New York: W. W. Norton & Company, 1996. Print.

Perry, Imani. "Of Degraded Talk, Digital Tongues, and a Commitment to Care." *Profession*. Ed. Rosemary G. Feal. United States: Modern Language Association of America, 2012. 17–24. Print.

Peterson, Carla L. *"Doers of the Word": African-American Women Speakers and Writers in the North (1830–1880)*. New Brunswick: Rutgers University Press, 1995. Print.

Quashie, Kevin. *The Sovereignty of Quiet: Beyond Resistance in Black Culture*. New Brunswick: Rutgers University Press, 2012. Print.

Réage, Pauline. *The Story of O*. New York: Ballantine Books, 2013. Print.

Reed, Ishmael. *Flight to Canada*. New York: Simon & Schuster, 1976. Print.

Richardson, Marilyn, ed. *Maria W. Stewart, America's First Black Woman Political Writer: Essays and Speeches*. Bloomington: Indiana University Press, 1987. Print.

Robinson, Cedric. *Black Marxism: The Making of the Black Radical Tradition*. Chapel Hill: University of North Carolina Press, 1983. Print.

Royster, Jacqueline Jones, ed. *Southern Horrors and Other Writings: The Anti-Lynching Campaign of Ida B. Wells, 1892–1900*. Boston: Bedford/St. Martin's, 1997. Print.

Rushdy, Ashraf. *Neo-Slave Narratives: Studies in the Social Logic of a Literary Form*. New York: Oxford University Press, 1999.

Salih, Sara, ed. *The History of Mary Prince, A West Indian Slave*. New York: Penguin Classics, 2000. Print.

Santamarina, Xiomara. *Belabored Professions: Narratives of African American Working Womanhood*. Chapel Hill: University of North Carolina Press, 2005. Print.

Schreiner, Samuel A., Jr. *The Trials of Mrs. Lincoln*. Lincoln: University of Nebraska Press, 2005. Print.

Smith, Valerie. "Black Feminist Theory and the Representation of the 'Other.'" *Feminisms: An Anthology of Literary Theory and Criticism*. Eds. Robyn R. Warhol and Diane Price Herndl. New Brunswick: Rutgers University Press, 2007. 311–25. Print.

———. *Self-Discovery and Authority in Afro-American Narrative*. Cambridge: Harvard University Press, 1991. Print.

Spillers, Hortense. "Mama's Baby, Papa's Maybe: An American Grammar Book." *Diacritics* 17.2 (1987): 64–81. Print.

Stiller, Richard. *The Spy, the Lady, the Captain, and the Colonel*. United States: Firebird Books, 1970. Print.

Stowe, Harriet Beecher. *Uncle Tom's Cabin*. Ware, Hertfordshire: Wordsworth Editions, 1995. Print.

Stover, Johnnie M. *Rhetoric and Resistance in Black Women's Autobiography*. Gainesville: University Press of Florida, 2003. Print.

Styron, William. *The Confessions of Nat Turner*. New York: Vintage International, 1993. Print.

Sundquist, Eric J. *To Wake the Nations: Race in the Making of American Literature*. Cambridge: Harvard University Press, 1993. Print.

Tate, Claudia. *Domestic Allegories of Political Desire: The Black Heroine's Text at the Turn of the Century*. New York: Oxford University Press, 1992. Print.

Vogel, Todd. *ReWriting White: Race, Class, and Cultural Capital in Nineteenth-Century America*. New Brunswick: Rutgers University Press, 2004. Print.

Walker, Alice. *In Search of Our Mothers' Gardens*. Orlando: Harcourt, Inc., 1983. Print.

Walker, Margaret. *Jubilee*. Boston: Mariner Books, 1999. Print.

Waters, Kristin, and Carol B. Conway, eds. *Black Women's Intellectual Traditions: Speaking Their Minds*. Burlington: University of Vermont Press, 2007. Print.

Waters-Dawson, Emma. "Psychic Rage and Response: The Enslaved and the Enslaver in Sherley Anne Williams's *Dessa Rose*." *Arms Akimbo: Africana Women in Contemporary Literature*. Eds. Janice Lee Liddell and Yakini Belinda Kemp. Gainesville: University Press of Florida, 1999. 17–31. Print.

Watkins, Mel. *On the Real Side: Laughing, Lying, and Signifying: The Underground*

Tradition of African-American Humor that Transformed American Culture, from Slavery to Richard Pryor. New York: Simon & Schuster, 1994. Print.

Weiss, Penny A. *Cannon Fodder: Historical Women Political Thinkers.* University Park, Pennsylvania: Pennsylvania State University Press, 2009. Print.

White, Cindy L., and Catherine A. Dobris. "The Nobility of Womanhood: 'Womanhood' in the Rhetoric of 19th Century Black Club Women." *Centering Ourselves: African American Feminist and Womanist Studies of Discourse.* Eds. Marsha Houston and Olga Idriss Davis. Cresskill. New Jersey: Hampton Press, Inc., 2002. 171–85. Print.

Williams, Patricia J. *The Alchemy of Race and Rights: Diary of a Law Professor.* Cambridge: Harvard University Press, 1992. Print.

Williams, Sherley Anne. *Dessa Rose.* New York: Quill/William Morrow, 1986. Print.

———. *Give Birth to Brightness.* New York: The Dial Press, 1972. Print.

———. "Meditations on History." *Callaloo* 22.4 (1999): 768–70. Web. 15 Mar. 2013.

Williams, Susan S. *Reclaiming Authorship: Literary Women in America, 1850–1900.* Philadelphia: University of Pennsylvania Press, 2006. Print.

Wilson, Harriet. *Our Nig; Or, Sketches from the Life of a Free Black.* United States: ReadaClassic.com, 2010. Print.

Wong, Sau-ling. "Diverted Mothering: Representations of Caregivers of Color in the Age of 'Multiculturalism.'" *Mothering: Ideology, Experience, and Agency.* Eds. Evelyn Nakano Glenn, Grace Chang, and Linda Rennie Forcey. New York: Routledge, 1994. 67–91. Print.

Young, Elizabeth. *Disarming the Nation: Women's Writing and the American Civil War.* Chicago: University of Chicago Press, 1999. Print.

Zafar, Rafia. *We Wear the Mask: African Americans Write American Literature, 1760–1870.* New York: Columbia University Press, 1997. Print.

Index

Black sweetness: Williams's positing of, as resistant site of collective fulfillment, 129, 164–65n16

Black women: articulating ways of knowing by and about, 144; contemporary state-sanctioned terror against, 143; as knowledge-producers, 10; on railroad cars, Cooper's attentiveness to cruelty to, 92

Blake (Delany), 108

Bland, Sandra, 143

Blues, Ideology, and Afro-American Literature (Baker, Jr.), 68

Body: as site of oppression, 151n5. *See also* Embodiment; Touch

Body-self: *Our Nig* as book about, 25

Book of Job: Keckly references, in *Behind the Scenes*, 65–67

Boyd, Rekia, 144

Brady, Mathew: portrait of Mary Todd Lincoln, 70, 71

Braiding: Williams's representation of act of, in *Dessa Rose*, 124–25

Braxton, Joanne, 62

Breastfeeding: interracial, in *Dessa Rose*, 125

Brightness tropes: in Keckly's *Behind the Scenes*, 76

Brooks, Daphne A., 14, 153n20

Brown, Jayna: on derivation of the term picaninny, 153n22

Brown, William Wells, 114

Brutalization of black women and girls: *Our Nig*, illusory notions of freedom, and, 26; state-sanctioned terror and, 143

Burleigh, H. T.: "Ethiopia's Paean of Exaltation" score by, 97

Burwell, Armistead, 53, 55

Burwell, Mary, 53

Butler, Octavia, 116

Byerman, Keith, 128, 149n2

Cable, George Washington, 90

Call-and-response singing: in *Dessa Rose*, 122

Camp, Stephanie M. H., 14, 37, 70

Canonical sociology: Ferguson on, 119

Capital: collusion of liberal empathy,

Christianity and, in Wilson's *Our Nig*, 23, 36, 47; fellow feeling colluding with, in *Our Nig*, 29

Capitalist privilege: liberalism and idealization of, 67

Carby, Hazel, 12, 21, 62, 63, 98, 99, 100

Care: insurgent, Williams's characterization of, in *Dessa Rose*, 129

Chesnutt, Charles W., 91

Child, Lydia Maria, 40

Childhood: *Our Nig* and manipulated trope of, 40–42

Choral self-definition: Cooper's acts of, 98

Christian, Barbara, 12, 20, 47, 114, 116, 146, 150n1

Christian education: Cooper posits, as remedy to racial acrimony, 85

Christianity: collusion of liberal empathy, capital and, in *Our Nig*, 23, 36, 47; fellow feeling colluding with in *Our Nig*, 29; radicalism of girl heroines contained via discourses of, 42–43

"Chronological surveys": Williams's eschewing of, 116

Citizenship: liberalism, emancipatory vision, and, 6

Civility: Cooper's paradigm of critical regard and, 105, 106; Cooper's reconceptualization of, 17, 86, 112; countering entrenched codes of, 12

Class and class privilege: called into question, Wilson's use of opacity and, 39; construction of American freedom around, 26–27; trope of childhood in *Our Nig* and, 41–42; Wilson's appropriation of "picaninny" trope and, 45. *See also* Privilege; Racial privilege

Closer to Freedom (Camp), 38

Club Movement, 161n23

Coherence, 6; countering entrenched codes of, 12; embodiment in Williams's narrative and, 136; liberal problematic, Wilson's conjuring of opacity, and, 23, 47; Williams's recent problematization of, 116

Coit, Jim: Sherley Anne Williams photographed by, 117

Collins, Patricia Hill, 12, 46, 47, 78, 106, 138

Regis M. Fox is assistant professor of English at Grand Valley State University. Her research has appeared in *Women's Studies: An Interdisciplinary Journal* and the *Journal of American Studies*, as well as in edited collections, including *A Determined Life: The Elizabeth Keckley Reader, Volume One*.

www.ingramcontent.com/pod-product-compliance
Lightning Source LLC
Chambersburg PA
CBHW021359090426
42742CB00009B/928